Gene Daly

THE FILMS OF
LANA TURNER

THE FILMS OF
LANA TURNER

BY LOU VALENTINO

THE CITADEL PRESS   SECAUCUS, NEW JERSEY

TO MOM AND DAD
AND TO L.T.
AND TO ALL THE OTHERS
WHO'VE BROUGHT SOME BEAUTY
INTO THE WORLD

For invaluable assistance the author wishes to express his gratitude to the following for giving freely of their knowledge, time and experience to make this book possible: Andrew Anthos; Fred Basten; Eva Bayne; Anne Berolzheimer; John Bowab; Clarence Sinclair Bull; Ben Carbonetto; David Chierichetti; Edward Clarke; John Cocchi; Shaun Considine; Joanne Cowen; James Cox; Kirk Crivello; Frank Edwards; Kevin Francis (Tyburn Film Productions); Edward Frank; Dore Freeman; Vic Ghidalia; Lester Glassner; Fran Goldstein; Diane Goodrich; Alex Gordon; Richard Gordon; Tom Huestis; Annelen Hughes; Walter Johnson; Neil Peter Jampolis; Tom Jones; Eleanor Karsten; John Kobal; Ellen Kostroff; Madison Lacy; Leonard Levine; Mervyn LeRoy; Beverly Linet; Moss Mabry; Doug McClelland; Dion McGregor; Robert Osborne; Toni Orlando; Adam Reilly; Gene Ringgold; Marjorie Rosen; Robert Rosterman; Diane Sears; Harry Tatelman; Joan Thursh; Vaughn Washington; Jim Watters; Douglas Whitney; Henry Willson; Lois Wilson; Sanae Yamazaki; and George Zeno.
Thanks must also be given to the companies that produced and distributed the films of Lana Turner and especially to the still photographers responsible for the photographs. If this book succeeds as a pictorial tribute to Miss Turner, it is primarily due to their genius.

First paperbound printing, 1979
ISBN 0-8065-0724-1

Copyright © 1976 by Lou Valentino
All rights reserved
Published by Citadel Press
A division of Lyle Stuart, Inc.
120 Enterprise Ave., Secaucus, N.J. 07094
In Canada: George J. McLeod Limited
73 Bathurst St., Toronto, Ont.
Manufactured in the United States of America by
Halliday Lithograph Corp., West Hanover, Mass.
Designed by Lou Valentino

LIBRARY OF CONGRESS CATALOGING IN PUBLICATION DATA
Valentino, Lou.
    The films of Lana Turner.
    1. Turner, Lana, 1921–   2. Moving-picture actors and actresses—United States—Biography. I. Title.
PN2287.T8V3   791.43′028′0924   76-26934

CONTENTS

FOREWORD
BY MERVYN LeROY

What a vivid recollection I have of my first meeting with Lana. Billy Wilkerson, the publisher of the *Hollywood Reporter*, had spotted her in a little soda place and sent her to Solly Baiano, a casting director for Warner Bros. At the time I was producing and directing pictures for Warner Bros., and I was looking for a sexy young girl to play a small but important part in a picture I was about to do called *They Won't Forget*. The problem was that she had to be more than just sexy; she had to be seductive and desirable, yes, but innocent and untouched by life as well.

I had already tested thirty girls and I was getting irascible. The combination of sex appeal and innocence is hard to find, believe me! Anyway, the phone rang and it was Solly. "Mervyn," he said, "I think we have the girl you are looking for. I'll send her over. Her name is Judy Turner."

I was sure that this Judy Turner would be just another disappointment. My secretary buzzed me. "A Miss Turner is here," she said. "Send her in," I said. I shuffled the pages on my desk, looking for a scene from the picture for her to read. She was supposed to be a teen-aged innocent who is murdered in the first few minutes of the picture.

I looked up. A girl with dark hair stood in the doorway, so nervous her hands were shaking. She had on a blue cotton dress. Her hair was impossible. It looked as if she had never put a comb through it. She wasn't wearing any makeup and she was so shy she could hardly look me in the face. Yet there was something so endearing about her that I knew she was the right girl. She had tremendous appeal, which I knew the audience would feel. The first thing I said to her was, "Do you want to sign a contract?" "I'll have to ask my mother," she answered. It was only when I had a contract drawn up putting Julia Jean Mildred Frances Turner under personal contract that she knew it wasn't all a dream.

The first day before the camera, she came through just as I knew she would. I felt sorry for her, and I knew audiences would too. Her shyness —and Lana was painfully shy—made me want to help her. She was an untutored kid, but she had a wonderful personality. Lana always had a bubbling, irrepressible sense of humor. She had it then, and she has it today. In those days, her humor showed itself by a carefree attitude. She wasn't conscious of the tremendous break that had come her way. She wanted to play and have fun like most youngsters. But I was taking her career seriously even if she wasn't. I knew she had great possibilities.

The first thing I did was to suggest that she change her name. And what a lucky name it turned out to be for her. I tried to help Lana in other ways too. Although her mother worked hard to provide her with shelter and clothes, there was very little room in their budget for luxuries. I recall once when Lana couldn't go to this big function that was being attended by everyone who was anyone in Hollywood because she didn't have a formal dress. I bought her one. I knew it was important that she be seen by all the right people.

Mervyn LeRoy and Lana Turner at Warner Bros. in 1937

As time went on I saw Lana mature. She had a mind that literally soaked up knowledge. She wanted to learn and she wanted to be a star. When I left Warners to go to Metro, I took her with me, but I gave her her release so she would be free to sign with Metro. I wanted her to find herself, to be somebody. Needless to say, she surpassed my wildest expectations. By the time we did films like *Johnny Eager* and *Homecoming* together, I could see how much Lana had learned about the business. Sure, luck played a big part in Lana's success story. But let me tell you about luck. It only happens to those who are ready for it. Success is never an 'accident.

Hollywood couldn't give talent if it wasn't already there, inside them, waiting to be developed, to be nurtured. What Hollywood *could* do was to bring that talent out into the open . . . so far out into the open that it could be projected on a screen sixty feet high!

Some years back, I wrote a book called *It Takes More Than Talent.* In it, I tried to tell how much more it takes to achieve success in Hollywood than mere talent. Star quality is a necessary ingredient, to be sure, but I have always maintained that you can't be a really fine actor or actress without heart. You also have to possess the ability to project that heart, that feeling and emotion. And you've got to

have a good amount of determination and courage. Gable had it. So did Tracy and Harlow and all our truly great stars. Lana? Yes, Lana had all of these qualities. And she still has them.

Mervyn LeRoy

Lana and Mervyn at a party in 1965

LANA

STAR AND LEGEND

At nine

Judy Turner at eight in San Francisco

"I've never known what it is I was supposed to have had. Something, obviously, otherwise I wouldn't have had so many fans; I wouldn't have survived so long on the screen. All I do know is that sex appeal isn't make-believe. It's not the way you look or the way you walk or the way you smile. It's the way you are."

—LANA TURNER

Hollywood, somebody once said, is a state of mind. Perhaps that's true, for what is Hollywood if not the magic conduit for dreams, the substantiation of perfection, our recollection of a Utopia where goddesses were crowned and villains punished and fantasy exalted? Today when we think of Hollywood, we flash back to the Garden of Allah, to Ciro's and the Trocadero and Mocambo; we relish those palatial soirées and breathtaking premieres attended by ermine-swathed starlets and tuxedoed men with square jawlines. Hollywood was the magnificent paradox—the lush screen innocence of 100 Busby Berkeley legs or a Judy Garland song or a Chaplin strut coupled with delicious whispers about what our idols were really like. But most of all, Hollywood meant the movies themselves whose barometers of appeal remained with those idols —fabulous creatures making small plots luminous

As a teenager

A Warner Bros. starlet at sixteen

and, for a while, small men's dreams within grasp. It's no coincidence that Hollywood rose and fell with its stars, and that the abolition of the star system preordained an end to that state of mind.

The men who built those empires of make-believe—Mayer, Zukor, Zanuck, Goldwyn, Warner, Cohn—instinctively realized that talent was their greatest commodity. And around 1912, when immigrant audiences were flocking to see the little blonde with the golden curls, Mary Pickford became our first star. As "America's Sweetheart" she brought magic to the screen. She had that certain something, a radiance, an affinity with the camera which differentiated between true stars and merely ubiquitous actors. Garbo had it, Dietrich, Monroe. Clara Bow had it and they called it "It." The studios couldn't create star quality, but since their very product and future depended on it, they could seek it out and nurture it to fruition. And they did this with grandiose efficiency.

The Golden Age of Hollywood is simply a tag evoking memories of those men and women whose glamour and perfection once seemed paramount. The men and women coddled within the star system rose from bit to feature player to headliner under careful tutelage from the parent company which had contracted them. Gods and goddesses learned to walk and talk in the bosom of the studio. They were groomed and designed not simply to

appeal to public taste, but to enhance their own natural assets. Diction was corrected, noses bobbed, ears pinned back. Hair colors changed, hairlines shifted, bosoms were remolded and teeth re-enameled. Dancers learned to sing. Singers learned to dance. Actors learned to "be." Studios invested in their properties and once a property paid off, every courtesy and protection was guaranteed—provided, of course, that the star remained grateful, loyal and obedient.

And the star usually did. Stardom was the great American Dream, the myth that could elevate plain

At the beginning of her career it was sweaters and more sweaters for Lana—and nobody was complaining

kids to living legends in what seemed like no time.
For women, especially, it was a twentieth-century
Horatio Alger possibility propelling them to the
heights. It promised money, fame, idolatry. The
small-town girl-next-door could touch romance; she
could trade in her vine-covered cottage for a stucco
palace in the hills of Beverly. And—as the fan
magazines told it—she might even be squired
around by princes and counts; she would wear, or
create, the latest fashions; she would know the love
and adoration of millions. Stardom held out a
fairy-tale invitation to the glitter of life, and
thousands of pretty, rosy-cheeked young dreamers
made the pilgrimage to Hollywood to be discovered.

Most met with disappointment. But one whose
discovery coincided with and implemented the
myth was a fair-skinned, brown-haired sixteen-
year-old from Idaho. Her name was Julia
Jean Mildred Frances Turner. Hollywood changed
it to Lana Turner and, within just a few years, she
became one of MGM's top box-office attractions.
Four decades later, Lana Turner is still a universal
symbol of glamour and a supreme example of the
quintessential Movie Star. Of all the film personalities who rose to fame under the star system, she
more than any other justly can be labelled Hollywood's own. Her story has become the classic
Hollywood story, for it comes complete with all the
romance and spectacular drama peculiar to the
movie capital.

Like another Cinderella, the beginning for Julia
Jean Turner was inauspicious. She was born on
February 8, 1921 in Wallace, Idaho.* Young
"Judy," her mother Mildred, and her father, Virgil
Turner, moved frequently from town to town,
wherever Mr. Turner could find work. Virgil
Turner tried to make a good life for himself and
his family by selling insurance, but he often found
it necessary to turn to hard labor in the mines or on
the docks. He even on occasion turned to bootleg-
ging. Because of this, the family changed names as
often as locations, and Lana recalls, "Two things I
remember particularly: I never knew for sure what
my name was, and my father danced with me."

Lana looks back at her father with love. As a
toddler she'd follow her parents' steps as they
whirled about the room. "Then my father would go
to a straight chair and do tap dances sitting down. I
stood in front and imitated him, and that's how I
learned to dance. I learned to dance naturally and

---

*Throughout her career, the year of Lana Turner's birth has
been listed as either 1920 or 1921. Early studio biographies
and editions of Who's Who, even photographs taken of
marriage certificates, support the latter date. In 1943, Current
Biography suddenly listed the year as 1920. Since that time,
biographers, depending upon which research material they
were using, have alternated between '20 and '21. Lana has
persistently maintained that the 1921 date is the correct one.
Over twenty-five years ago, she reasoned, "Why would I lie
for one year?"

(Associated Press Wirefoto)

HAS "IT." Lana Turner, 17, Los Angeles
high school girl and film player,
will be groomed by studio as "It" girl of 1939.

Girl Discovered At Soda Fountain Gets Film Career

HOLLYWOOD April 8. — (By
United Press.)—Lana Turner spied
by a movie talent scout while she
was attending Hollywood High
School, went to work today under
a contract paying her $250 a week.

With the prospect of starring
roles, she was signed to a MGM
contract. Because she is only 17
years of age, the contract must be
approved in Superior Court.

easily and, as I learned years later, very well indeed because my father was genuinely good at it. It was always reported that as a girl I went to the best dancing schools. The fact is that all I ever knew about dancing I learned from him before I was nine years old."

The Turners moved to San Francisco at the beginning of the Depression, and most of Judy's early family memories were happy. Although her parents eventually separated, they never divorced and the Turners remained close.

But on December 15, 1930, tragedy struck: Virgil Turner was found dead on the streets of San Francisco, a robbery victim. A friendly, congenial, good-looking man with a soft Southern accent, Turner was only thirty-six when he died, and it was shortly after his unsolved murder that the weaving

As an MGM starlet publicity photos continued to be an important part of the Turner buildup. Holiday art, such as those illustrated on these pages, was a favorite way of promoting an up-and-coming beauty

of his only daughter's destiny began.

To support herself and her child, Mildred Turner took a job in a small beauty parlor. Because she worked long hours, she had no way to take care of Judy, so she sent the child to live with some friends in Modesto, California. There, without her mother's knowledge, Judy was mistreated and regarded as a "scullery maid." "A cheap Cinderella with no hope of a pumpkin," remembers Lana.

When Mrs. Turner discovered her daughter's situation, the two promptly were reunited in San Francisco. Although they were so poor they sometimes went without food for days, they managed to stay alive. Eventually, mother and daughter moved to Sacramento where Judy attended a Catholic

By the 40s, Lana's name had become a household word

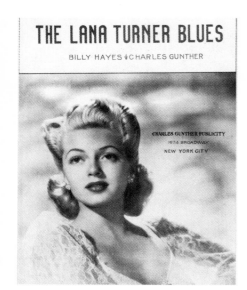

Songs were written about her . . .

Airplanes were named for her . . .

. . . and her image was reproduced on thousands of commercial products

For the youngsters there was a series
of paper dolls and paint books that
carried Lana's name

school run by the Dominican Sisters. "I plagued the sisters with demands that I be made a nun," Lana once stated. "I don't know what foreknowledge they had, but they smiled and discouraged me."

Mrs. Turner's work prospects in Sacramento proved less than promising, however, so mother and daughter continued their nomadic existence by moving back to San Francisco. For a while Judy dreamed about dress designing, but in the middle of her fifteenth year fate imposed other plans. The fog hovering over San Francisco had irritated Mildred Turner's health to such an extent that she was advised by a doctor to move to the warmer climate of Los Angeles. There, she found work in another beauty shop and her daughter enrolled at Hollywood High School.

At fifteen, Judy Turner was five-foot-three, flawlessly built, with auburn hair, large gray-blue eyes, ivory skin and a dimpled smile. One of her classmates was Nanette Fabray, who has since described the effect the teen-ager made on Hollywood High: "She was the most incredibly beautiful girl we had ever seen. Even the teachers stared at her. She'd

walk down the hall, looking straight ahead while all the other kids gawked at her. She was only fifteen, but even then she had the bearing of a princess. We all *knew* she would be a movie star."

Another famous alumna of the school is Alexis Smith, who has said, "Lana was the talk of the school when she first came in. She had a marvelous look about her."

Hollywood High was just a few blocks from Hollywood and Vine and the gilded dreams of dime-store girls and Park Avenue debutantes. And, like every other mother and daughter who lived close to the movie studios, Mildred Turner could not help entertaining the notion that one day Judy might land a job in motion pictures. But they were pipe dreams, nothing more. Lana herself has confessed, "It would have seemed absurd. I had never acted. I had never danced, or tried to do either even *semi*professionally. People didn't stop me on the street and say, 'Ah! What a pretty girl! You ought to be in pictures.'"

But one morning in January 1936, it did happen. And for Judy Turner of Wallace, Idaho, it was the beginning of a legend that has been told and retold, distorted and even denied, over the years. Lana Turner's own account follows:

One morning when the rigors of a typewriting class were too much to take, I slipped across the street and perched on a stool at a soda fountain on Sunset Boulevard.* I used my meager lunch money to console myself with a cold drink. The manager and soda jerk was an old friend. He saw me often because I cut classes often. We spoke, he made my drink, then he responded to a beckoning black-haired man with a mustache. They talked and looked at me. I squirmed uncomfortably and sucked at my soda. The manager came back. "Judy," he said, "Mr. Billy Wilkerson over there is a friend of mine. He's all right. He wants me to introduce him to you."

I was scared out of my wits. I had never been picked up before, even under the auspices of a soda jerk. I gurgled into my straw and shook my head. "No," I said.

"Aw, come on, Judy. Mr. Wilkerson don't mean any harm. He's a real nice fellow. This ain't what you think it is." I hadn't thought it was anything, but I'd heard about slick Hollywood wolves who picked up little girls and led them into lives of shame. "No," I said.

Mr. Wilkerson came over anyway. He made a bow and handed me his card. "I'm Billy Wilkerson, publisher of *The Hollywood Reporter*," he said. "How would you like to be in pictures?"

How would you like to be in pictures! Even a kid from Wallace, Idaho, knew better than that. How corny could this guy get? "No thanks," I said primly. Mr. Wilkerson smiled. "I understand," he said kindly. "You don't know me or anything about me. But suppose you take this card. It has my address on it. Could you and your mother come to see me at my office?"

"With my mother?" I gasped. That was a new twist. That night when I told the story to Mother and a close friend they had three different reactions. At first they laughed. Then they looked at me with new eyes and were frightened. Then they grew curious. They went out and bought a copy of the *Reporter*, saw Mr. Wilkerson's name and decided, after a conference that lasted through many cups of coffee, that they would take baby by the hand and go together to see the odd and probably terrible man who thought Judy ought to be in pictures.

For that fateful meeting, Lana recalls, "I was primped like a pup at a dog show, of course, and I must have looked like a bumpkin indeed to a man who was used to associating with all the great beauties of Hollywood. But he was still convinced and still patient." Wilkerson's next move was to guide mother and daughter over to the Zeppo Marx Agency where Henry Willson, its young vice-president, decided to gamble on the fledgling. Along with his assistant, Solly Baiano (who later became casting director for Warner Bros.), Willson offered the youngster this first bit of advice: "Don't overdress."

Contrary to popular belief, Lana Turner was not an instant success. She did get some work as an extra—in David O. Selznick's *A Star Is Born*—but little else materialized and more than one studio rejected her for a contract. Finally, Solly Baiano arranged an interview for her at Warners where director Mervyn LeRoy was looking for a teen-age girl to portray a murder victim in *They Won't Forget*, one of the many sociological dramas the studio was producing in the 1930s. "I'm sure Mervyn said more, but I recall only one word," informs Lana. "Walk," he commanded.

---

*Although long established that the site of this happening was at Sunset Boulevard and Highland Avenue, directly across from Hollywood High, the legend's most notable variance through the years is the name of the drug store, malt shop or café (as it has been alternately described) where Judy Turner and Billy Wilkerson met. Lana Turner herself has no recollection of its name—not surprisingly, since her tenure at the school lasted no more than a month and a half before she was swept into the maelstrom of the film industry. She doesn't even recall precisely what she was drinking. "But," she says, "it had to be a nickel drink because I couldn't afford any other."
Early newspaper and magazine articles (including Niven Busch's in-depth article on the actress's discovery in *Life*, December 23, 1940) identify the spot as the Top Hat Malt Shop. However, in the mid-1940s, it shifted to Schwab's Pharmacy, a drugstore peopled by movie hopefuls and bit players. Since it was the ideal spot to be "discovered," the Lana Turner soda fountain legend was transferred to Schwab's—probably by a Schwab's publicity man—in order to serve as inspiration to the young unknowns who frequented the place. No matter that Schwab's was located a good two miles from Hollywood High and, therefore, geographically inaccurate. Today Schwab's drugstore is the essence of halcyon Hollywood and remains one of the landmarks that visitors invariably come to see—primarily because of its fame as the spot where Lana Turner was discovered!
In recent years, however, with Hollywood myths exploding, the incident has been placed at Currie's Ice Cream Parlor across from Hollywood High. Yet, records existing in Los Angeles today, while confirming that Currie's was one of a chain of ice cream parlors operating in Los Angeles 1936–37, clearly establish that the only Currie's in the Hollywood district at that time was located at Beverly Boulevard and Vermont Avenue, far from Hollywood High.
The same records, however, indicate that there was indeed a business establishment on the corner of Sunset and Highland then: Top's Cafe, located at 6750 Sunset Boulevard, directly across from the high school. Since the name of this restaurant closely parallels that of the one in the initial discovery stories, it seems safe to assume that Top's Cafe was the real landmark. Today, a Texaco gas station stands on the corner spot once occupied by Top's.

Lana Turner, cover girl

With Louis B. Mayer

He hired her.

He also suggested a name change. Judy Turner became Lana Turner, and on February 22, 1937, the California courts approved her contract calling for a starting salary of $50 and escalating to $600 a week over seven years. LeRoy then gave the tyro a sweater to wear and a brief but pivotal role as, coincidentally, a sexy schoolgirl. The highlight of Lana's screen footage consisted of a seventy-five-foot dolly shot of her walking through the streets of a small Southern town. But that one scene had a tumultuous effect on moviegoers. At the preview of *They Won't Forget,* high school and college boys whistled and whooped. Suddenly Hollywood had given birth to its first "Sweater Girl"—and a star was on her way.

Indeed, Lana's brief appearance in *They Won't Forget* made an impact not only on her but on the sweater industry. Lana brought sweaters into vogue. Every American girl built her wardrobe around them. One observer claimed that "More sheep were shorn for wool in the years that followed than in all history, for sweaters became the rage." In fact, Lana initiated a fetish for bosoms augmented by Jane Russell in the '40s and Monroe, Mansfield, Loren and all the other sexpots of the '50s. By 1948, 4,500,000 "breast pads" or falsies were sold largely as a result of this new Hollywood focus.

When the world fell in love with its new sweater sweetheart in 1937, the young actress, barely a woman, was distinctly uneasy with her new image. Years later, Lana explained:

I did not see myself on screen until the preview of *They Won't Forget* at Warner Bros.' Hollywood Theatre. Mother and I went together and sat in the rear, goggling at the movie stars whose names we knew, wondering what it would feel like when baby came on screen. We thought I might have been cut out, and I was so nervous by this time, I rather hoped I had.

Then, out of the darkness and hush of the big theatre, a girl came on screen. She walked slowly down the street, then away. She wore a tight sweater and her breasts bounced as she walked. She wore a tight skirt, too, and her buttocks bounced as she walked. She moved sinuously, undulating fore and aft, but with a kind of coltish grace. Mother and I scrooched down in our seats.

Someone in the audience whistled. There were also some gasps. Then The Thing was gone. I understood later why this girl was there and why she was a Thing. She was the motive for the entire picture. She was the girl who got raped. She had to look like a girl men would like to rape . . . The girl on the screen looked innocent, but also like a blossom waiting to be plucked. She was enough to start a reaction leading up to a murder all right. But she certainly did not seem to be me.

Mother and I crept out of the theatre and stumbled into a cab, not knowing what to say to each other. I held myself very self-consciously, trying not to bounce. Of course I knew I had a bosom. But I had assumed that it was stock equipment for girls. All the girls I knew were adequately supplied. I knew I had a rear, too, because I sat on it and tugged my skirt down over it, but at fifteen it had certainly not occurred to me that my derriere (a word I did not know then) was anything a $2,500-a-week Hollywood cameraman would want to train a lens on.

For quite a while I was ashamed to face people. I also found it embarrassing to turn my back on them.

But the Turner embarrassment didn't last too long, for the Turner career had been launched. Studio press agents began building her up as "America's Sweater Girl," and even before her film was released in June 1937, Mervyn LeRoy saw to it that she was spotted in a series of small roles that projected her assets to the best advantage.*

*In recent years, *Four's a Crowd* (Warner Bros., 1938) has appeared in a number of Lana Turner filmographies. For the benefit of the many frustrated Turner fans who have searched in vain for her appearance in this film in its showings on television or at reissue houses, Lana is *not* in the movie. The actress herself denies working in it and Mervyn LeRoy insists that he never arranged for her to appear in the picture. Both Turner and LeRoy had in fact moved from Warners to MGM in January, 1938, even before *Four's a Crowd* began shooting at the former studio on February 2, 1938 (under the working title *All Rights Reserved*).

In addition to repeated screenings of the film, I have checked contractual records at Warner Bros.; the key still books; Hollywood trade papers of the period; and other source material at both the Lincoln Center Library for Performing Arts in New York City and the Academy of Motion Picture Arts and Sciences in Los Angeles—and there is no evidence of her association with the project.

The part of Mary Clay in *They Won't Forget* was just the first of a number of nubile adolescents Lana would portray during the first years of her film career. Years later, her youthful screen image was to be perfectly recalled by Francis Wyndham of *The Times* (London): "Wearing sweater and skirt, insolently hunched over an ice cream soda, she exuded a homespun glamour in the late 1930s that was peculiarly American. Both frail and tough, she appealed to the masculine protective instinct and at the same time promised danger."

In 1938, when LeRoy moved from Warners to MGM, he shepherded his prodigy along with him. Within the gates of the largest, swankiest dream factory, Lana worked and learned. The size and

importance of her roles grew with each picture, and MGM assigned her to rigorous elocution, dramatic and dancing lessons. At the same time, she lightened the color of her hair to a bright red. During this apprenticeship period, Lana attracted attention in films like *Love Finds Andy Hardy*, *Rich Man Poor Girl*, *Dramatic School* and *Calling Dr. Kildare*. Eventually, after leading parts in minor but effective items like *These Glamour Girls* and *Dancing Co-Ed*, studio chief Louis B. Mayer decided she should be groomed for real stardom.

MGM's expert professional machinery began attending her needs with special care. Beauticians from Hairdressing experimented with hairstyles and coloring until they found those most complimen-

Lester Glassner

On May 24, 1950 Lana was immortalized in cement at Grauman's Chinese Theatre in Hollywood

With Judy Garland on the set of THE BAD AND THE BEAUTIFUL

With Clark Gable on the set of ADVENTURE

A dressing room chat with Joan Crawford

tary to her face. Wardrobe was instructed to use special care in dressing her. A publicity representative taught her how to handle herself with the press. The studio's number one portrait artist, Clarence Bull, took hundreds of photographs of Lana, which then were distributed to movie magazines as well as to newspapers across the country. The vast but precise system left nothing to chance. Once the studio molded their star into an image and showcased her in important films, it would then be up to the public to embrace or turn its back on her.

Lana wasn't just embraced, she was practically suffocated by her fans' devotion. Even as a starlet, titles and honors were bestowed on her, especially by the college youth of the nation—the girls who wished they could look like her, and the boys who wished those girls could, too. Graciously accepting such titles as the "Ideal Date," "Miss Wunky Woo," "The Sweetheart of Phi Kappa Psi" (and Sigma Nu, Sigma Chi, Beta Theta Pi and thirty-six other college fraternities) was part of the publicity grind the studio had mapped out for her. Walter Winchell dubbed Lana "America's Sweater Girl Sweetheart." Mickey Rooney called her "Baby Glamour." *Pic* coined the phrase "Lan-allure" and another publication referred to her as the "Sextasy Girl." Lana was not yet old enough to vote, and she hadn't yet reached major stardom, but already her name was synonymous with glamour.

Ziegfeld Girl, in 1941, marked a turning point in the actress's career. To play the role of an ill-fated show girl, Lana lightened her hair to a golden blonde. She looked lovelier than ever, so blonde she has stayed—except for a few later screen appearances when the parts called for her to be a brunette. But most importantly, *Ziegfeld Girl* was the film that brought her full-fledged stardom.

Lana has been quoted as saying: "No one considered me an actress. No one except me, and I kept this new conviction strictly to myself. For once I studied my part long and faithfully, determined to make my Ziegfeld girl not merely a clotheshorse and decoration but, if possible, a human being. I do not suggest that I wholly succeeded, but it's interesting that as we went along, my role was expanded ... I realized then that acting is not merely certain technical tricks that can be learned, as important as they sometimes are, but the sum total of your experience and your observation. I think that once you know *who you are* in your part, more than half your acting battle is won. Then and only then can you put yourself into the part, selecting the experiences and attitudes that you have lived or observed to draw the picture you want."

Lana won critical acclaim for *Ziegfeld Girl*. And the moment she began taking herself seriously, so did MGM. In the space of a year, the studio cast

With her longtime makeup man, Del Armstrong, on the set of THE PRODIGAL

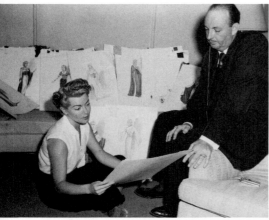

her opposite its three biggest leading men—Clark Gable, Spencer Tracy and Robert Taylor. She emerged MGM's most romantic heroine and most publicized star. Lana Turner endorsed more beauty ads than any other movie star of the day. Radio comics dropped her name more frequently, too. The most popular gag: one comic says to another, "Anything you say will be held against you." His partner replies, "Lana Turner!" Comic strips parodied her with characters called Tana Lerner, Lana Turnip, Bana Burner, among others. Songs were written about her. Comic books and paper dolls reproduced her image. She was one of World War II's favorite pin-ups, and the Air Force even named a plane after her. It was the kind of mass hysteria which boosted box-office appeal, and MGM was delighted that their property was proving so valuable.

The 1940s were golden years for Lana. As a bona fide star from the very beginning of the decade, almost the entire output of her films during this period were star vehicles, handsomely cast and mounted in the best Metro manner. If the scripts were sometimes less substantial than the production values, it mattered little as far as moviegoers—and Turner fans especially—were concerned. This was an era of romance between gods and goddesses of the screen—and an audience of mortals. A continuing passion which made people all over the world care enough to come back again and again to see those same stars in their next films, and the ones after that. In Lana's case, she beguiled her public with a persona that was antithetical, and thus hypnotic, in the same way that other great contradictory personalities of the screen did. For Lana Turner on one hand suggested a modern-day, angel-faced Circe; she could also be the cool, submissive beauty whose poise cloaked a wild and passionate interior. Never quite the lady but never cheap, warm and friendly but unattainable, she held a fascination for both men and women. Aside from the obvious physical appeal, perhaps her most potent asset was an almost quivering vulnerability. Later on, another sex sorceress, Marilyn Monroe, would have a similar soft, wounded quality.

MGM provided the ideal climate for Lana's growth as a performer. Due to her success in *Ziegfeld Girl*, her box office had risen considerably and the studio quickly cast her in a trio of fast and sexy hits that showcased her beautifully—*Honky Tonk, Johnny Eager, Somewhere I'll Find You.* Love, Hollywood Style, was the key to such films and the romantic atmosphere that pervaded them struck a responsive chord in a public in the midst of a war.

Between 1943 and 1948, she was seen in an assortment of tailored, mass-appeal entertainments. There was the marshmallow fluff (*Slightly Dan-*

Beautiful clothes have always been an important ingredient of Lana's films.
The original costume sketches below are the creations of four top designers Miss Turner
has worked with during her career

Irene, MARRIAGE IS A PRIVATE AFFAIR   *Helen Rose*, LATIN LOVERS

Walter Plunkett, DIANE   *Edith Head*, LOVE HAS MANY FACES

A star both on-screen and off, Lana's private life has always been front page news. The Turner husbands:

ARTIE SHAW

STEPHEN CRANE

HENRY J. "BOB" TOPPING

LEX BARKER

FRED MAY

ROBERT EATON

RONALD DANTE

gerous, Keep Your Powder Dry); all-star escapism (*Week-End at the Waldorf*); and picturizations of best-selling novels (*Marriage Is a Private Affair, Cass Timberlane*). She also lent her charisma to multimillion-dollar epics (*Green Dolphin Street*) and costume extravaganzas (*The Three Musketeers*).

But her most significant role of that decade came in 1946 with *The Postman Always Rings Twice*, the film version of James M. Cain's steamy, ironic murder novel. Here Lana slipped into a genre which Marjorie Rosen in her book, *Popcorn Venus*, defines as that in which "the fantasy female and fatal woman are embodied as one." If MGM, the studio that vehemently supported "taste" and "refinement," often veiled Lana's on-screen sensuality in vague suggestion, *Postman* gave her the opportunity to display it in a manner that she had never been allowed before. The picture also provided her with one of the meatiest dramatic roles of her career opposite one of her favorite co-stars, John Garfield. And just as her sweaters had given a new look to the previous decade, it was in 1946 that Lana set another fashion trend: the platinum-tressed actress's startling appearance in the white shorts and bare midriff of *The Postman Always Rings Twice* began the vogue for women's shorts.

At the same time, white became the color most associated with Lana.

With a huge following and a succession of money-making films to her credit, she sailed into the 1950s an undisputed superstar. Her status at this time can be exemplified by writer Geoffrey McBain's ode in *Cosmopolitan*: "What is a Lana Turner? *Who* is a Lana Turner? Lana Turner is a name in lights on a thousand grubby Main Streets. Lana Turner is a long, low, libidinous whistle on the wetted lips of America. She is the four-by-six glossy that serves as barracks wallpaper from Tokyo to Heidelberg and in the cabins of all the ships at sea. She is the pick-up a guy will never stop hoping to make until senility overtakes him. She is the girl a girl can always think she is, until the house lights come up. She is love with a stranger; the girl you didn't marry; the chapter Havelock Ellis forgot to write; and she is yours whenever you want her, for forty cents plus tax . . . She is, in short, a Hollywood press release come to life."

By 1950, Lana was earning a salary of $5,000 a week. She was also approaching thirty and her screen image had become increasingly sophisticated. The high-powered sex appeal of the '40s was still unmistakably there, but the emphasis now was on beauty and femininity. In both her films and her publicity photos she was the epitome of sleek allure —impeccably gowned, perfectly manicured, not a hair out of place. Although a new blonde sex symbol named Marilyn Monroe had captured the center spotlight, Lana continued to hold the attention of the public. And the honors continued to pour in—in July 1951, the Academy of Contemporary Arts, an organization of painters, sculptors and illustrators, voted her "the most glamourous woman in the history of international art."

For the most part, the Turner vehicles of the early '50s traversed ground familiar from the previous decade; their primary function was to serve as a series of plushly designed star showcases. With Love still the leitmotif of her films, she graced soap operas (*A Life of Her Own*); more fluff (*Latin Lovers*); happily-ever-after musicals (*The Merry Widow*); and a couple of European-made ventures (*Flame and the Flesh, Betrayed*). Later, on loanout from MGM for the first time, she battled the elements at both Warners (*The Sea Chase*) and 20th Century-Fox (*The Rains of Ranchipur*); as well as weathering historical drama (*Diane*) and a biblical potboiler (*The Prodigal*) back at her home studio.

In 1952 Lana contributed a genuine characterization to MGM's *The Bad and the Beautiful*, a superb drama about the motion picture industry. Directed by Vincente Minnelli, who in his recent memoir extolled her "brilliant" performance as a Diana Barrymore-ish, alcoholic actress, it won five Academy Awards and remains one of Lana's best pictures.

Movies like *The Bad and the Beautiful* were scarce, however. MGM, assuming that anything Lana appeared in would draw an audience, had begun to choose her vehicles carelessly, and it showed in the grosses. Like Grable and Hayworth and Crawford and Davis and all the other prominent female players then, Turner, of course, did have her own faithful following that attended her films ritualistically, indifferent to their merit or critical reception. When the fans plunked down their money at the box office, they were there to see *her* more than the movies; the characters she played and the pictures themselves were almost incidental. When the vehicle surrounding her appearance turned out to be a rewarding one, it was icing on the cake.

But change was overtaking the industry. Dore Schary replaced Louis B. Mayer at Metro. By mid-decade, the tried-and-true formulas which had worked so well and for so long for many personalities nurtured under the star system were showing signs of faltering. The great mass audience was discovering new means of "escape." Television had already so severely cut into Hollywood's market that to lure patrons back the industry was trying

new ploys: 3D; Cinerama; CinemaScope; science fiction; horror thrillers and motorcycle melodramas. And as taxes soared and box-office receipts dwindled, first-magnitude, high-salaried stars were breaking loose from the paternal studio system which had been their home for years.

Early in 1956, Lana ended her contractual association with MGM. The parting was by mutual agreement. She was now thirty-five and her career needed a change of direction. Since she had been MGM's Golden Girl for nearly eighteen years, her departure had industryites wondering how she would fare without the security and protection of a major studio.

The answer came late the next year with the release of *Peyton Place*, the film version of Grace Metalious' best-seller. Produced by 20th Century-Fox, it marked Lana's debut as a free-lance actress. The Turner image that greeted patrons of this blockbuster was different from anything Lana heretofore had projected. For the first time, she appeared as the mother of a teen-ager—a woman past her youth, restless, searching for love and happiness. Under the direction of Mark Robson, Lana's performance won her an Oscar nomination. In addition, the role signalled the course her career would take in the next few years.

In 1959 producer Ross Hunter added the final touch to this new image. An advocate of old-fashioned glamour, Hunter combined beauty, tears and Lana Turner for a series of immensely popular, ultra-glamourous "women's pictures," in which the star portrayed sophisticated but troubled matrons suffering the soignée agonies of the rich. The first of their films together was a remake of the Fannie Hurst tear-jerker, *Imitation of Life*, for Universal.

Lana and Tyrone Power were the most publicized romantic match of 1947

Producer Ross Hunter and director Douglas Sirk discuss the script of IMITATION OF LIFE *with Lana*

Embellished with Technicolor, luxurious clothes and jewels, the picture was released in the spring of 1959, and although highbrow critics labelled the results "rhinestone reality," it was balm to millions of moviegoing women. *Imitation of Life* grossed $9 million in its initial U.S. run and, for quite a few years thereafter, Turner and Hunter clung tenaciously to this magic formula. In 1966, when the "woman's picture" genre had virtually played itself out, it was Turner and Hunter who drew the final curtain with their joint production of *Madame X.*

When this fourth remake of the classic mother-love saga reached theatres, Lana was a veteran of fifty films while her career had spanned almost thirty years. It was during this period that writer Alyce Canfield, in a study of the mysteries of stardom, offered her theory on the Turner durability:

At forty-five, she is the most glitteringly upholstered survivor of the World War II love goddesses. It's true her stardom has rested more in her beauty than in the distinction of the films in which she has appeared. Yet Turner's most positive quality has actually been her vulnerability. It provided a sharp contrast to her sophisticated allure and, more than any other single factor, it is this potent blend of glamour and vulnerability that has allowed Turner's career to endure while so many of her cinema sisters have either retired, faded or else are languishing on the vine.

Turner has another great advantage over her contemporaries. Her name means only one thing: Star. She wears it as brilliantly as she wore her sweaters. She is the glitter and glamour of Hollywood; a symbol of the American Dream fulfilled. Because of her, being discovered at a soda fountain has become almost as cherished an ideal as

being born in a log cabin has been. To reject her is to reject the Dream itself.

Perhaps another factor essential to Lana's endurance as a star was the public's long-time fascination with her private life. Over the decades, in fact, her public and private lives became so closely linked that many moviegoers responded as if the two were one.

If Garbo's legend thrived on secrecy, the legend of Lana Turner flourished on front pages from Brooklyn to Beirut. There were few secrets between her and her public. At Lana's peak, her simple, straightforward, and very romantic attitudes about life and love supplied irresistible copy for bored housewives, lonely spinsters and star-struck teenagers whose restlessness found an ideal outlet in her vivid lifestyle. In the heyday of the fan magazines, she was portrayed as the walking, breathing Movie Star; the corn-fed kid skipping through the American Dream with relish; the good-natured girl whose heart ruled her head;* the movie star who *enjoyed* being a movie star.

Rarely a week went by without a magazine or a Sunday supplement carrying pictures of her making a blinding entrance at a premiere with her latest beau or featuring a by-lined article revealing her beauty secrets or her recipe for romance. Her hairstyles, her look, her flair for the most spectacular clothes were quickly copied by her legions as they breathlessly awaited the next movie, the next romance, the next headline. Turner fans didn't have to go to the movies to search out and emulate their favorite; all they had to do was pick up a magazine† or a newspaper. For, in addition to the heroines of her films, Lana Turner offered her public another infinitely glamourous and exciting role—herself. Her public image was best summed up by one fan who said, "Lana Turner seems to do in real life all the things every girl would like to do —if she had the opportunity."

---

*Lana Turner's husbands: musician Artie Shaw (married February 13, 1940—divorced September 12, 1940); broker-actor Stephen Crane (married July 17, 1942—marriage annulled February 4, 1943—remarried March 14, 1943—divorced August 21, 1944); tin-plate heir Henry J. ("Bob") Topping (married April 26, 1948—divorced December 16, 1952); actor Lex Barker (married September 7, 1953—divorced July 22, 1957); rancher Fred May (married November 27, 1960—divorced October 15, 1962); businessman Robert Eaton (married June 22, 1965—divorced April 1, 1969); nightclub hypnotist Ronald Dante (married May 9, 1969—separated six months later but not divorced until January 26, 1972). Stephen Crane, today one of Los Angeles' most successful restaurateurs, is the father of Lana's only child, Cheryl Christina Crane, born July 25, 1943.

†So popular was Lana Turner among the fan magazine set that in 1949, the readers of *Modern Screen* voted her their number one female favorite—despite the fact that she had no films released that year. In another poll taken the same year, *Quick* named her "the largest seller of movie fan magazines in the business." And on November 27, 1955, on a nationwide television show saluting motion picture periodicals, she received an award from the Dell Publishing Company as "the star who has appeared on the most fan magazine covers."

Of course, columnists like Louella Parsons and Hedda Hopper revelled in the Turner lifestyle. Wrote Miss Parsons in 1952: "Lana was seen today driving onto the MGM lot in her low-slung white Jaguar, upholstered in white leather with a silver monogram on the door—just to make it more effective she was dressed all in white, a dazzling sight for both MGMers and visiting tourists.

"Lana always has a way of attracting attention whenever she appears. It's not so much her beauty as a certain healthy charm and, if you'll pardon me, a sex appeal that she has for every one of the male sex who even looks at her. Moreover, she is a great showwoman, and an actress off the screen as well as on. She knows just what to do to keep her fans interested and alive to her potentialities as a star. More than any actress I know she revives that marvelous showmanship that used to make Hollywood the most exciting city in the world."

While the press continued to supply up-to-the-minute progress reports on all phases of Lana's off-screen doings, it was inevitably the romantic side of her private life that most intrigued the public. Particularly since her name was linked with such industry figures as Victor Mature, Tony Martin, Fernando Lamas, Turhan Bey, Peter Lawford and even Frank Sinatra and Howard Hughes. Although some of these "romances" were studio-inspired, a few were the real thing. In the latter category was a much-publicized idyll with Tyrone Power, and during 1947 Turner and Power were easily the handsomest couple in the movie capital.*

Suddenly, the American Dream turned into a nightmare.

On April 4, 1958, Lana's fourteen-year-old daughter, Cheryl Crane, fatally stabbed her mother's suitor, Johnny Stompanato, when, during a violent quarrel between the couple, she allegedly heard him threaten to beat and disfigure her mother. Like something out of a Lana Turner movie, a lengthy, sensational court trial ensued, with the final verdict justifiable homicide. It was the darkest chapter in the Turner saga; a period in her life the actress will not discuss today.

Professionally, life has been much easier for Lana Turner. There have been good pictures and bad, ups and down, champions and detractors. But through it all she's never been anything less than a Star.

---

*Looking back in 1974, Lana Turner said of Tyrone Power: "He was a beautiful person, possessing not just outer beauty but sensitivity and gentleness . . . .That was a happy and wonderful time, my time with Tyrone."

With Bob Hope, entertaining the troops in Korea

Presenting Red Buttons his Best Supporting Oscar for SAYONARA. *Lana had been nominated that same year for* PEYTON PLACE

A 1938 publicity portrait of Lana and her mother, Mrs. Mildred Turner

Lana and her daughter, Cheryl, in 1945

The threesome at an invitational press preview of MADAME X in 1966

Like most beautiful women whose initial claim to fame rested primarily on their physical attributes, she has often been underrated as an actress. Because she was brought up with a shrewd awareness of what the American public wanted of her, she restricted herself to the lush vehicles that had catapulted her to the top and kept her there. Occasionally breaking away for a *Bad and the Beautiful*, a *Peyton Place* or a *Madame X*, she could surprise her severest critics by being remarkably effective.

Almost all of her directors—from Mervyn LeRoy to Tay Garnett, from Vincente Minnelli to Douglas Sirk—have voiced highest praise for her professionalism and hard-working attitude.

Said John Farrow, her director on 1955's *The Sea Chase*: "She doesn't need much coaching or preparation. There isn't any need for this long Actors Studio type warmup that a lot of young actors and actresses feel they need today. The reason for this is that they have had very little acting training and are trying to compensate for that lack by calling for weeks of rehearsal before the shooting of a movie starts. Lana knows her lines and the character she is supposed to play, and she's ready to go whenever

production begins. There is nothing like a top old pro."

Jerry Wald, who produced *Peyton Place*, once told the press he felt her longtime association with a sweater actually had been a handicap to Lana the actress. "Hollywood doesn't easily accept the fact that a star can have great sex appeal and still be a fine dramatic actress," said Wald. "Academy voters favor the Shirley Booths, the Katharine Hepburns, the Anna Magnanis. These are superbly skilled performers—but they haven't had to live down the reputation of once having been a pin-up queen.

"The movie industry has always thrived on manufactured stars; personalities who are the products of high-voltage publicity campaigns. Quite often these personalities develop into real acting pros, such as Lana, and the very studios which made them colorful and controversial fail to recognize the talent potential they possess."

Perhaps the greatest tribute that has ever been paid Lana Turner is her long hold on the public. As a top box-office attraction, she outlasted all of her peer love goddesses; and in 1966, when *Variety* published its list of all-time top-grossing features and the stars associated with them, Lana ranked seventh among all the female participants.

Her popularity with ticket-buyers has frequently surprised Lana. Several years ago, columnist Sidney Skolsky wrote about a Turner film that, despite its critical lambasting, was cleaning up. Said Lana to Skolsky: "What would I have been with *good* pictures?"

Forty years have passed since Judy Turner was discovered sitting at that soda fountain. Since that oft-recounted moment and Lana's subsequent champagne days at both MGM and Universal, the motion picture business has virtually been reshaped. No area has escaped change—management, talent guilds, labor unions, distribution, exhibition; and, most significantly of all, the films themselves. The Mayers and the Warners have been replaced by blue-jeaned executives; the Garbos and the Gilberts by "character" types turned stars, often talented yet also often undistinguishable from one another. The glamour and romance of yesterday have given way to themes of unexpurgated sex and violence. And the breakup of the studio system has permanently eliminated that carefully executed maneuver known as the creation of a star.

Present-day predilections, of course, have greatly affected the role of woman in films. Today's crop of actresses—with rare exception—no longer carry on a subtle love affair with the public the way the Turners and the Crawfords did. Now, with the best roles being written for men, Hollywood's modern heroines are depicted, more often than not, as whores, psychotics, ax murderesses or sex-starved misfits. Consequently, because of her adamant unwillingness to adapt to the prevailing attitude, Lana Turner's film roles in recent years have been extremely limited. While more and more of her contemporaries have accepted "cameo" film assignments while awaiting that rare suitable larger role, she has refused to settle for anything less than her customary star billing.

Lana's screen work since the demise of the "woman's picture" has consisted of minor and lit-

Signing autographs during a cross-country promotional tour for MADAME X

tle-seen efforts; yet, the nature of the pictures she chose permitted her to retain familiar trappings. Indeed, although one of them—a British-made production called *Persecution*—is the closest she's come to the horrific film school tackled by so many of her veteran sisters of the silver screen, even here she was extravagantly gowned by Berman's of London. ("Forsaking glamour is like forsaking my identity. It's an image I've worked too hard to attain and preserve," she observed.)

While biding her time cinematically, she has kept her name before the public in other areas of the entertainment field. Guest appearances on television, while irregular, have been attention-getters, and a few years ago she became one of the first big film names to enter the medium on a weekly basis. Although her widely touted, multimillion-dollar series, Harold Robbins' *The Survivors*, ultimately proved a costly non-survivor, the mountain of publicity surrounding its birth and its demise made it in its own way as momentous as any of her successes. And the experience was hardly a loss: Lana resurfaced with a clear million dollars for her efforts.

Shrewd investments such as the deal she had on *The Survivors* have made her financially secure for life.* Her decision to keep herself busy, however, resulted in an unexpected triumph.

Early in 1971, producers Lee Guber and Shelley Gross offered her the starring role in a summer stock production of the romantic comedy, *Forty Carats*, which would tour for ten weeks throughout the East. In the long-running show on Broadway, Julie Harris had created the lead part of the forty-year-old woman in love with a twenty-two-year-old man.

Lana made her stage debut in *Forty Carats* on June 8, 1971, in Shady Grove, a Washington, D.C. suburb, surprising disbelievers—including, no doubt, a number of Hollywood glamour girls who had failed in their own stage attempts. Not only did she fulfill a strenuous ten-week tour in which all of the shows were performed "in-the-round," calling for many difficult ramp entrances and exits, but she managed a surprisingly fine performance—no mean feat for a "studio product" who for thirty-five years

---

*Lana Turner's comfortable financial status was realized, oddly enough, at the latter part of her career rather than during her salad days at MGM. She had participation rights in each of the three pictures she made with Ross Hunter, and from *Imitation of Life,* the most successful of these, she is said to have earned $1,750,000. Her cut-of-the-gross contract for the film was set up in the form of a trust fund giving her an income for life.

Until just a few years ago, Lana had a ranch in the Malibu Hills for the breeding of race horses. Several raced in the $100,000 Derby at Hollywood Park, of which Mervyn LeRoy is one of the club's owners. At present she owns only one of these horses—Grey Host, who is three-fourths brother to Kelso and was recently a prize-winner at Santa Anita.

In addition to playing the stock market, she is heavily invested in real estate and has a couple of subdivisions going.

never knew what it was like to act before a live audience—". . . not even at Hollywood High; I wasn't there long enough before I was put into pictures."

Although many other actresses had already offered their versions of the play either on Broadway or in touring companies, the Turner production was redesigned as a showcase for a Hollywood queen and presented the star in over a dozen lavish costume changes. Wherever the play toured, Lana's audiences clamorously endorsed her interpretation. Critic Richard L. Coe described the opening night as "a salute to the reign of Louis B. Mayer and Mervyn LeRoy at Metro," adding: "No fool, Lana. She knows her audience and there they were Tuesday night lining the highway a mile this side of Shady Grove to join the first night of her two-week visit. Came applause time and the house rose as though the Marine Band had gone into 'Hail to the Chief.' It was quite a reception."

The *Forty Carats* tour was another lucrative venture for Lana. In addition to her salary of $17,500 a week, she was accorded the grand manner treatment by the show's producers, who picked up the tab for her personal entourage of hairdresser, makeup man, maid, chauffeur and limousine. Since then, she has had a number of Broadway offers. Lana's first love, however, remains the motion picture medium, and she is optimistic that the industry will soon swing away from violent, promiscuous themes and that scenarists will once again be writing stories for women. One of her pet peeves these days is the great emphasis on nudity in what she refers to as "toilet" movies. "I think men are more intrigued by a little mystery," she says. "Keep 'em guessing just a bit. Even though I wore a tight sweater in *They Won't Forget*, I never took it off."

Just as Hollywood has changed, so have the personal values of its erstwhile sweater girl. Instead of the palatial residences of the past, Lana Turner is presently ensconced in a twenty-story high-rise penthouse apartment in the Century City section of Los Angeles. Very much her own woman these days, she doubts she'll marry again.

During a recent London interview, a young reporter asked about her former husbands. "Look," she said, "I had seven husbands. And why? I wanted it signed, sealed and delivered. Lots of women know lots of men. I married mine. If I met someone now, I don't think I'd do the paperwork again. There's no point. I can't have any more children—I should have had a dozen, not just one*—a relationship has got to be more than just sex for me. Don't misunderstand. I'm still very female. Very. But now I think with my head more than my heart . . . But I'll go to my grave a romantic. Because for me romance is very beautiful; the *most*

beautiful thing."

Of her lifestyle, then and now, she admitted: "When I was a playgirl, honey, I *played*. I was here, there and everywhere living it up. And what's more we had the vitality to see us through the day or night without the aid of either pot or pep pills. I think we were luckier than the kids today.

"Do I miss it all now? Not any more. I don't go to parties because I've had all that in the past. I don't go to big social functions because they're a bore. I'm happy with the few very close friends that I have and I don't need any of that social swing anymore."

Lana's social life these days has been limited indeed—much to the chagrin of the fans who have for years doted on the spectacular style of her public appearances. When her name does crop up on a guest list it is primarily on behalf of charity functions like the recent benefit for Phoenix House, the drug-abuse treatment center in New York. At events such as this, however, she is still followed by strained necks in a crowd, she still creates a sensation making her entrance and she still has that command of the public's interest that only a superstar possesses. It should also added that, in her fifties, she still wears a sweater better than many a starlet half her age.

As one of the best known figures of the World War II pin-up brigade, she has never stopped receiving mail from ex-servicemen who once decorated their foxholes and barracks with her photos. One veteran of the European campaign recalls: "I'm a paunchy, middle-aged businessman now with three children and a nice house in the suburbs, but I was just a green kid during the war. I used to carry Lana's picture in my wallet. It was torn from some movie magazine. I was in a rifle company, and I remember on cold miserable days, especially during the drive through France in 1944–45, taking out her crumpled picture and looking at it in the foxhole with the snow falling down.

"Guys would have favorite pin-ups, like they had best ball clubs, and every time we stopped for a few days somewhere, Lana and Betty Grable and Rita

---

*Cheryl Crane is a graduate of the Cornell Hotel and Restaurant Management School. Of her daughter, Lana comments: "Cheryl is now living with my mother in the San Fernando Valley. It's a nice house and they both have their own floors. My mother, who was just four days short of seventeen when I was born is one hell of a wonderful woman. The three of us are close, with Mother as pivot.

"Although we see a good deal of each other, Cheryl is independent and very happy with her career as general manager of her father's chain of restaurants . . . I call her Miss Executive . . . She has always celebrated her birthday. But recently, when July 25 was approaching and I asked her what she wanted, she said she wasn't having another birthday. She was turning thirty, you see, and was in shock. Well, I was in shock, too. A thirty-year-old daughter! Incredible!

"When two human beings go through a tremendous emotional experience as we did—it either cracks them apart or brings them closer together. Cheryl and I became closer."

In the Sunset Boulevard offices of her Eltee Productions in 1966

Hayworth and some of the others would go up on the wall."

During another war, the sweater sweetheart again found herself the inspiration for GI smiles. In 1967, Lana undertook a three-week good will tour of Vietnam under auspices of the Hollywood Overseas Committee and the U.S.Q. as part of its "Operation Handshake." Instead of boosting morale through

her pin-ups, she did her bit two decades later by talking to the boys in the hospitals and in the fields. Some of the news stories on her trip noted that she paid every penny of her own expenses, including the cost of carloads of film for the soldiers and lipstick for the nurses and WACs. Upon her return, she was presented with an official U.S.O. citation commending her "for patriotic service in providing entertainment to members of the Armed Forces."

Lana considered it "provocative" rather than impertinent when a reporter asked her if her audience of seventeen- to nineteen-year-olds recognized her. "I really wasn't too sure," she said, "because, let's face it—the younger kids didn't even get a chance to stay home and watch the late, late show on TV. But," she added firmly, "the older ones—they knew me, all right!"

Although she remembers with great affection her years under Louis B. Mayer at MGM, Lana has little interest in today's nostalgia craze. Unlike Norma Desmond, the fictional screen queen of *Sunset Boulevard*, this real-life screen queen has retained few mementos of the past. "I never look back, I always look ahead . . . All that interests me is today—and tomorrow."

Occasionally, though, to satisfy her fans she will recall the golden past for them via magazine articles or television interviews. Where once she was portrayed as the Eternal Romantic, writers today depict her as the Supreme Survivor—of changing industry trends; of personal misfortune; of the Hollywood "rat race" and the very system that developed her.

Making a spectacular entrance at a fund-raising benefit in New York City. Her escort is director John Bowab

Since today the registrars of births worldwide probably hold thousands of girls named Lana, one of the questions interviewers most frequently ask is—where did the name originally come from? Her reply: "Mervyn LeRoy said Judy Turner sounded too much like a chorine, so we went through a book of names from A to Z but nothing was right. Then out of a clear sky—I've taken an oath on this—I said, 'How about Lana?' And Mervyn said, 'How would you spell it?' I found out later that it means wool in Spanish, which was kind of cute because of all that sweater jazz, but I didn't know it then. Also, it's a Spanish slang word for money, which is cute, too. Later, I changed it legally."

Lana delights in exploding press agents' myths, such as the story that she wears the famous sweater which shot her to fame at least once during each picture. "It would be a great trick if I could do it. In the first place I couldn't find the sweater if my life depended on it. I got it from the Warner Bros. wardrobe department for the picture, and afterwards I gave it right back. I haven't seen it since. Besides," she laughs, "who cares? It was just a dumb old sweater. But what was in it is still walking around, thank God!"

Not long ago Lana expounded on other related matters:

THE STAR SYSTEM AND THE MGM YEARS

I was dancing at the Trocadero and Ciro's every night and going to Miss MacDonald at the Little Red Schoolhouse at Metro every day. It was a cockeyed situation. There were girls who were prettier, more intelligent, just as talented. Why didn't they make it? It's a question of magic. You have it or you don't, I guess, and the lucky ones have had it. They brought us along slowly. I posed for the dumbest Valentines!

Nowadays, young actresses and actors make one picture and they are billed as stars. Why, when we were at MGM, we worked years before anybody called us stars. I don't consider those years as bondage. I'm very grateful for them. I like to think they gave me a basic foundation.

THE '40s

The '40s were great, but they were also war years, and there was nothing fabulous about that. But we all did what we could, selling bonds, selling kisses or anything we could. What I do remember about the '40s is that we worked damn hard, all of us. But

I myself don't really relate to any particular era.

WORKING WITH CLARK GABLE, HER FAVORITE CO-STAR

Ours was a wonderful, chemical rapport that came over on film. Such a dear man. We were working together on *Somewhere I'll Find You* when his wife Carole Lombard died in that plane crash. Of course, filming stopped. In those days the major studios had compassion for a shocking situation that involved their people. But now it's "Keep shooting, no matter what." Clark and I had a closeness without intimacy. There was a dear loving for him, but never an affair.

THE DISADVANTAGES OF BEING A STAR

Whoever started the idea that we are public property? We give the public performances, glamour and a dream. But we are all human beings and we should have moments that are our own. If I were just an ordinary working girl and someone asked me some of the questions I've been asked, I'd say, "Get lost, Buster!" But I just take a deep breath and try to answer. I resent stupid questions, but I can't do anything about the Lana Turner image. I've lived with it too long.

SEEING HERSELF IN OLD MOVIES ON TV

Seeing myself on the TV screen is like going through an old album, looking at pages of old photographs. Like everyone who does this, it brings back memories and results in mixed emotions. Most of the films had good stories, and I had great co-stars. I always knew Clark was good, but I didn't realize how good until I saw him recently in *Honky Tonk*. Clark *was* Rhett Butler. In fact Clark convinced me he *is* Rhett Butler.

THE MOTION PICTURE BUSINESS TODAY

I do love the business. It has been very good to me. But there are times when I almost want to apologize for the industry. Films used to leave something to the imagination, so moviegoers could do a little work and exercise their emotions. Now it's done for them; they are no longer participants.

And where are the stories for women? Writers are not writing for women anymore, and when you've lost your women audiences, you've had it. Women used to walk out of a theatre saying, "Wasn't that beautiful?" And when they ran the vacuum around the house the next day, they relived the picture. Now they walk out of a nightmare! We all have our own personal problems. Why should we spend very good money to go and see someone else's problems? This is an entertainment business—let's give the public back their dreams!

WHY NO AUTOBIOGRAPHY

The last offer was for $150,000. I told them, "Thank you so much, gentlemen, but the answer is no." Why? Because I'm still living. God has other things in store for me.

RETIREMENT

Retire? Why should I retire? I've still got too many juices working!

Despite the setbacks in her career, despite the unhappy marriages and the tragedies in her private life, Lana Turner has retained that kind of strength and good humor which has consistently won her public support and adoration everywhere. On April 13, 1975, a standing-room-only crowd of 1,200 filled New York's Town Hall to pay tribute to the star. The evening was one of a periodic series devoted to Legendary Ladies of the Screen, and some of the audience had traveled from as far away as London to attend. Lana's predecessors in the series included Bette Davis, Joan Crawford and Rosalind Russell, but it was generally agreed that the reception accorded Hollywood's former sweater girl was the most enthusiastic of them all.

Publicist-host John Springer opened the program quoting a recent magazine article which described the honoree as one of the most exciting women in the world, who lived a life more dramatic than any part she ever played. Springer's introduction was followed by a ninety-minute compilation of film highlights from seventeen of Lana's movies. The clips began with Lana bouncing down that street in *They Won't Forget* and traced her gallery of screen heroines through *Madame X*. All of the footage was fervently received, with perhaps the biggest response going to the scenes from *Ziegfeld Girl* and *The Postman Always Rings Twice*.

After the final clip, Lana's famous car-hysteria scene from *The Bad and the Beautiful*, the veteran actress walked on stage to a standing ovation. Wrote critic John Cuttenden, "Her white dress was cut low, the sleeves sparkling with silver. At fifty-four, she still walks in beauty." Apologizing for her obvious but disarming nervousness, Lana explained, "I haven't had that much experience with wonderful, live people." But one man called out, "Lana, we love you! We're your friends!" And the crowd applauded, shouting its agreement.

In the hour that followed, Lana answered questions submitted in advance by the audience. She thanked Mervyn LeRoy, who first put her under contract and whose guidance during the early stages of her career was invaluable. Credit was also given to director Robert Z. Leonard, who recognized her acting potential and had her role enlarged in the milestone *Ziegfeld Girl*.

There were anecdotes about co-stars Clark Gable and John Garfield and directors Vincente Minnelli and Douglas Sirk; a brief acknowledgment of her love for Tyrone Power; and an up-to-the-minute report on her daughter, Cheryl. Lana also included a tribute to the memory of Judy Garland: "Judy was the greatest . . . correction . . . Judy *is* the greatest!"

Not all of her comments were laudatory. Diatribes were aimed at director Otto Preminger, whose methods of working led her to withdraw from the cast of 1959's *Anatomy of a Murder*, and at those members of the press who have been unkind to her over the years—"I wonder how they sleep at night? Don't they see the vultures they are?"

Later, Lana was asked: if she had a choice, would she relive her life the same way? "Yes," she answered, "because my life is so ordained, so controlled by destiny, fate. Every part of my life was planned for me. How could I change it?"

And what actress would she choose to play her if Hollywood ever put the Lana Turner story on film? The star leaned forward, looked squarely at the audience and replied, "She hasn't been born yet!"

"And Miss Turner may not be mistaken at that," opined Leonard Maltin in *Nostalgia Illustrated*. "As the collection of film clips showed, she was more than just a great beauty. From the start she had great presence, and a fresh spontaneity that matured into genuine talent."

Proper showcases may be few and far between in these male-oriented film days, but Lana Turner is one actress who doesn't have to work hard at keeping her legend alive. As her Town Hall appearance indicated, there are few, young or old, unfamiliar with that special first name that spells glamour, sex appeal and international celebrity. As the *Los Angeles Times'* Charles Champlin wrote a few years ago, "It must be as hard for her as for us to recollect a Hollywood of which Lana Turner was not a part."

Quite possibly the reason the public has never tired of its romance with Lana is because she is their golden link between the old Hollywood and the new. If she has outgrown the role of love goddess to GIs and red-blooded American boys, she still exists as an object lesson. For women, she remains the fantasy creature they identified with in their youth; and for young people she exemplifies the razzle-dazzle style of Hollywood at its peak.

Asked what she would like to be remembered for, Lana Turner answers, "I just want to be remembered as a sensitive woman who tried to do her job, that's all . . . I would like to think that in some small way I have helped preserve the glamour and beauty and mystery of the movie industry."

In February 1976 Lana appeared at a Hollywood photo exhibit honoring great still photography of the past. Here she poses with one of her most glamorous 1943 portraits

Daughter Cheryl was also present at the exhibit

Frank Edwards

LANA

HER FACE

AND FIGURE
THROUGH THE YEARS

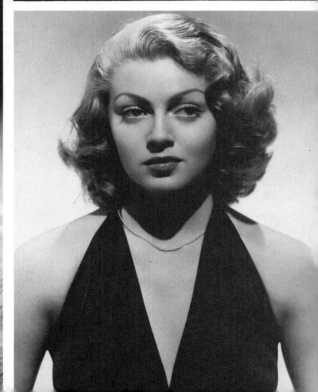

LANA

HER FILMS

A STAR IS BORN

A DAVID O. SELZNICK PRODUCTION FOR UNITED ARTISTS RELEASE
1937

Fredric March and Janet Gaynor, the stars of
A STAR IS BORN, *peer down at a very young
Lana Turner here in one of her earliest Warner
Bros. studio portraits. Sixteen years old and
fresh off a soda fountain stool, Lana worked as
an extra in the Selznick film. Unfortunately,
in this, her very first encounter with moviemaking, the camera never focused on her face!*

CAST

JANET GAYNOR, *Esther Blodgett/later Vicki Lester;* FRED-
RIC MARCH, *Norman Maine;* ADOLPHE MENJOU, *Oliver
Niles;* MAY ROBSON, *Lettie;* ANDY DEVINE, *Danny
McGuire;* LIONEL STANDER, *Libby;* ELIZABETH JENNS,
Anita Regis; EDGAR KENNEDY, *Pop Randall;* OWEN
MOORE, *Casey Burke;* J. C. NUGENT, *Theodore Smythe;*
CLARA BLANDICK, *Aunt Mattie;* A. W. SWEATT, *Esther's
Brother;* PEGGY WOOD, *Miss Phillips;* ADRIAN ROSLEY,
Harris; ARTHUR HOYT, *Ward;* GUINN WILLIAMS, *Posture
Coach;* VINCE BARNETT, *Otto Friedl;* PAUL STANTON,
Academy Awards Speaker; FRANKLIN PANGBORN, *Billy
Moon;* ROBERT EMMET O'CONNOR, *Bartender at Santa
Anita;* OLIN HOWLAND, *Rustic;* IRVING BACON, *Station
Agent;* CLARENCE WILSON, *Justice of the Peace;* JONA-
THAN HALE, *Night Court Judge;* PAT FLAHERTY, *Cuddles;*
DR. LEONARD WALKER, *Orchestra Leader in Hollywood
Bowl;* FRANCIS FORD, KENNETH HOWELL, CHRIS-PIN
MARTIN, *Prisoners;* MARSHALL NEILAN, *Bert;* CHARLES
WILLIAMS, *Asst. Cameraman;* SNOWFLAKE, *Witness;*
CLAUDE KING, DAVID NEWELL, BUD FLANNIGAN (DENNIS
O'KEEFE), *Party Guest Bits;* CAROLE LANDIS, LANA
TURNER, *Extras at Santa Anita Bar.* (Note: Warner Bros.
remade *A Star is Born* in 1954 with JUDY GARLAND as
Esther Blodgett and JAMES MASON as Norman Maine. In
1976, the same studio produced a rock version of the story
with BARBRA STREISAND and KRIS KRISTOFFERSON.

CREDITS

Director, WILLIAM A. WELLMAN; Producer, DAVID O.
SELZNICK; Screenplay, DOROTHY PARKER, ALAN CAMP-
BELL and ROBERT CARSON; From the story by WILLIAM A.
WELLMAN and ROBERT CARSON; Photography (Techni-
color), W. HOWARD GREENE; Set Decorations, LYLE
WHEELER with Associate EDWARD-BOYLE; Sound, OSCAR
LAGERSTROM; Editors, HAL C. KERN and ANSON STEVEN-
SON; Costumes, OMAR KIAM; Music, MAX STEINER; Spe-
cial Effects, JACK COSGROVE; Assistant Director, ERIC
STACEY; Designed in Color by LANSING C. HOLDEN; Run-
ning time, 111 minutes.

NOTES ABOUT THE FILM

In 1936, when he interviewed Lana Turner, Henry
Willson was twenty-one and the youngest vice-president
of a talent agency. "She was no quick sensation," he
recalled. "She worked hard and had a lot of disappointments. Trade paper publisher Billy Wilkerson saw
her at that soda fountain and sent her to the agency
where I worked. Her name was Judy Turner. She came
in all decked out in her aunt's borrowed furs and jewelry. After school she worked in a little lingerie shop on
Hollywood Boulevard for $ 12.50 a week. I'd go to the
principal of Hollywood High to get her excused from

class. Then with her books under my arm we'd make the rounds of the studios. I took her to Paramount but they didn't see anything in her. At Fox they didn't see any spark in her personality. What they should have done was put her in a part that fit her personality until she learned how to act. That's what makes a star."

Willson heard that RKO needed dancers for *New Faces of 1937*. Lana insisted that she could dance and "my boy friend can play the piano for me." The boy friend turned out to be Mickey Rooney. "She was cute and graceful, but she didn't get the part," says Willson. Finally, she did manage to get some work as an extra in David O. Selznick's *A Star Is Born*. She was paid twenty-five dollars for the bit but Selznick later rejected her for a contract.

Coincidentally, the heroine of *A Star Is Born* is a movie-struck farm girl, who goes to Hollywood and starves bravely trying to get work as an extra. Ultimately, she wins her big chance through an accidental meeting with the Peck's Bad Boy of the film colony. After they marry, there is no stopping her rise or his descent, so the husband gallantly bows out via suicide and the wife discovers there is no warmth in the spotlight's glare.

It's one of the most brilliant Hollywood-on-Hollywood films ever made and Janet Gaynor and Fredric March in the leads gave outstanding performances. Although it certainly had its precursors, it is one of the industry's earliest and most astonishing attempts at disrobing before the public. *The New York Times* hit it right on the button when they called *A Star Is Born* "the most accurate mirror ever held before the glittering, tinseled, trivial, generous, cruel and ecstatic world that is Hollywood."

Approximately ninety minutes into the film, there's a sequence that takes place at the bar of the Santa Anita racetrack. Fredric March and Lionel Stander have just engaged in a fight and a huge crowd is milling around them. Among the horde of extras used in this scene is Lana Turner, doing her very first film work. Carole Landis, who was also just beginning her career, is

somewhere in there as well. It's a typical movie mob scene, however; the action is fast and frenetic and neither Turner nor Landis can be easily spotted.

In Lana's case, a man named Mervyn LeRoy—and a sweater—would soon bring her into better focus.★

Arrow points to Lana (back to camera), one of a bunch of extras in the racetrack sequence of A Star Is Born. *Chief protagonists in the scene are Fredric March (face covered, hand to head) and Lionel Stander.*

THEY WON'T FORGET

A FIRST NATIONAL PICTURE FOR WARNER BROS. RELEASE
1937

CAST

CLAUDE RAINS, *Andy Griffin;* GLORIA DICKSON, *Sybil Hale;* EDWARD NORRIS, *Robert Hale;* OTTO KRUGER, *Gleason;* ALLYN JOSLYN, *Bill Brock;* LANA TURNER, *Mary Clay;* LINDA PERRY, *Imogene Mayfield;* ELISHA COOK, JR., *Joe Turner;* CY KENDALL, *Detective Laneart;* CLINTON ROSEMOND, *Tump Redwine;* E. ALYN WARREN, *Carlisle P. Buxton;* ELISABETH RISDON, *Mrs. Hale;* CLIFFORD SOUBIER, *Jim Timberlake;* GRANVILLE BATES, *Detective Pindar;* ANN SHOEMAKER, *Mrs. Mountford;* PAUL EVERTON, *Governor Mountford;* DONALD BRIGGS, *Harmon;* SYBIL HARRIS, *Mrs. Clay;* TREVOR BARDETTE, *Shattuck Clay;* ELLIOTT SULLIVAN, *Luther Clay;* WILMER HINES, *Ransom Clay;* EDDIE ACUFF, *Drugstore Clerk;* FRANK FAYLEN, *Reporter;* LEONARD MUDIE, *Judge Moore;* HARRY DAVENPORT, HARRY BERESFORD, EDWARD McWADE, *Confederate Soldiers;* I. STANFORD JOLLEY, *Courtroom Extra.*

CREDITS

Producer and Director, MERVYN LEROY; Screenplay, ROBERT ROSSEN and ABEN KANDEL; From the novel *Death in the Deep South* by WARD GREENE; Photography, ARTHUR EDESON; Art Direction, ROBERT HAAS; Editor, THOMAS RICHARDS; Gowns, MISS MACKENZIE; Music and Arrangements, ADOLPH DEUTSCH; Musical Director, LEO F. FORBSTEIN; Running time, 95 minutes.

NOTES ABOUT THE FILM

In 1937, Mervyn LeRoy and Warner Bros. hurled at the screen a stick of cinematic dynamite in the shape of one of one of the most scorching indictments against prejudice and political corruption ever to emerge from Hollywood. It was titled *They Won't Forget.* This stirring and uncompromising drama was selected by the National Board of Review as one of the ten best pictures of the year. Howard Barnes in the *New York Herald Tribune* described it as "a work of art," and *Life* added it to the "meagre handful of U.S. cinema classics."

Despite the critical acclaim at the time of its release, *They Won't Forget* is ironically best remembered today for being the picture that launched the career of Lana Turner and made the term Sweater Girl an American idiom. This was the film in which Lana, then under personal contract to producer-director LeRoy, made her "official" screen debut. Here she performed not as an "extra" player (as in *A Star is Born*), but in a small but pivotal featured role. Among the cast members, she is billed sixth although her name does not appear on the screen until the final roll of credits at the end of the film.

They Won't Forget's inception as a motion picture dates back to a Ward Greene novel called *Death in the Deep South.* In 1915, Greene was a reporter covering

With Edward Norris

With Linda Perry

the Leo Frank murder case for the Atlanta *Journal*. A northern Jew had been convicted of killing a boy. After reviewing the case's circumstantial evidence, Georgia's Governor granted the condemned man a reprieve. But Southern prejudice against Northerners fired mob frenzy to lynching. Later, the man's innocence was established. The tragedy unnerved Greene and remained in his thoughts for so long a time that he decided to write a book on a similar theme. In 1936, he hired a room at New York's Waldorf-Astoria hotel and wrote his novel in three weeks. Warner Bros. bought the film rights and turned the property over to Mervyn LeRoy, who had among his credits, *I Am a Fugitive from a Chain Gang*, one of the most vital social documents ever filmed.

Principal photography on *They Won't Forget* began on March 6, 1937 under the working title *The Deep South*. The scenario by Robert Rossen and Aben Kandel

As the beautiful but ill-fated Mary Clay

followed, more or less faithfully, the Greene novel: A young northerner, Robert Hale, is the new teacher of a business college class of young women in a small Southern town. One of his attractive pupils, Mary Clay, is found murdered in the school building on a holiday afternoon when Hale is known to have been in his classroom. A Negro janitor, Tump Redwine, also is in the building at the time of the slaying.

Andy Griffin is then introduced—a politically ambitious district attorney, eager for a break that will thrust him into the spotlight of publicity. Griffin sees in the murder of Mary Clay the opportunity he craves. But for his desire for higher office, it is clear that he would have tried to fasten the killing on the janitor. He feels now, however, he must use something more likely to arouse popular feeling.

Through Bill Brock, a newspaper man, he learns that Mary Clay was fond of her teacher, Hale. In Hale, Griffin sees a likely victim, a newcomer with no influential friends in the community to help him or be displeased by his prosecution. He begins to investigate Hale's movements, is able to establish that the teacher was in the school building when the murder was done, later that there is a bloodstain on his coat. This stain, Hale insists, resulted when a barber cut him while shaving.

Feeling in the city runs high against Hale, mounts swiftly as he is indicted, then put on trial. The case stirs up so much attention that a New York newspaper, championing Hale's cause sends both a detective, Laneart, and a smart lawyer, Gleason, to take a hand. This interference only lifts the feeling against Hale to a higher pitch.

Finally, despite the fact that the case against the accused is flimsy, that the barber who cut him obviously lies on the stand for fear of his townsmen's wrath if he testifies for the accused, Hale is convicted and sentenced to death. The Governor, appealed to by Hale's loyal wife, braves public opinion and commutes the sentence to life imprisonment. But while Hale is being taken to prison, a furious mob led by Mary Clay's three brothers halts the train and lynches him. The picture ends with Brock, the reporter, saying to the D.A., "You know, Andy, now that it's all over, I wonder if Hale really did it," and Griffin replies, "I wonder, too!"

In *They Won't Forget*, Lana Turner is the beautiful, ill-fated Mary Clay. Her sole costume in the film consists of a tight-fitting wool sweater, an equally tight skirt and a pair of dangerously high spiked heels. A saucy beret completes the outfit, and from the first moment she appears—sexy, dimpled and as fresh as clover—she is utterly irresistible. ("Like a flower, she was . . ." is the way a cast member later described her.)

A popular notion has long existed that Lana's appearance in this film consists of a single, non-speaking trot across the screen, and nothing more. On the contrary, a viewing of *They Won't Forget* today reveals that she has as many as eighteen lines of dialogue and fairly dominates the film's first twelve minutes until her character is murdered. She is first seen in a classroom; then the action shifts to a scene at a drugstore soda fountain, quickly followed by a long, seventy-five-foot tracking shot as the camera pursues her through the crowded streets where a parade is in progress. Finally, she works her way back to the school and into an empty classroom to pick up her vanity case ("I don't feel dressed without my lipstick," Mary proclaims earlier in the film). Her murder is never shown but she has a striking close-up as she stands at her desk and her face responds with instinctive fear to the ominous footsteps

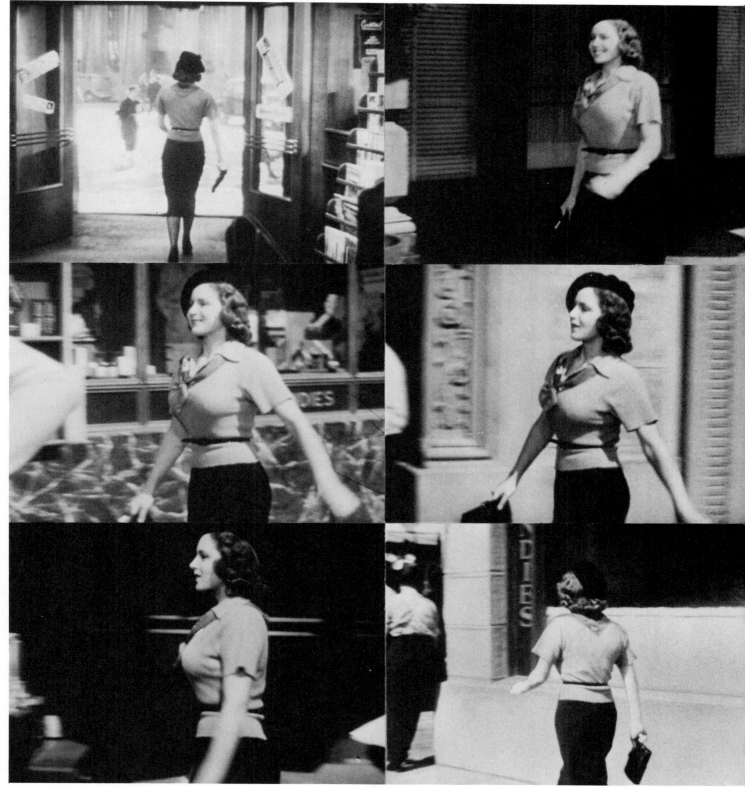

Frame enlargements of Lana's famous walk across the screen in THEY WON'T FORGET

in the corridor. With split-second timing, her image lap-dissolves into an explosive burst of muskets at the Memorial Day celebration. Through this clever bit of symbolism the audience is told that she has met her untimely end.

Mervyn LeRoy recalls it was his idea that Lana be garbed in a sweater for her role. "First of all," he says, "sweaters and schoolgirls are almost synonymous. It was very important that the girl in our story have what they call 'flesh impact.' She had to *make* it look like it was a

Studying the script on the set

Cameraman Wesley Anderson shoots some test closeups of Lana

Posing with her first film contract

With director Mervyn LeRoy

Between scenes on an outdoor set

PICTURE IN THE DEEP SOUTH
NAME LANA TURNER
CHARACTER MARY CLAY
WARDROBE CHANGE #1
SET WORN IN {INT. CLASSROOM
{INT. DRUG STORE
SCENES EXT. PARADE
EXT. BUXTON BLDG
DATE TESTED FEB. 19—'37
CAMERAMAN HICKOX

In this rare wardrobe test shot, Lana is wearing a costume that was later rejected in favor of the much sexier sweater and skirt eventually used in the film

sex murder. You'll notice we never used the word 'rape' in the screenplay. We couldn't say things like that in those days. I figured that a tight sweater on a beautiful young girl would convey to the audience everything we couldn't say outright.''

LeRoy was right. In the now famous scene where Mary Clay hurriedly walks through the streets of the Southern town, cinematographer Arthur Edeson's camera catches Lana—fore and aft—from virtually every angle. Smiling broadly as she walks, almost flaunting her youth and beauty, this moment in the film better than any other epitomizes that magic combination of childlike innocence and knowing sexuality projected so well by the young Lana Turner. With a chin-lifted, high-heeled, sweater-straining strut, she literally bounces across the

screen. This depiction of sexual suggestion generated many a male whistle in 1937 and, not until sixteen years later—with Marilyn Monroe in *Niagara*—did another screen walk elicit as much audience enthusiasm. Says director LeRoy: ''When Lana walked down the street, her bosom seemed to move in a rhythm all its own. Later, when I added the musical score to the picture, I made sure that the composer emphasized that rhythm with his music. During the parade scene, the band was playing *Dixie* and it worked out quite well.''

It was also LeRoy's decision to use a cast comprised largely of relative unknowns. With the exception of Claude Rains (superb, as the district attorney) and Otto Kruger, major roles in *They Won't Forget* were held by little-known players: Gloria Dickson came from a

Now take a story so great it touches every human life, give it to the director who has made the most powerful pictures in Hollywood history, bring it to life with actors who are the people they're playing – and you have one of the world's great pictures! – YOU HAVE

"THEY WON'T FORGET"

EDWARD NORRIS
Socialite, traveler, newspaperman . . . combines good looks, personality, charm, great ability.

GLORIA DICKSON
Blonde acting prodigy . . . discovered in Pasadena . . . rocketing to stardom in one picture!

LANA TURNER
16 years old . . . discovered in Hollywood High school . . . signed to live role of high school girl!

with **CLAUDE RAINS**
Otto Kruger

A MERVYN LEROY PROD'N

A First National Picture Presented by Warner Bros.

Produced by the man who gave you 'Public Enemy', 'I Am A Fugitive', 'Anthony Adverse'!

LANA TURNER
TALK AND DIE!
UNTIL NOW THEIR LIPS WERE FROZEN WITH FEAR!

THEY WON'T FORGET
with CLAUDE RAINS OTTO KRUGER

An original 1937 ad for THEY WON'T FORGET. When the picture was reissued in 1956, Lana was billed as the star of the film

Federal Theatre Project in Los Angeles; Allyn Joslyn from the New York stage production of *Boy Meets Girl;* Edward Norris had been in Hollywood for four years, most of which time he spent under contract to Metro without getting anywhere. All of these players scored decisively in a uniformly excellent cast which included Elisha Cook, Jr., Clinton Rosemond, Elizabeth Risdon, Trevor Bardette, Frank Faylen and many others.

In lauding *They Won't Forget* and its director, the fine work of its cast did not go unnoticed by the critics. "The girl in the sweater" (whose name several reviewers had trouble remembering) drew considerable comment. In the New York *Daily Mirror*, Kenneth McCaleb wrote, almost prophetically: ". . . a girl named Lana Turner exits from the screen much too early to suit me; I want to see more of her and have no doubt that I shall,

for she looks to me like a natural." And *The Hollywood Reporter* noted: "Short in playing time is the role of the murdered schoolgirl, but as played by Lana Turner it is worthy of more than passing note. This young lady has vivid beauty, personality and charm." ★

THE GREAT GARRICK

A WARNER BROS. PICTURE

1937

CAST

BRIAN AHERNE, *David Garrick*; OLIVIA DE HAVILLAND, *Germaine*; EDWARD EVERETT HORTON, *Tubby*; MELVILLE COOPER, *M. Picard*; LIONEL ATWILL, *Beaumarchais*; LUIS ALBERNI, *Basset*; LANA TURNER, *Auber*; MARIE WILSON, *Nicolle*; LINDA PERRY, *Molee*; FRITZ LEIBER, *Horatio*; ETIENNE GIRARDOT, *Jean Cabot*; DOROTHY TREE, *Mme. Moreau*; CRAIG REYNOLDS, *M. Janin*; PAUL EVERTON, *Innkeeper of Adam and Eve*; TREVOR BARDETTE, *M. Noverre*; MILTON OWEN, *Thierre*; ALBERT VAN DEKKER, *LeBrun*; CHESTER CLUTE, *M. Moreau*; HARRY DAVENPORT, *Innkeeper of Turk's Head*; JACK NORTON, *Drunken Gentleman*; FRITZ LEIBER, JR., *Fortenbras*; CORBET MORRIS, *Osric*. (Note: HENRY O'NEILL, frequently credited for this film, did work in the picture but his role as Sir Joshua Reynolds was deleted from the final print.)

With Linda Perry and Marie Wilson

With Edward Everett Horton, Brian Aherne, Marie Wilson and Linda Perry

With Edward Everett Horton, Marie Wilson, Melville Cooper and Linda Perry

CREDITS

Director, JAMES WHALE; Personally Supervised by MERVYN LeROY; Screenplay, ERNST VAJDA (Based on Vajda's Story *Ladies and Gentlemen*); Photography, ERNEST HALLER; Art Direction, ANTON GROT; Sound, C. A. RIGGS; Editor, WARREN LOW; *Costumes*, MILO ANDERSON; *Makeup*, PERC WESTMORE; Music and Arrangements, ADOLPH DEUTSCH; Musical Director, LEO F. FORBSTEIN; Assistant to Mr. LeRoy, WILLIAM CANNON; Assistant Director, SHERRY SHOURDS; Running time, 89 minutes.

NOTES ABOUT THE FILM

In *The Great Garrick*, her second film at Warners, Lana's Sweater Girl charms were hidden—almost—under a wealth of wigs and costumes and beauty patches circa 1750. Mervyn LeRoy produced this farcical period piece as his fourth independent production at the studio.

Based upon a legendary exploit of David Garrick, the great English actor, the screenplay was the work of the Hungarian scenarist, Ernst Vajda. Instead of presenting Garrick in a straight biographical film record, Vajda's scenario offered an amusing series of circumstances that "might have happened." At the start of the film, a rumor has reached the ears of the members of the Comedie Française that the English actor had boasted in his farewell speech at the Theatre Royal in Drury Lane, that he was going to Paris to teach the Frenchmen how to act.

The French players, thinking that Garrick has insulted them, decide to teach him a lesson. They take over an inn where Garrick must stop on his way to Paris, and by assuming the parts of landlord, servants and guests, do their best to scare him out of his wits. But Garrick is warned of the plot in advance, turns the tables on his tormentors, and in doing so finds romance with a beautiful stranger.

Although its sophisticated concept was clearly not designed for the masses, *The Great Garrick* was richly produced, very well performed and the comedy was reasonably amusing. Brian Aherne contributed a bravura portrayal of the eighteenth-century actor in his younger days and Olivia de Havilland made a charming heroine.

Largely relegated to background action, Lana was Auber, a cute-as-a-button member of the Comedie Française, who assumes the disguise of a tavern maid as her part of the plot against Garrick. Although her on-screen footage was greater than in *They Won't Forget*, Lana's impact in this one was decidedly less showy. The script, for instance, limited her to only three lines of dialogue and an excessive amount of giggling and squealing in the best tradition of Marie Wilson (who also happened to be in the cast). But the company she was in was the very best—James Whale directing, Ernest Haller on the camera, Milo Anderson for costuming—and she was learning the business. ★

With Craig Reynolds

THE ADVENTURES OF MARCO POLO

A SAMUEL GOLDWYN PRODUCTION FOR UNITED ARTISTS RELEASE

1938

CAST

GARY COOPER, *Marco Polo;* SIGRID GURIE, *Princess Kukachin;* BASIL RATHBONE, *Ahmed;* ERNEST TRUEX, *Binguccio;* ALAN HALE, *Kaidu;* GEORGE BARBIER, *Kublai Khan;* BINNIE BARNES, *Nazama;* LANA TURNER, *Nazama's Maid;* STANLEY FIELDS, *Bayan;* HAROLD HUBER, *Toctai;* H. B. WARNER, *Chen Tsu;* EUGENE HOO, *Chen Tsu's Son;* HELEN QUAN, *Chen Tsu's Daughter;* SOO YONG, *Chen Tsu's Wife;* MRS. NG, *Chen Tsu's Mother;* LOTUS LIU, *Visahka;* FERDINAND GOTTSCHALK, *Persian Ambassador;* HENRY KOLKER, *Nicolo Polo;* HALE HAMILTON, *Maffeo Polo;* ROBERT GREIG, *Chamberlain;* GRANVILLE BATES, REGINALD BARLOW, THEODORE VON ELTZ, *Venetian Businessmen;* DIANE TOY, *Kaidu Entertainer;* HARRY KERUA, *Kaidu Guard;* GRETA GRANSTEDT, *Kaidu Maid;* WARD BOND, *Mongol Guard;* JASON ROBARDS, *Messenger;* HARRY CORDING, DICK RICH, JOE WOODY, LEO FIELDING, *Kaidu Officers.*

CREDITS

Director, ARCHIE MAYO; Producer, SAMUEL GOLDWYN; Associate Producer, GEORGE HAIGHT; Screenplay, ROBERT E. SHERWOOD; From the story by N. A. POGSON; Photography, RUDOLPH MATE; Art Direction, RICHARD DAY; Set Decorations, JULIA HERON; Musical Director, ALFRED NEWMAN; Sound, OSCAR LAGERSTROM; Editor, FRED ALLEN; Costumes, OMAR KIAM; Assistant Director, WALTER MAYO; Special Effects, JAMES BASEVI; Running time, 104 minutes.

NOTES ABOUT THE FILM

"Sam Goldwyn telephoned one morning," recalls Mervyn LeRoy, "to tell me he had a good part for Lana in his next film, *The Adventures of Marco Polo.* She was free at the moment and I thought the experience working in a large-scale production would be good for her, so I sent her over to see him."

Goldwyn had just attended a screening of *They Won't Forget* and was captivated by Lana's youthful beauty. The impression she left was apparently strong enough to make him forget his entire stable of gorgeous Goldwyn Girls, any one of whom could easily have filled the role he had in mind.

A loan-out deal for Lana's services was then arranged and she joined the cast of this very ambitious Goldwyn production which, the producer announced, would be approached as a "thirteenth-century fantasy, replete with humor, romance and spectacle." Goldwyn gave the picture a ranking box-office star in the popular Gary Cooper and assigned to the script Robert E. Sherwood, whose treatment was on the broad side with the

emphasis, except for a rattling good climax, more on comedy than on action.

The story unfolds as Marco Polo, in company with his trusted bookkeeper, Binguccio, leaves Venice for China to negotiate trade agreements between the two nations. They go through storms, shipwrecks and much hardship until, bedraggled, they finally arrive in Pekin, their destination. During the course of the story, Marco discovers, in the order named, the wonders of a stringy substance called "spaghett," a mysterious exploding powder and the beautiful daughter of the Kublai Khan.

He also meets Ahmed, the Khan's villainous counselor, who contrives to have Marco sent as a spy to the

With Alan Hale

enemy camp of Lord Kaidu. With Marco gone, Ahmed overthrows the Khan and takes over his powers. Marco, however, gains the friendship of Kaidu and the support of his army in saving the throne of Kublai Khan from Ahmed.

The climax is well worth waiting for: Marco rushing into the palace in time to stop the wedding ceremony between Ahmed and the Princess; Ahmed falling into a pit of hungry lions; and Marco restoring peace and winning the Princess.

Lana's role consisted of two brief scenes neither of which, unfortunately, were with the picture's star, Gary

Cooper. She comes on midway into the film when Lord Kaidu sees in Marco a chance for release from his marital slavery, and orders him to keep his wife amused, so that he might carry on with her beautiful handmaiden The latter part is the role that Goldwyn assigned to Lana and although the film boasted "a cast of thousands," she luckily was not buried among the crowds. Her two scenes are played within the confines of a tent as she vamps Kaidu, played by Alan Hale. Done up as an appetizing Oriental siren, she has four lines of dialogue and a couple of provocative closeups before Hale's screen wife, Binnie Barnes, invades their love nest and breaks up the party.

Although critics were divided on Goldwyn's treatment of *Marco Polo*, it did well enough at the box office to warrant a national reissue seven years later. When it reached theatres for the second time, in October 1945, Lana was by then a household name and the ads for the reissue were rigged to make it appear that she was Cooper's co-star. Originally, the honor fell to lovely Sigrid Gurie (the film's Princess), a Goldwyn "discovery" that fizzled out. ★

With Alan Hale

With Binnie Barnes and Alan Hale

LOVE FINDS ANDY HARDY

A METRO·GOLDWYN·MAYER PICTURE

1938

A publicity photo with cast members Ann Rutherford, Judy Garland, Douglas McPhail, Lana, Cecilia Parker, Betty Ross Clarke, Lewis Stone, Fay Holden and Mickey Rooney. (All of McPhail's footage in the film later wound up on the cutting room floor)

CAST

LEWIS STONE, *Judge James Hardy*; MICKEY ROONEY, *Andrew Hardy*; JUDY GARLAND, *Betsy Booth*; CECILIA PARKER, *Marian Hardy*; FAY HOLDEN, *Mrs. Hardy*; LANA TURNER, *Cynthia Potter*; ANN RUTHERFORD, *Polly Benedict*; MARY HOWARD, *Mrs. Tompkins*; GENE REYNOLDS, *Jimmy MacMahon*; DON CASTLE, *Dennis Hunt*; BETTY ROSS CLARKE, *Aunt Milly*; MARIE BLAKE, *Augusta*; GEORGE BREAKSTON, *"Beezy"*; RAYMOND HATTON, *Peter Dugan*; FRANK DARIEN, *Bill Collector*.

CREDITS

Director, GEORGE B. SEITZ; Producer, CAREY WILSON (Uncredited); Screenplay, WILLIAM LUDWIG; From the Stories by VIVIEN R. BRETHERTON; Based on the Characters Created by AURANIA ROUVEROL; Photography, LESTER WHITE; Art Direction, CEDRIC GIBBONS with STAN ROGERS and EDWIN B. WILLIS; Sound, DOUGLAS SHEARER; Wardrobe, JEANNE; Editor, BEN LEWIS; Musical Score, DAVID SNELL; Vocal Arrangement, ROGER EDENS; Songs: "Meet the Beat of My Heart," "It Never Rains But What It Pours," Words and Music by MACK GORDON and HARRY REVEL; "In Between," Words and Music by ROGER EDENS; Running time, 91 minutes.

NOTES ABOUT THE FILM

When MGM released *A Family Affair* in 1937, there was little thought that the studio had just launched a series that would ultimately earn millions of dollars at the box office. Based on characters created for a minor Broadway play called *Skidding*, the plot concerned the trials and tribulations of the Hardys, a one hundred percent American family residing in the mythical midwestern town of Carvel. The charm and unpretentiousness of *A Family Affair* so completely captured public approval that the studio quickly spun out a series of Hardy films that helped make Mickey Rooney—as Andy Hardy, the son—a household name.

Among the vast legions of Hardy enthusiasts was William Ludwig, a young New York lawyer, who had moved west on the advice of his physician. Through friends, he got a job at MGM in the junior writing department, did some copy reading and submitted synopses and rough treatments, all for thirty-five dollars a week. He saw a Hardy Family picture, liked the theme, got to work and delivered a lot of original ideas around a Vivien Bretherton story the studio owned. Three weeks later, he submitted a final screenplay.

The film that resulted was *Love Finds Andy Hardy*, the fourth and many feel, the best, in the popular series. It was also the film that began Lana Turner's long tenure as a contract player at MGM. When Mervyn LeRoy moved over from Warners to the home of Leo the Lion, he took with him Lana and Fernand Gravet, both of whom he had under personal contract. They arrived at the studio just as *Love Finds Andy Hardy* was being cast.

One of the characters in the screenplay was Cynthia Potter, the erratic, feather-brained vamp of Carvel High. More than 200 girls were interviewed for the part, but it was Lana's test that eventually won her the role. Cynthia, as described in the script, is the type of girl who won't swim because it would wet her hair—and "special hair like mine is a responsibility." She doesn't like tennis —it gives big muscles. What she does like to do is kiss —and with great frequency. So often, in fact, that it leaves poor Andy questioning his masculinity. In frustration, he eventually asks of his sympathetic, knowing father: "D'ya think there's anything wrong with a guy that don't want a girl to kiss him all the time?"

As the story unfolds, Andy is buying a car without his dad's knowledge and he needs eight dollars to pay the final installment. So when Polly, his girl, goes away for the holidays Andy makes a deal to squire an absentee pal's girl, Cynthia, to the Christmas Eve dance for the required eight dollars. Things get sticky when Polly returns unexpectedly, finds that Andy has now fallen for Cynthia and breaks off with him. Front and center into the plot comes Betsy Booth, the little girl next door, to help Andy through his troubles. She contrives to get him to take her to the big dance and is the hit of the show with her singing (Garland, at her very best, sang three numbers in the film). On the next day, Betsy reconciles Andy and Polly and happiness is restored in time for Christmas celebration.

Although the character "Cynthia Potter" never reappeared in any of the 12 remaining Hardy Family films, there were occasional attempts to resuscitate her. In *Andy Hardy Meets Debutante* (1940), she's pictured on the cover of the school newspaper as "the most beautiful girl in Carvel." Five years later, in *Love Laughs at Andy Hardy*, her photo popped up once more, enshrined in Andy's room amidst an army of past loves. In each instance, then-current studio portraits of Lana were used to depict Cynthia so that an effective timespan was achieved.

In 1958, MGM released *Andy Hardy Comes Home* as an epilogue of sorts in which the now middle-aged Andy daydreams about the women in his youth. In it, two complete Cynthia sequences from *Love Finds Andy Hardy* were utilized as flashbacks. ★

With Mickey Rooney

With Mickey Rooney

With Mickey Rooney

With Judy Garland and Mickey Rooney

THE CHASER

A METRO·GOLDWYN·MAYER PICTURE
1938

A 1938 portrait of Lana taken during the making of THE CHASER

NOTES ABOUT THE FILM

In 1938, when *The Chaser* was released, the ads for the film proclaimed: "Watch Out for a Gorgeous Girl!" The lady in question was Ann Morriss, a young actress making her screen debut as the film's leading lady, and for whom MGM had high hopes. But for movie buffs viewing *The Chaser* today in its not-too-frequent television showings the "Watch Out for a Gorgeous Girl" slogan offers connotations of another sort since Lana Turner appears in the film, unbilled, for a few brief seconds.

Seldom alluded to in her studio biographies or press releases issued after mid-1938, *The Chaser* was Lana's second film under her new MGM contract. When the picture completed its quickie production schedule on June 29, 1938, her name was listed eleventh in the

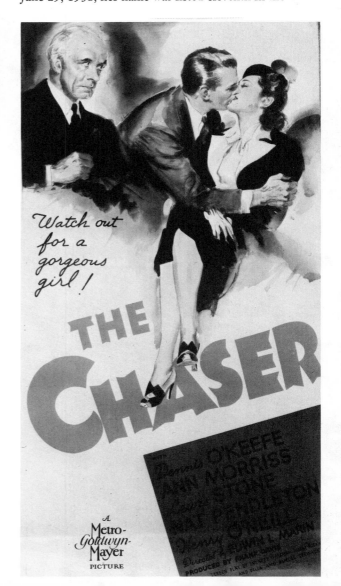

CAST

DENNIS O'KEEFE, *Thomas Z. Brandon;* ANN MORRISS, *Dorothy Mason;* LEWIS STONE, *Dr. Prescott;* NAT PENDLETON, *"Floppy" Phil;* HENRY O'NEILL, *Calhoun;* RUTH GILLETTE, *Mrs. Olson;* JOHN QUALEN, *Lars;* ROBERT EMMETT KEANE, *Simon Kelly;* JACK MULHALL, *Joe;* IRVING BACON, *Harvey;* PIERRE WATKIN, *Mr. Beaumont;* BARBARA BEDFORD, *Brandon's Secretary;* EDDIE ACUFF, *Photographer;* SELMER JACKSON, *Judge;* BARBARA PEPPER, *Mabel;* LANA TURNER, *Miss Rutherford.*

CREDITS

Director, EDWIN L. MARIN; Producer, FRANK DAVIS; Screenplay, EVERETT FREEMAN, HARRY RUSKIN and BELLA and SAM SPEWACK; From an Original Story by CHANDLER SPRAGUE and HOWARD EMMETT ROGERS; Photography, CHARLES LAWTON, JR.; Art Direction, CEDRIC GIBBONS with RANDALL DUELL and EDWIN B. WILLIS; Wardrobe, DOLLY TREE; Assistant Director, RICHARD GREEN; Editor, GEORGE BOEMLER; Running time, 75 minutes.

With Dennis O'Keefe in a scene that was cut from the film

official supporting cast as "Miss Rutherford, a divorcee." The role she played consisted of one brief but effective scene as a client of lawyer Dennis O'Keefe.

By the time the film reached movie houses (it was processed, edited and rushed into theatres less than two months after shooting had been completed), Lana's one big scene was gone from *The Chaser.* In tightening the film's pace, Miss Rutherford, an extraneous character to begin with, wound up on the cutting room floor. Consequently, Lana's screen billing was removed.

Filmed just five years earlier as *The Nuisance* with Lee Tracy and Madge Evans, *The Chaser* was an exposé of ambulance chasers who plan fake damage cases and the unscrupulous methods resorted to by big corporations in order to track them down. The hero, Thomas Brandon, is a young ambulance-chasing lawyer who determines to have vengeance, as well as profit, from the traction company responsible for his first defeat at the bar. Calhoun, the traction company lawyer, plants pretty

Dorothy Mason at the scene of a streetcar wreck with instructions to get the goods on Brandon. Which she does, finally, then promptly falls in love with him and marries him overnight so she can't testify against her husband. When Dorothy is put in jail for perjury, Brandon uses some unscrupulous methods of his own to spring her before the final fade-out clinch.

Early in the film, as Dennis O'Keefe enters his office and greets his secretary, there is a clear view of the clients awaiting appointments. One of them—the most conspicuous, it should be added—is Lana. Garbed in the outfit illustrated in the above photo, her legs crossed provocatively as she reads a magazine, Lana never gets to keep her appointment with O'Keefe since her ensuing footage was cut. But a now-you-see-her, now-you-don't shot of her still remains in the final film. If your local late-late show ever programs *The Chaser*, be advised to "Watch Out for a Gorgeous Girl." In this instance the reference is *not* to leading lady Ann Morriss. ★

RICH MAN, POOR GIRL

A METRO·GOLDWYN·MAYER PICTURE
1938

CAST

ROBERT YOUNG, *Bill Harrison;* LEW AYRES, *Henry Thayer;* RUTH HUSSEY, *Joan Thayer;* LANA TURNER, *Helen Thayer;* RITA JOHNSON, *Sally Harrison;* DON CASTLE, *Frank;* GUY KIBBEE, *Pa.;* SARAH PADDEN, *Ma;* GORDON JONES, *Tom Grogan;* VIRGINIA GREY, *Selma;* MARIE BLAKE, *Mrs. Gussler.*

CREDITS

Director, REINHOLD SCHUNZEL; Producer, EDWARD CHODOROV; Screenplay, JOSEPH A. FIELDS and JEROME CHODOROV; Based on the Play *White Collars* by EDITH ELLIS; Story, EDGAR FRANKLIN; Photography, RAY JUNE; Art Direction, CEDRIC GIBBONS with GABRIEL SCOGNAMILLO and EDWIN B. WILLIS; Sound, DOUGLAS SHEARER; Musical Score, DR. WILLIAM AXT; Wardrobe, DOLLY TREE; Editor, FRANK E. HULL; Running time, 72 minutes.

NOTES ABOUT THE FILM

Rich Man, Poor Girl, based on the play *White Collars,* was an amusing, if unpretentious, satire on socialism centering around a screwy, *You Can't Take It with You*-type family. An earlier version, filmed in 1929 under the title *The Idle Rich,* was one of William DeMille's few directorial efforts in talking pictures and had Conrad Nagel, Leila Hyams and Bessie Love in the leads.

The Joseph A. Fields and Jerome Chodorov screenplay for the 1938 remake surrounded the original boy-meets-girl plot with subtle digs at both the upper and middle classes. Robert Young played a rich young man in love with his secretary, the oldest daughter in a

With Gordon Jones, Don Castle and Robert Young

With Guy Kibbee, Sarah Padden, Robert Young, Lew Ayres, Rita Johnson, Ruth Hussey and Don Castle

With Lew Ayres

large, poor family. Before accepting his proposal, she wants to make sure he won't mind her screwy relatives, members of the poor but proud white-collar class. To prove that he is really one of them, Mr. Young moves in to share their poverty and toil. Before the picture ends, the girl's family has won the rich hero over to the bourgeoisie, and in the process they learn a few facts of life themselves. One is that money is nice to have.

In the role of the heroine's ambitious jitterbug sister, Lana had her best featured spot to date. She did a rhumba in one scene, paraded around in a scanty slip in another and tossed off wisecracks like: "Nothing but a fire will help that parlor" and "Love is wonderful but it can't survive seven people for one bathtub." *Variety* called her "a promising youngster" and Metro, ever aware of the popularity of their current family series, billed her in the ads as "the 'kissing bug' of Andy Hardy."

Rich Man, Poor Girl had a tight, four-week shooting schedule and began production under the title *It's Now or Never.* ★

A first meeting for future co-stars Clark Gable and Lana Turner as Gable visits director Reinhold Schunzel on the set of RICH MAN, POOR GIRL

DRAMATIC SCHOOL

A METRO·GOLDWYN·MAYER PICTURE

1938

With Jean Chatburn, Ann Rutherford, Dorothy Granger and Virginia Grey

CAST

LUISE RAINER, *Louise Mauban;* PAULETTE GODDARD, *Nana;* ALAN MARSHAL, *Andre D'Abbencourt;* LANA TURNER, *Mado;* ANTHONY ALLAN (JOHN HUBBARD), *Fleury;* HENRY STEPHENSON, *Pasquel, Sr.;* GENEVIEVE TOBIN, *Gina Bertier;* GALE SONDERGAARD, *Madame Therese Charlot;* MELVILLE COOPER, *Boulin;* ERIK RHODES, *Georges Mounier;* VIRGINIA GREY, *Simone;* ANN RUTHERFORD, *Yvonne;* HANS CONRIED, *Ramy;* RAND BROOKS, *Pasquel, Jr.;* JEAN CHATBURN, *Mimi;* MARIE BLAKE, *Annette;* CECILIA C. CALLEJO, *La Brasiliana;* MARGARET DUMONT, *Pantomimic Teacher;* FRANK PUGLIA, *Alphonse;* DOROTHY GRANGER, *Fat Girl;* ESTHER DALE, *Forewoman in Factory;* BARBARA WEEKS, BERYL WALLACE, ONA MUNSON, *Girl Students;* DICK HAYMES, EDWARD ARNOLD, JR., JOHN SHELTON, RICK VALLIN, *Boy Students;* MINERVA URECAL, *Rose (Boulin's Secretary);* FLORENCE LAKE, *Factory Worker.*

CREDITS

Director, ROBERT B. SINCLAIR; Producer, MERVYN LEROY; Screenplay, ERNST VAJDA and MARY McCALL, JR.; From the Hungarian Play *School of Drama* by HANS SZEKELY and ZOLTAN EGYED; Art Direction, CEDRIC GIBBONS with GABRIEL SCOGNAMILLO; Set Decorations, EDWIN B. WILLIS; Photography, WILLIAM DANIELS; Sound, DOUGLAS SHEARER; Music, FRANZ WAXMAN; Gowns, ADRIAN; Editor, FREDRICK Y. SMITH; Running time, 80 minutes.

NOTES ABOUT THE FILM

After a trio of programmers, this was Lana's first appearance in one of Metro's top quality attractions—expensively cast, handsomely mounted, and worthy of a booking at New York's prestigious Radio City Music Hall. *Dramatic School* resembled in many respects 1937's highly successful *Stage Door,* which also concerned itself with the dreams and aspirations of a group of would-be Duses and Bernhardts. Although it lacked the penetrating wit of the earlier film and consequently suffered in comparison, *Dramatic School* was still a vast improvement over many of the vehicles Luise Rainer was accepting at the time and much obvious thought and care went into its tasteful production. It was Mervyn LeRoy's first film under his new MGM pact and, ironically, Miss Rainer's last at the studio which helped her to win two successive Academy Awards. Miss Rainer played Louise

Mauban, a student in a Parisian drama school, who is wrapped up in her burning ambition to be a great actress. A poor girl, she must work nights in a factory in order to attend school during the day. To explain her tiredness to her classmates and to satisfy her romantic nature, Louise concocts a fictitious love affair with a marquis. Her classmates, discovering she has never even met him, arrange a meeting between them but, at a party given to humiliate her, the marquis pretends the romance is real and lifts Louise from poverty to a life of luxury.

Before long, however, the marquis tires of her and Louise is left with only her burning ambition. Brokenhearted, she goes on to triumph in the school's production of *Joan of Arc* and eventually comes to the realization that acting is not only her life, but her love. In the final scene, when the marquis returns repentant, Louise forgives him but sends him away.

Adapted from an original Hungarian stage play, *Dramatic School* afforded Miss Rainer an actress's field day. In addition to a lengthy *Joan of Arc* rendition, the scenario permitted her a crack at the balcony scene from *Romeo and Juliet.* Paulette Goddard shared co-starring billing as a scheming classmate and prominent among the assorted aspirants were Virginia Grey and Ann Rutherford. (Ona Munson, soon to create a memorable Belle Watling in *Gone with the Wind,* also worked in the film but little of her footage appears in the released version.)

Lana's role was small but noticeable and her billing quite good (fourth). As one of the heroine's catty colleagues, she is possibly the bitchiest of them all, and to prove it, midway into the film she venomously spills a glass of champagne on one of Miss Rainer's loveliest Adrian gowns. Although still in her teens here, Lana is costumed and made up somewhat older for the role to keep in step with her senior co-stars; and she shows a great deal of confidence in handling her lines, which are almost exclusively caustic comments aimed at the other cast members.

When viewed today, *Dramatic School* is perfect fodder for film buffs, thanks to a rich supporting cast that included Gale Sondergaard as a jealous instructress who loses patience while trying to coach Miss Rainer through Juliet; Genevieve Tobin as a celebrated musical comedy star; and Margaret Dumont (the Marx Brothers' favorite foil), less befuddled than usual as a teacher of pantomime. Strictly a coincidence—albeit an amusing one—was the fact that Robin Page (Maxine Marx, daughter of Chico and then a fledgling actress) played one of Miss Dumont's students. Two other prominent members of her class included the young Dick Haymes and Edward Arnold, Jr., the son of the actor. ★

With Jean Chatburn, Virginia Grey, Ann Rutherford, Paulette Goddard, Alan Marshal and Luise Rainer

With Virginia Grey, Paulette Goddard, Luise Rainer, Dorothy Granger and Ann Rutherford

With Ann Rutherford, Hans Conried, Virginia Grey, Jean Chatburn and Paulette Goddard

A METRO·GOLDWYN·MAYER PICTURE
1939

CAST

LEW AYRES, *Dr. James Kildare;* LIONEL BARRYMORE, *Dr. Leonard Gillespie;* LARAINE DAY, *Mary Lamont;* NAT PENDLETON, *Wayman;* LANA TURNER, *Rosalie;* SAMUEL S. HINDS, *Dr. Stephen Kildare;* LYNNE CARVER, *Alice Raymond;* EMMA DUNN, *Mrs. Martha Kildare;* WALTER KINGSFORD, *Dr. Walter Carew;* ALMA KRUGER, *Molly Byrd;* HARLAN BRIGGS, *James Galt;* HENRY HUNTER, *Harry Galt;* MARIE BLAKE, *Sally;* PHILLIP TERRY, *Bates;* ROGER CONVERSE, *Joiner;* DONALD BARRY, *Collins;* REED HADLEY, *Tom Crandell;* NELL CRAIG, *"Nosey";* GEORGE OFFERMAN, JR., *Nick;* CLINTON ROSEMOND, *Conover;* JOHNNY WALSH, *"Red";* AILEEN PRINGLE, *Mrs. Thatcher;* HORACE MCMAHON, *Fog Horn.*

CREDITS

Director, HAROLD S. BUCQUET; Producer, LOU OSTROW (Uncredited); Screenplay, HARRY RUSKIN and WILLIS GOLDBECK; From an Original Story by MAX BRAND; Art Direction, CEDRIC GIBBONS with GABRIEL SCOGNAMILLO; Set Decorations, EDWIN B. WILLIS; Sound, DOUGLAS SHEARER; Photography, ALFRED GILKS and LESTER WHITE; Musical Score, DAVID SNELL: Editor, ROBERT J. KERN; Wardrobe, DOLLY TREE; Running time, 86 minutes.

NOTES ABOUT THE FILM

Made for only a few hundred thousand dollars and devoid of the lavish production elements and high-pressure promotional publicity associated with Metro product, the Dr. Kildare group of films was another series that turned out to be enormously profitable for MGM. *Calling Dr. Kildare* was the second of the Kildare films dealing with the youthful, idealistic medic and his irascible but kind-hearted mentor, Dr. Gillespie. Like its predecessor, *Young Dr. Kildare*, the film that inaugurated the series,* it had the same fresh, invigorating entertainment qualities and was just as heartily received.

This time Kildare probes a bullet wound, donating his own blood to his patient whose hideaway and circumstances surrounding it he keeps secret from hospital and police records. This is because he has become enamored of the victim's red-haired sister, Rosalie, who is actually playing him for a fool to protect her brother from arrest for a headline murder. At the same time, Rosalie is unaware that her boy friend—who provides her lavish apartment, the elegant clothes and the roadster—is the man who committed the crime and wounded her

---

*The Metro series was inspired by Paramount's *Internes Can't Take Money* (1937) with Joel McCrea in the role of Dr. Kildare.

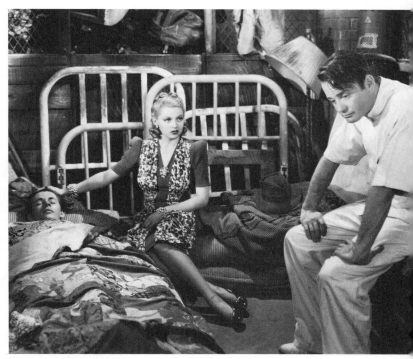

With George Offerman, Jr., and Lew Ayres

With Lew Ayres

With Laraine Day and Lew Ayres

With Lionel Barrymore

—Laraine Day and Lana Turner." The studio's star-building campaign on behalf of Miss Day, who began in films under her real name of Laraine Johnson, included a name change and the success of *Calling Dr. Kildare* did much to establish her as "Laraine Day." It was the first of seven appearances in the series for Miss Day, whose refreshing wholesomeness was ideal for the role of nurse Mary Lamont.

Lana's assignment, on the other hand, gave her a perfect opportunity to display her baby-doll sexuality. Rosalie, who draws the doctor away from ethical practice and nearly ruins his budding career, was in a manner a grown-up version of Andy Hardy's troublesome Cynthia Potter. The character also served as the model for all Turner shady ladies of the future—sexy, yet basically vulnerable; faithless, but regenerative in the end. Rosalie's character is established early in the film when she tells Kildare with a certain disarming honesty: "I'm city people. I like great big shiny limousines and orchids in a vase. I love the cold wind whipping around a skyscraper —and a sable coat to keep it out." Equipped with a long red hairdo, flashy clothes and dialogue like that, Lana couldn't help but attract audience attention.

Even sedate publications like *The Family Circle* noticed her, commenting: "Lana Turner goes glamourous on us, and she needn't take a back seat to any of the other glamour girls." *The Hollywood Reporter* thought she was "a bit uncertain in early scenes" but added "she warms to her work and registers with excellent effect in later chapters." And *Variety* opined: "Laraine Day is excellent . . . while Lana Turner is a fine type as the gal who nearly leads him astray. Both players are to be heard from." ★

brother. Facing dismissal from the hospital and possible loss of his medical license on account of his secret treatments, Kildare unearths the murderer, earns full pardon and the additional respect of Dr. Gillespie.

Like the Hardy films, the Kildare series was a great testing ground for aspiring young contract players. *Calling Dr. Kildare* showcased not one, but two such hopefuls, a fact that Metro vehemently boasted of in the film's ads: ". . . watch these exciting new MGM beauties

THESE GLAMOUR GIRLS

A METRO·GOLDWYN·MAYER PICTURE
1939

A publicity photo spotlighting the young cast members of THESE GLAMOUR GIRLS. *Top row: Tom Brown, Richard Carlson, Lew Ayres, Sumner Getchell, Peter (Lind) Hayes and Owen Davis, Jr. Bottom: Ann Rutherford, Jane Bryan, Lana, Anita Louise, Marsha Hunt and Mary Beth Hughes*

With Sumner Getchell

With Lew Ayres

CAST

LEW AYRES, *Philip S. Griswold;* LANA TURNER, *Jane Thomas;* TOM BROWN, *Homer Ten Eyck;* RICHARD CARLSON, *Joe;* JANE BRYAN, *Carol Christy;* ANITA LOUISE, *Daphne Graves;* MARSHA HUNT, *Betty Ainsbridge;* ANN RUTHERFORD, *Mary Rose Wilston;* MARY BETH HUGHES, *Ann Van Reichton;* OWEN DAVIS, JR., *Greg Smith;* ERNEST TRUEX, *Alumnus;* SUMNER GETCHELL, *"Blimpy";* PETER (LIND) HAYES, *Skel Lorimer;* DON CASTLE, *Jack;* TOM COLLINS, *Tommy Torgler;* HENRY KOLKER, *Mr. Griswold;* DENNIE MOORE, *Mavis;* MARY FORBES, *Mrs. Van Reichton;* NELLA WALKER, *Mrs. Graves;* ROBERT EMMETT KEANE, *Mr. Wilston;* TOM KENNEDY, JAMES PIERCE, *Bouncers;* GLADYS BLAKE, *Cashier;* JOHN KELLY, *Sailor;* DAVE OLIVER, *Cabby;* LEE BENNETT, ROD BACON, RUSSELL WADE, *College Boys;* ARTHUR Q. BRYAN, *Dance Customer.*

CREDITS

Director, S. SYLVAN SIMON; Producer, SAM ZIMBALIST; Screenplay, JANE HALL and MARION PARSONNET; Photography, ALFRED GILKS; Art Direction, CEDRIC GIBBONS with HARRY MCAFEE; Set Decorations, EDWIN B. WILLIS; Sound, DOUGLAS SHEARER; Wardrobe, DOLLY TREE; Editor, HAROLD F. KRESS; Musical Score, EDWARD WARD and DAVID SNELL; Vocal and Orchestral Arrangements, WALLY HEGLIN; Song: "Loveliness." Music by EDWARD WARD, Lyrics by BOB WRIGHT and CHET FORREST; Running time, 79 minutes.

NOTES ABOUT THE FILM

During Lana's red-headed-ball-of-fire phase, writers like Anita Loos frequently described her as "a young Clara Bow." Appropriately enough, when *These Glamour Girls*, her second film of 1939, was released, it was likened to a sort of undergraduate, sub-deb version of Miss Loos's *The Women* and the frizzy-haired heroine she played was not unlike those typified by Miss Bow: the warm and unself-conscious sexpot who cuts across cultural boundaries to grasp her future and win her hero's heart.

Jane Hall wrote this satire on social snobbishness for *Cosmopolitan*, and then collaborated with Marion Parsonnet on the screenplay, which helped retain the breeziness that characterized the original. The story centered around a group of wealthy collegiates attending an exclusive Eastern college. Into one of their typical elbow-bending evenings comes Jane Thomas, a taxi-dancer, who accepts the drunken proposal of Philip Griswold, a senior, to attend the school's annual weekend of house parties. Later, in a more sober state, he promptly forgets that he invited her.

When Jane arrives at the college, Phil sees her and the events come back to him. He apologizes and tries to convince her to leave because he knows she will only be humiliated by the other girls. But Jane decides to stay on and she soon runs into a feminine free-for-all with a half-dozen debutantes who resent her intrusion. At one point, when they try to insult her, Jane tells the whole crowd of debutantes off.

As the house parties proceed, she really takes things over by staging a dance that is such a sensation she has all the boys flocking to her side. Needless to say, in the end the taxi-dancer has completely triumphed over the debs by being the most popular girl of the weekend. She not only upsets their social applecart but walks off with glamour boy Griswold, the college's most eligible bachelor.

Lew Ayres, riding on the crest of his Kildare popularity, co-starred with Lana for the third time. Prominent among his classmates were Richard Carlson, Tom Brown and Peter (Lind) Hayes (the latter Lana's partner in a lively, clear-the-floor dance sequence). The debutantes were represented by Ann Rutherford and Mary Beth Hughes as stereotyped bluebloods of the "dizzy" variety; Jane Bryan, an impoverished socialite who hopes to marry for money; Anita Louise (in an off-beat "heavy" role) as an ultra-sophisticated snob; and Marsha Hunt, quite good as a prom guest who kills herself when she finds her popularity waning.

These Glamour Girls is the film that gave Lana her first star billing in the principal feminine role and quite a few critics—including Bosley Crowther of *The New York Times*—felt she was ready for it. Said *Boxoffice*: "Young blades especially may be expected to do nipups over a ball of fire named Lana Turner, attractive, spirited and apparently going places." Abroad, The *London Evening News* commented: "With considerable justification, Metro thinks it has a great new exponent of glamour in Lana Turner. Beautiful, full of life, impish and sensitive, she is now well on her way to stardom."

Director S. Sylvan Simon had a few words to offer on the subject himself. In an interview given during the making of the film, he told a reporter, "I venture to predict that in another year Lana Turner will be one of the biggest stars on the screen." ★

With Dennie Moore

With Lew Ayres

DANCING CO-ED

A METRO·GOLDWYN·MAYER PICTURE
1939

CAST

LANA TURNER, *Patty Marlow;* RICHARD CARLSON, *"Pug" Braddock;* ARTIE SHAW, *Himself;* ANN RUTHERFORD, *Eve;* LEE BOWMAN, *Freddy Tobin;* THURSTON HALL, *H. W. Workman;* LEON ERROL, *"Pops" Marlow;* ROSCOE KARNS, *Joe Drews;* MARY BETH HUGHES, *"Toddy";* JUNE PREISSER, *"Ticky" James;* MONTY WOOLLEY, *Professor Lange;* CHESTER CLUTE, *Braddock;* ETHELREDA LEOPOLD, *Flapjack Waitress;* BARBARA BEDFORD, *Secretary's Voice;* MINERVA URECAL, *Woman's Voice on Radio;* EDWARD ARNOLD, JR., ROBERT WALKER, *Students.*

CREDITS

Director, S. SYLVAN SIMON; Producer, EDGAR SELWYN; Screenplay, ALBERT MANNHEIMER; Based on a Story by ALBERT TREYNOR; Photography, ALFRED GILKS; Art Direction, CEDRIC GIBBONS with HARRY McAFEE; Set Decorations, EDWIN B. WILLIS; Sound, DOUGLAS SHEARER; Wardrobe, DOLLY TREE; Editor, W. DONN HAYES; Musical Score, EDWARD WARD and DAVID SNELL; Dance Direction, GEORGE KING; Artie Shaw Instrumentals: "Back Bay Shuffle," "At Sundown," "I'm Yours," "Nightmare," "Stealin' Apples," "Racket Rhythm"; Song, "Jungle Drums" by ERNESTO LECUONA, CARMEN LOMBARDO and CHARLES O'FLYNN; Running time, 84 minutes.

NOTES ABOUT THE FILM

Dancing Co-Ed gave Lana top billing for the first time in her brief, two-year career. Originally slated as a vehicle for Eleanor Powell, this was the studio's most determined effort yet in their campaign to hoist Lana to stardom. Although *Co-Ed* was another in their series of college programmers, its vigorous direction and snappy dialogue made it faster and funnier than many of Metro's bigger-budgeted comedies. And it was a great "leg show" to boot (as the picture on the opposite page will testify).

Based on an *American* magazine story that appeared under the same title in the September 1938 issue, this very lively yarn built its foundation on a press agent stunt. Lana played Patty Marlow, a professional dancer who is planted in a midwestern college by a publicity director for Monarch Pictures. The idea is to start a nationwide hunt, via a radio program, to find a dancing co-ed to star in a forthcoming film.

So, accompanied by Eve, the press agent's secretary (Ann Rutherford had this role, replacing Virginia Grey who had been set originally), Patty enrolls in the school and waits to be "discovered" by the publicity man, who's giving phony screen tests at colleges throughout the country. In the meantime, Pug Braddock, the crusading editor of the school paper, becomes convinced that the

contest is a fake and intends to expose it. When Patty and Pug fall in love, Patty tells all, and Pug tries to prevent her appearing at the contest by having her kidnapped. A surprise finish has Eve, the secretary, winning the contest and the chance for Hollywood stardom, and Patty happily renouncing her career for marriage.

With Artie Shaw

With Ann Rutherford

Pug has a couple of his friends kidnap Patty

Artie Shaw, then America's "King of Swing" (and who later became Lana's first real-life husband) was literally dragged into the story by his clarinet, contributing a flock of his most famous numbers, including two written especially for the picture, "Stealin' Apples" and "Racquet Rhythm." The latter number prompted an intricate tap routine, one of three surprisingly polished numbers Lana did in the film, working under George King, the dance director who coached Clark Gable for *Idiot's Delight.*

Reviews for *Dancing Co-Ed* indicated that Metro's intentions for the film had been successfully realized. *The Hollywood Reporter* called Lana "a new Metro-Goldwyn-Mayer star and one destined to reach as far in selling tickets as any this great company has ever pro-

duced. *Dancing Co-Ed* definitely *makes* Lana Turner, and when you see the picture we believe you will agree with us that the little lady has been launched." The critic for the *Chicago Herald-American* agreed: "*Dancing Co-Ed* makes a full-fledged star out of Lana Turner, who has been knocking at the door for some time now without anybody answering. In my book, from now one, this kid can't miss." And this from *Silver Screen*: " . . . you've seen her spotted here and there in a couple of unimportant pictures. But in *Dancing Co-Ed* she is the star, and after one reel of the youthful and shapely Lana, it's safe to bet your bank account that little Miss Turner is going places fast. She has plenty of personal attractions, she's most easy on the eyes, she has more s-e-x appeal then any gal in the business." ★

With Richard Carlson, Ann Rutherford, Artie Shaw, Lee Bowman, June Preisser and Roscoe Karns

TWO GIRLS ON BROADWAY

A METRO·GOLDWYN·MAYER PICTURE
1940

CAST

Lana Turner, *Pat Mahoney;* Joan Blondell, *Molly Mahoney;* George Murphy, *Eddie Kerns;* Kent Taylor, *"Chat" Chatsworth;* Richard Lane, *Buddy Bartell;* Wallace Ford, *Jed Marlowe;* Otto Hahn, *Ito;* Lloyd Corrigan, *Judge;* Don Wilson, *Announcer;* Charles Wagenheim, *Bartell's Assistant;* Carole Wayne, *First Girl;* Hillary Brooke, *Second Girl;* Hal K. Dawson, *Clerk;* Arthur O'Connell, *Reporter.*

CREDITS

Director, S. Sylvan Simon; Producer, Jack Cummings; Screenplay, Joseph Fields and Jerome Chodorov; Based on a Story by Edmund Goulding; Photography, George Folsey; Art Direction, Cedric Gibbons with Stan Rogers; Set Decorations, Edwin B. Willis; Sound, Douglas Shearer; Wardrobe, Dolly Tree; Editor, Blanche Sewell; Musical Presentation, Merrill Pye; Musical Director, Georgie Stoll; Musical Arrangements, Walter Ruick; Orchestrations, Leo Arnaud and George Bassman; Dance Directon, Bobby Connolly and Eddie Larkin; Songs: "My Wonderful One Let's Dance" by Nacio Herb Brown, Arthur Freed and Roger Edens; "Broadway's Still Broadway" by Harry Revel and Ted Fetter; Running time, 73 minutes.

NOTES ABOUT THE FILM

After a headlined marriage and cover stories in both *Life* and *Look* just weeks apart, the America of 1940 was so Lana Turner–conscious that MGM's ad campaign for her next film, *Two Girls on Broadway,* shouted: "The Girl They're All Talking About! She Puts 'It' Back on the Screen!" And despite the strong presence of two veteran co-stars, Joan Blondell and George Murphy, Lana was top-billed over them, with her face and figure dominating the poster art.

Two Girls on Broadway was an unpretentious reworking of an old favorite, *Broadway Melody of 1929,* the popular pioneer of early sound-film days. In the new version, Turner, Blondell and Murphy formed the triangle that Anita Page, Bessie Love and Charles King had in the earlier film. No one was fooled, least of all *The New York Times'* Bosley Crowther who wrote: "With Lana Turner figuring prominently in the doings, it is fairly safe to predict that none of the patrons at Loew's Criterion will bother to inquire this week where and when they have seen *Two Girls on Broadway* before. There is an indefinable something about Miss Turner that makes it a matter of small concern."

The story: Turner, Blondell and Murphy play three ambitious young people from the sticks who storm Broadway together. Joan is just about to buy the furniture for the apartment she has rented for George and herself, following their wedding, when she learns that George has fallen in love with kid sister Lana. Lana is all for sacrificing herself by marrying Kent Taylor, a playboy with five ex-wives, but Joan gets her sacrifice in first and leaves the way clear for the other two.

S. Sylvan Simon, just turned thirty and one of Hollywood's youngest feature directors, was by now an old hand at guiding Lana—*Two Girls on Broadway* was their third successive film together. Two new songs especially written for the film were "My Wonderful One Let's Dance" by Nacio Herb Brown, Arthur Freed and

With Joan Blondell

With Kent Taylor

Roger Edens, and "Broadway's Still Broadway" by Harry Revel and Ted Fetter, both of which called for dance routines that required quite intricate footwork on Lana's part. If nothing else, *Two Girls on Broadway* bears conclusive evidence that had Metro chosen to continue her training along those lines, she could have had a very prominent musical career. Here she was, of course, fortunate enough to have as strong a partner as George Murphy, who had just held his own with Fred Astaire, no less, in *Broadway Melody of 1940.* The grace and precision of the Turner–Murphy team is worth the entire weight of *Two Girls on Broadway,* especially in the

With George Murphy in the "My Wonderful One, Let's Dance" number

With Kent Taylor, Joan Blondell and George Murphy

With Kent Taylor

THE GIRL THEY'RE ALL TALKING ABOUT!

Lovely Lana, America's Blonde Bonfire, in her hottest, most daring role!

LANA TURNER
JOAN BLONDELL
GEORGE MURPHY

TWO GIRLS ON BROADWAY

An M-G-M Picture with
KENT TAYLOR · WALLACE FORD

PREVIEW TODAY
plus last times
"PAROLE FIXER"

1st N. Y. SHOWING!
LOEW'S CRITERION
B'WAY & 45th ST.

dazzling "My Wonderful One" production number which utilized a spectacular revolving stage and a large number of dance extras. Bobby Connolly, a new recruit to Metro after many successful years at Warners, staged the number with Merrill Pye and Eddie Larkin in a way that belied the film's modest budget.

Said *The Hollywood Reporter*: *Two Girls on Broadway* seems to be a fairly entertaining bit of fluff, important only in one respect. It proves Lana Turner is the gal Fred Astaire should be dancing with if MGM wants to duplicate the old Astaire–Rogers sizzle."

Irene Thirer of the *New York Post* had thoughts along the same lines: "Their lithe grace and terpsichorean capabilities as a team in tap and glide is something which rates hurrahs . . . If you didn't see their faces, they might easily be Fred Astaire and Ginger (or Eleanor) going through their impressively intricate

routines. Miss Turner (Mrs. Artie Shaw) is certainly in for a bright screen future, and her public (which filled the Criterion to capacity yesterday) is mighty glad that she isn't really going to retire to domesticity—as she revealed in jest, during her honeymoon here."

Two Girls on Broadway was released under the title *Choose Your Partner* in Great Britain where just months earlier Lana's *Dancing Co-Ed* had also undergone a name change—to the more provocative *Every Other Inch a Lady.* ★

WE WHO ARE YOUNG

A METRO·GOLDWYN·MAYER PICTURE
1940

CAST

LANA TURNER, *Margy Brooks;* JOHN SHELTON, *William Brooks;* GENE LOCKHART, *C. B. Beamis;* GRANT MITCHELL, *Jones;* HENRY ARMETTA, *Tony;* JONATHAN HALE, *Braddock;* CLARENCE WILSON, *R. Glassford;* IAN WOLFE, *Judge;* HAL K. DAWSON, *Salesman;* JOHN BUTLER, *Mr. Peabody;* IRENE SEIDNER, *Mrs. Weinstock;* CHARLES LANE, *Perkins;* HORACE MCMAHON, *Foreman;* TRUMAN BRADLEY, *Commentator;* DON CASTLE, *Clerk;* GRADY SUTTON, *New Father;* RICHARD CRANE, *Bellhop;* CHARLES MCMURPHY, *Mover;* RALPH DUNN, ED DEARING, *Policemen.*

CREDITS

Director, HAROLD S. BUCQUET; Producer, SEYMOUR NEBENZAHL; Story and Screenplay, DALTON TRUMBO; Art Direction, CEDRIC GIBBONS with WADE B. RUBOTTOM; Set Decorations, EDWIN B. WILLIS; Music, BRONISLAU KAPER; Sound, DOUGLAS SHEARER; Photography, KARL FREUND; Wardrobe, DOLLY TREE; Editor, HOWARD O'NEILL; Running time, 80 minutes.

As Margy Brooks

NOTES ABOUT THE FILM

Early in 1940, MGM surprised the college boys of America by casting their Number One Dream Girl in a straight dramatic, nonglamourous role. The picture was called *We Who Are Young* and in it Lana played a young housewife. Instead of the red-headed ball-of-fire of films like *Dancing Co-Ed,* for *We Who Are Young* Lana was transformed into a rather wistful brunette with an easy naturalness about her. The sex appeal was still there, however, even more appealing because it was under wraps.

We Who Are Young was based on a story by Dalton Trumbo. Although not one of Metro's Grade-A efforts, the film was a good little programmer that benefited from, in addition to Trumbo, the crack technical contributions of photography by Karl Freund, musical scoring by Bronislau Kaper and direction by Harold S. Bucquet of the popular *Dr. Kildare* series. Seymour Nebenzahl, the European producer who turned out *M* and *Mayerling,* handled the production chores on the picture as his initial Hollywood venture.

Trumbo's screenplay, although an original, could not help recalling such earlier love-against-the-odds themes as *Bad Girl, Saturday's Children* and even King Vidor's *The Crowd.* The story focused on a boy and girl employed by the same firm who get married in a burst of youthful optimism. Inevitably, they face all the annoyances that beset poor young couples in the big city—doctor's bills, loan sharks, and relief, until success smiles on them (in the form of benefactor Gene Lockhart). The picture's climax has the husband stealing an automobile when labor pains beset his pregnant wife. Accompanied by a police escort, they make it in time to Bellevue where the final reel had Lana giving birth to twins (for the record, her first young mother role).

In her New York *Daily News* review, Kate Cameron said: "Lana Turner, who has not been much more than a glorified sweater model on the screen up to now, is handing out a surprise over at the Criterion Theatre . . . Metro-Goldwyn-Mayer decided to deglamourize their young star and, to prove that she could get along without a sweater, they assigned her to a role that required real acting ability. Lo and behold! She turns in a fine performance."

And *Time* commented: ". . . surprisingly, Lana Turner turns into a dramatic actress of some talent, hiding her most publicized charms behind a simple gingham house dress."

Metro's promotional campaign for *We Who Are Young* included a theatre contest, offering guest tickets as prizes, in which patrons were asked to fill out a questionnaire asking "Do you prefer Lana Turner glamourous or dramatic?" Early results evidently favored the former image for by the time *We Who Are Young* opened in New York City, the dignified ad campaign used in the film's initial showings had been drastically revised. Substituted was the more familiar approach featuring the Lana of old—reclining in a clinging satin nightgown, with the ad copy reading: "Modern Youth in Search of All the Answers! Lana Turner, the Blazing Blonde in her most daring role!" ★

With John Shelton in her first "mother" role

Above and below: with John Shelton (playing a role originally intended for Lew Ayres)

ZIEGFELD GIRL

A METRO·GOLDWYN·MAYER PICTURE
1941

CAST

JAMES STEWART, *Gilbert Young;* JUDY GARLAND, *Susan Gallagher;* HEDY LAMARR, *Sandra Kolter;* LANA TURNER, *Sheila Regan;* TONY MARTIN, *Frank Merton;* JACKIE COOPER, *Jerry Regan;* IAN HUNTER, *Geoffrey Collis;* CHARLES WINNINGER, *"Pop" Gallagher;* EDWARD EVERETT HORTON, *Noble Sage;* PHILIP DORN, *Franz Kolter;* PAUL KELLY, *John Slayton;* EVE ARDEN, *Patsy Dixon;* DAN DAILEY, JR., *Jimmy Walters;* AL SHEAN, *Al;* FAY HOLDEN, *Mrs. Regan;* FELIX BRESSART, *Mischa;* ROSE HOBART, *Mrs. Merton;* BERNARD NEDELL, *Nick Capalini;* ED McNAMARA, *Mr. Regan;* MAE BUSCH, *Jenny;* RENIE RIANO, *Annie;* JOSEPHINE WHITTELL, *Perkins;* SERGIO ORTA, *Native Dancer;* ANTONIO AND ROSARIO, *Specialty Dancers;* JOYCE COMPTON, *Miss Sawyer;* HARRIET BENNETT, NINA BISSELL, ALAINE BRANDEIS, GEORGIA CARROLL, VIRGINIA CRUZON, PATRICIA DANE, MYRNA DELL, LORRAINE GETTMAN (LESLIE BROOKS), FRANCES GLADWIN, CLAIRE JAMES, LOUISE LA PLANCHE, MADELEINE MARTIN, VIVIEN MASON, ANYA TARANDA, JEAN WALLACE, IRMA WILSON, *Showgirls;* RUTH TOBEY, *Betty Regan;* GINGER PEARSON, *Salesgirl;* FRED SANTLEY, *Floorwalker;* GEORGE LLOYD, *Bartender;* ROSCOE ATES, *Theatre Worker;* REED HADLEY, *Geoffrey's Friend;* ARMAND KALIZ, *Pierre;* AL HILL, *Truck Driver;* DONALD KIRKE, *Playboy;* RAY TEAL, *Pawnbroker;* BESS FLOWERS, *Patron in Palm Beach Casino;* JOAN BARCLAY, *Actress in Slayton's Office;* SIX HITS AND A MISS, *Singers.*

CREDITS

Director, ROBERT Z. LEONARD; Producer, PANDRO S. BERMAN; Screenplay, MARGUERITE ROBERTS and SONYA LEVIEN; Original Story, WILLIAM ANTHONY McGUIRE; Photography (Sepia), RAY JUNE; Art Direction, CEDRIC GIBBONS with DANIEL B. CATHCART; Set Decoration, EDWIN B. WILLIS; Sound, DOUGLAS SHEARER; Editor, BLANCHE SEWELL; Gowns and Costumes, ADRIAN; Makeup, JACK DAWN; Hair Stylist, LARRY GERMAIN; Musical Numbers Directed by BUSBY BERKELEY; Musical Direction by GEORGIE STOLL; Musical Presentation by MERRILL PYE; Vocals and Orchestrations, LEO ARNAUD, GEORGE BASSMAN and CONRAD SALINGER; Songs: "You Stepped Out of a Dream" by NACIO HERB BROWN and GUS KAHN; "Minnie from Trinidad" by ROGER EDENS; "I'm Always Chasing Rainbows" by HARRY CARROLL and JOSEPH McCARTHY; "Whispering" by JOHN SCHONBERGER, RICHARD COBURN and VINCENT ROSE; "Mr. Gallagher and Mr. Shean" by EDWARD GALLAGHER and AL SHEAN; "Caribbean Love Song" by RALPH FREED and ROGER EDENS; "You Never Looked So Beautiful Before" by WALTER DONALDSON; "Laugh? I Thought I'd Split My Sides" by ROGER EDENS; "You Gotta Pull Strings" by HAROLD ADAMSON and WALTER DONALDSON; Running time, 131 minutes.

With James Stewart

NOTES ABOUT THE FILM

In 1936, MGM produced *The Great Ziegfeld*, the spectacular film musical depicting the life and loves of the famous showman. It was nominated for seven Academy Awards, won three of them (including Best Picture), and cleaned up at the box office.

A sequel was inevitable and in May 1938, the same studio announced that *Ziegfeld Girl* was being readied for production. This time the focus was to be on the producer's gallery of fabled beauties. William Anthony McGuire, who wrote the original story for the '36 film, performed the same duties on *Ziegfeld Girl* and pencilled in as its stars were four of Metro's top feminine contractees: Joan Crawford, Eleanor Powell, Margaret Sullavan and Virginia Bruce.

There were delays in production, however, and more than two years passed before *Ziegfeld Girl* was ready for filming. By then, all of the aforementioned ladies were either busy with other assignments or else off the project entirely.

When *Ziegfeld Girl* finally went before the cameras in October 1940, a new and equally glittering array of stars had been assembled. Among them was Lana Turner playing the role of Sheila Regan, a showgirl whose moral fiber fails to hold up under the glare of the spotlight and who nose-dives to inevitable disaster. Sheila was Lana's most important assignment to date. The part had high spirits, recklessness, glitter and much of the same youthful brashness that had made Joan Crawford the toast of every frat house in the country during the titillating Twenties. There were many other prominent characters in the film, of course, but *Ziegfeld Girl's* central theme revolved around Sheila's rise and fall and whether she was strutting like a peacock through lavish production numbers, counting her minks and diamonds, or soaking in a bubble bath of DeMille-like elegance, it

was Lana's movie all the way. The final reels of the film
contain a drunken episode where she's beaten up by an
ex-prizefighter; a plunge from a stage before a horrified
audience; a ten-minute sickbed scene; and last, but not
least, a sensational demise in black chiffon in the film's
big dramatic climax.*

Ziegfeld Girl marked the first major turning point in

Lana's career. As a result of her performance, the powers at MGM elevated her to full-fledged stardom. After *Ziegfeld Girl*, there were no more "series" films or college programmers on Lana's movie agenda. It was also the film that first presented her as a blonde, the decisive shade which would soon become a Turner trademark†

With Hedy Lamarr and Judy Garland

Ziegfeld Girl was produced by Pandro S. Berman —his first production in his new post at MGM (Berman had just moved over to the Culver City lot after a long and successful tenure at RKO)—and directed by Robert Z. Leonard, who had been at the helm of *The Great Ziegfeld*. The story centered on three heroines, chosen out of hundreds for glorification by the off-screen Ziegfeld (who never appears in the film). There is Susan Gallagher, a young vaudeville performer; Sandra Kolter, the wife of a penniless musician; and Sheila Regan, a department store elevator operator.

Susan, forced to break up a vaudeville act with her father in order to further her own career as a Ziegfeld player, quickly graduates to singing stardom. She falls in love with Sheila's brother, Jerry, as well, and eventually experiences the great thrill of seeing her father make a comeback in one of her shows. Sandra, on the other hand, has an affair with singing star Frank Merton, although her love for her husband never really falters. When she comes to her senses, she leaves the show and returns to her husband, who in time wins his chance as a concert violinist.

Sheila is the one who allows the glamour of show business to go to her head. Her jump from Flatbush to Park Avenue, from running a department store elevator to jewels, wealth and stage-door-Johnnies, includes the tossing aside of her truck driver boyfriend Gil Young for the suave attentions of Geoffrey Collis, a socialite. Sheila goes from bad to worse and finally loses her job in the show when she goes on while drunk. She hits the skids, leads a dissolute life and returns to her Brooklyn home ill, where Gil finds her. He had been serving a jail term for driving a liquor truck for bootleggers, the means from which he hoped to be able to give Sheila the

———————————

*Lana has often said that the role of Sheila Regan, originally just a supporting one, grew in size as the shooting of the film progressed; that each day she would be handed new scenes not in the original script. The epitome of the Doomed Showgirl, Sheila is said to have been a composite of Lillian Lorraine, Jessie Reed and several other ill-starred real-life beauties glorified by the famous showman.

†In this early phase of her life as a fair-haired sex goddess, Lana had not yet adopted the full blonde shade which would most win the favor of her public. As Sheila in *Ziegfeld Girl*, her hair is a red-blonde—almost a golden shade—and throughout the film, Sheila's boyfriend, Gil, refers to her as "Red."

With Hedy Lamarr

With Renie Riano

With
Eve Arden

With
Dan Dailey

luxuries she craved. The two make up their differences and plan marriage when she recovers.

But Sheila cannot bear to miss the opening of the new Ziegfeld show and she leaves her sickbed to attend. At the theatre, when she sees the girls walking down the typical Ziegfeld stairs the way she used to, it's more than she can stand. Dazed, she leaves the balcony, starts down the stairs to the foyer—but collapses. Taken backstage, where she is reunited with some of her old friends, the film ends with Sheila's voice fading into nothingness as the music of the show swells into its finale.

Ziegfeld Girl was released in April 1941 and if it was not quite up to the Oscar-winning standards of *The Great Ziegfeld*, it was at least a bargain buy for moviegoers, bursting with the stuff of which successful audience pictures are made. MGM poured into the movie just about everything in the way of production possibilities—an opulence that's almost overwhelming; dazzling, often bizarre Adrian costumes; ear-filling music and eye-filling photography (lensed in a new two-tone sepia process); and an impressive array of important players.

James Stewart, with a recent Oscar-winning performance under his belt (for *The Philadelphia Story*) drew top billing for the comparatively brief role of Sheila's boyfriend; Judy Garland belted out four num-

Sheila goes from bad to worse after she is fired from the Follies. Forced to hock her jewelry (left), she soon becomes a familiar face in the cheap speakeasys around town

bers and gave a characteristically versatile performance in a role that helped to establish her screen coming-of-age (Garland's rendition of "I'm Always Chasing Rainbows" is one of the film's most touching moments); Hedy Lamarr as a showgirl was quite possibly more beautiful than she's ever been; Tony Martin sang "You Stepped Out of a Dream," the picture's hit tune (now a standard); and there were dozens of vital incidental characterizations by everyone from Eve Arden to the "ever-popular" Mae Busch (as a wardrobe mistress).

Although neither of *Ziegfeld Girl*'s two super-colossal production numbers are as imaginative as Busby Berkeley's work in his early '30s musicals at Warners, they are still typical of the screen techniques he originated. Interestingly enough, when the film ran overlong, one new and expensively staged number—"We Must Have Music," featuring Judy Garland and Tony Martin —was deleted from the picture. One year later, however, MGM utilized this footage in its entirety in a short subject (entitled, not coincidentally, *We Must Have Music*) which explained the function of a movie studio's music department.

Ziegfeld Girl will always be fondly remembered by Lana Turner fans, for this key film in the early Turner output displays the first great evidence of her development as a glamourous star personality. As a result of Robert Z. Leonard's insight, care and sensitivity in directing her, Lana's Sheila Regan won critical praise. If there were few comparisons to Bernhardt or Duse, it was nonetheless unanimously agreed that she contributed a very effective performance.

Since *Ziegfeld Girl* had been so obviously slanted in Lana's favor, *Time*'s critic did not seem unjustified when he labelled the picture "a glorification of Lana Turner." The reviewer for *Kinematograph Weekly* shared *Time*'s opinion and wrote: "The part is her big chance and she

takes it. All the hopes, disillusionment and the follies of youth are crystallized in her vital, memorable, glamourous and appealing performance."

The more conservative *New York Times* had this to say: ". . . it is the perilously lovely Miss Turner who gets this department's bouquet for a surprisingly solid performance as the little girl from Brooklyn."

For many, the single most stunning moment in *Ziegfeld Girl* comes during the film's ultra-dramatic final moments. It is the scene where Lana, as the ailing, drink-ridden ex-Ziegfeld beauty, attends a performance of the Follies. Dreaming of herself a success once more, she descends a staircase in the theatre lobby. Head held high, a smile on her lips and dragging her coat behind her, she finally collapses like a dying swan. Performed to the accompaniment of a rousing background rendition of "You Stepped Out of a Dream," this poignant sequence is one of the most memorable climaxes ever put on film and a tribute to the combined respective talents of actress Turner, director Leonard and the MGM music department. Although his contribution can be considered minor, some credit for the success of the scene must go to "Doc" Roemer, the MGM gymnasium trainer who spent most of his time boxing with male stars. Roemer was the gentleman who had the pleasure of teaching Lana how to crumble and fall without breaking any of her lovely—and heavily insured—bones. Reportedly, twenty-six takes and rehearsals of that fall were required before director Leonard was satisfied.

Note: A sequence from *Ziegfeld Girl* (featuring Lana and Renie Riano) was used for a scene that takes place in a movie theatre in MGM's *Down in San Diego* (1941). And in Andy Warhol's *Women in Revolt* (1971), transvestite Candy Darling did an impression of Lana from the film.★

Lana's Big Moment in ZIEGFELD GIRL: *the famous staircase scene in the final reel of the film*

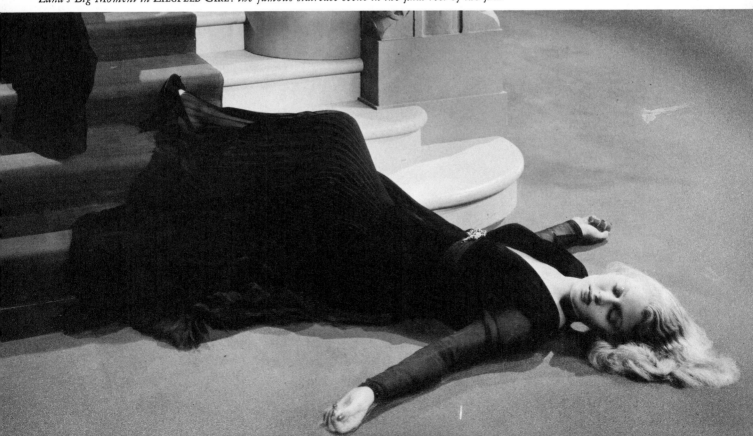

DR. JEKYLL AND MR. HYDE

A METRO·GOLDWYN·MAYER PICTURE
1941

CAST

SPENCER TRACY, *Dr. Harry Jekyll/Mr. Hyde;* INGRID
BERGMAN, *Ivy Peterson;* LANA TURNER, *Beatrix Emery;*
DONALD CRISP, *Sir Charles Emery;* IAN HUNTER, *Dr. John
Lanyon;* BARTON MACLANE, *Sam Higgins;* C. AUBREY
SMITH, *The Bishop;* PETER GODFREY, *Poole;* SARA ALL-
GOOD, *Mrs. Higgins;* FREDERIC WORLOCK, *Dr. Heath;*
WILLIAM TANNEN, *Interne Fenwick;* FRANCES ROBINSON,
Marcia; DENIS GREEN, *Freddie;* BILLY BEVAN, *Mr.
Weller;* FORRESTER HARVEY, *Old Prouty;* LUMSDEN HARE,
Colonel Weymouth; LAWRENCE GRANT, *Dr. Courtland;*
JOHN BARCLAY, *Constable;* DORIS LLOYD, *Mrs. Marley;*
GWEN GAZE, *Mrs. French;* HILLARY BROOKE, *Mrs.
Arnold;* MARY FIELD, *Wife;* AUBREY MATHER, *Inspector.*

CREDITS

Producer and Director, VICTOR FLEMING; Screenplay,
JOHN LEE MAHIN; Based on the Novel by ROBERT LOUIS
STEVENSON; Photography, JOSEPH RUTTENBERG; Set Dec-
orations, EDWIN B. WILLIS; Art Direction, CEDRIC GIB-
BONS with DANIEL B. CATHCART; Sound, DOUGLAS
SHEARER; Editor, HAROLD F. KRESS; Special Effects,
WARREN NEWCOMBE; Montage Effects, PETER BALL-
BUSCH; Music, FRANZ WAXMAN; Dance Direction, ERNST
MATRAY; Gowns, ADRIAN; Men's Wardrobe, GILE STEELE;
Makeup, JACK DAWN; Running time, 127 minutes.

NOTES ABOUT THE FILM

This adaptation of Robert Louis Stevenson's tug of
war between the good and the evil in the soul of a
Harley Street physician was a conversation piece when it
was released in 1941. Foremost among its controversies
was the decision of director Victor Fleming to cast
against type. Fleming's theory was that the surprise
element would be an asset to the film. The first real
surprise came with the casting of Spencer Tracy in the
dual title role (in May 1940, MGM had announced that
the film would soon roll with Robert Donat in the lead).

Yet even more of a stir was caused by the casting of
Tracy's two leading ladies, Ingrid Bergman and Lana
Turner. It was assumed that Miss Bergman, who had
been admirably noble in her three previous American
films, would play Beatrix, Dr. Jekyll's well-bred fiancée
and Lana would play Ivy Peterson, the barmaid victim
of Hyde's bestialities. But it was quite the other way
around. Bergman was so anxious to play a "bad girl" for
a change that Fleming reversed their roles.

With Lana riding the crest of her newly won stardom

*Frame enlargements of Lana
(alone, and with Ingrid Bergman)
in the transformation scenes*

With Spencer Tracy

enlargements. Unlike the makeups affected by both John Barrymore (1920) and Fredric March (1932) in the previous filmings, Tracy played Hyde with the smallest application of makeup, his transformation relying more on facial expressions. A symbolic montage with Freudian overtones—brilliantly conceived and easily the high point of a film that excelled in every technical department—accompanied Tracy's change to Hyde. One

With Donald Crisp

as a result of her success in *Ziegfeld Girl*, it seemed only fair that Miss Bergman should now have her moment of glory, which she did, since her performance as Ivy was a perfect showcase for her talents (oddly enough, the meaty role of the luckless barmaid, which did so much for Miss Bergman as well as for Miriam Hopkins in an earlier [1932]version, is one that doesn't even exist in the original Stevenson novel).

Lana's casting here was primarily for dress-up-the-picture purposes and another move on the studio's part to spot her in only their most ambitious productions. But whatever the shortcomings of her role,* her beauty (exceptional in this case, in Adrian's billowy nineteenth-century gowns) and her star presence were a decided asset to *Jekyll and Hyde*'s box office.

(In a recent *New York Times* interview, Katharine Hepburn revealed that the Turner–Bergman castings occasioned one of her few career disappointments. "Spencer wanted me to play both the good and the bad girls and the studio wouldn't let him have his way," said Miss Hepburn. "They thought he was crazy. He maintained that the good side of Jekyll would see the good girl, and the bad side would see the bad, but that they really were the same.")

To add further intrigue to the production, Tracy's scenes as Hyde were filmed behind closed sets and not one still photo of him in makeup was issued although one week after the film's release, *Life* managed to publish pictures of Tracy as Hyde by using frame

---

*In earlier film versions, Jekyll's fiancee has been portrayed by Martha Mansfield (1920) and Rose Hobart (1932).

exciting segment of the montage offered a not too remote suggestion of flagellation, as Tracy appeared on a chariot beating in exultation two horses, a white one and a black one, which ultimately evolve into Turner and Bergman. Peter Ballbusch executed these montage sequences and Joseph Ruttenberg's expert lensing of them won him an Oscar nomination.

The plot: Dr. Jekyll is engrossed in the scientific experiments to separate the evil from the good in men's souls. His fiancee, Beatrix Emery, supports his theory but little encouragement is given him by his colleagues. Returning from a dinner party where he has shocked his friends with his ideas, Jekyll encounters Ivy Peterson, a cheap barmaid. Jekyll is attracted to the girl in spite of himself. That night he drinks his own potion and becomes Mr. Hyde, his evil self.

When Beatrix accompanies her father to the Continent, Jekyll, lonely and frustrated in his work, turns to Hyde more and more frequently. He finds Ivy again, keeps her with him through fear and, in a frenzy, murders her. Beatrix returns, but too late. No longer can Jekyll control his transformation into Hyde. As Hyde, he murders her father, is wounded in the ensuing police chase, and through death is released from his evil self.

In reviewing the film, *Variety* said: "*Dr. Jekyll and Mr. Hyde*, although twice before produced, once in sound, is standard material, offering a wide gamut for an actor . . . The promise, however, of something superlative in film making, in the combination of the star, the Robert Louis Stevenson classic and Victor Fleming's direction, is not completely fulfilled. The fact is, that in the evident striving to make *Jekyll* a "big" film, by elaborating the theme and introducing new characters and situations not found in the original story or earlier stage or screen adaptations, some of the finer psychological points are dulled. John Lee Mahin's script is overlength, running two hours and seven minutes. Nevertheless, it has its highly effective moments. . . ."

Reviews for *Jekyll and Hyde*—and for Tracy's interpretation—were, like *Variety*'s, mixed at best, but aided by a shrewd ad campaign and an eager curiosity on the part of the public, it had a strong box-office following and was one of Metro's biggest money-makers of the year. In 1954, thirteen years after its original release, MGM put the film into distribution again. Paired with the Joan Crawford starrer, *A Woman's Face*, and hypoed by a new ad campaign, the program was sold as a "shocker" package.★

As Beatrix Emery

HONKY TONK

A METRO·GOLDWYN·MAYER PICTURE
1941

With Clark Gable

CAST

CLARK GABLE, *"Candy" Johnson;* LANA TURNER, *Elizabeth Cotton;* FRANK MORGAN, *Judge Cotton;* CLAIRE TREVOR, *"Gold Dust" Nelson;* MARJORIE MAIN, *Mrs. Varner;* ALBERT DEKKER, *Brazos Hearn;* HENRY O'NEILL, *Daniel Wells;* CHILL WILLS, *The Sniper;* VEDA ANN BORG, *Pearl;* DOUGLAS WOOD, *Governor Wilson;* BETTY Blythe, *Mrs. Wilson;* HARRY WORTH, *Harry Gates;* LEW HARVEY, *Blackie;* DOROTHY GRANGER, SHEILA DARCY, *Saloon Girls;* CY KENDALL, *Man With Tar;* RAY TEAL, *Poker Player;* ESTHER MUIR, *Blonde on Train.*

A publicity shot showing Lana looking over still photos of Clark Gable and his past screen loves

With Clark Gable

CREDITS

Director, JACK CONWAY; Producer, PANDRO S. BERMAN; Screenplay, MARGUERITE ROBERTS and JOHN SANFORD; Photography, HAROLD ROSSON; Art Direction, CEDRIC GIBBONS with EDDIE IMAZU; Set Decorations, EDWIN B. WILLIS; Music, FRANZ WAXMAN; Editor, BLANCHE SEWELL; Sound, DOUGLAS SHEARER; Gowns, KALLOCH; Men's Costumes, GILE STEELE; Hair Styles for Claire Trevor, SYDNEY GUILAROFF; Running time, 104 minutes.

NOTES ABOUT THE FILM

MGM's decision to co-star Lana with Clark Gable was not only a box-office natural, but a fan's romantic dream come true. There were, of course, other more or less steady screen teams at the time but none of them quite had the sex-appealing chemistry that Gable and Turner offered.

As part of a splashy publicity campaign heralding the event, *Life* ran a Gable–Turner cover, which was one of that publication's largest-selling issues of 1941. Said *Life*: "Never mind the story of *Honky Tonk*. It is strictly synthetic. Its gold miners and saloon toughs, its bad men and shady ladies are there only to provide a colorful Wild West background for more fundamental business. And that business is a series of sizzling bed-room scenes in which, in a variety of dress and undress, Clark Gable and Lana Turner make love. For Gable, this means another rough and rowdy part like Rhett Butler, the kind of sardonic, hell-raising rogue that has kept him an irresistible box-office magnet. For Turner, now graduated from sweaters to nightgowns, it means the topmost rung in her meteoric four-year climb to success. For cinema fans, it means the birth of a hot new starring team."

Gable and Turner first met back in 1938, a year after the untimely death of Jean Harlow. Gable had been shooting *Too Hot to Handle* when the front office called and asked him to do a reading with their new seventeen-year-old contract player, whom they thought could be groomed for the same type of roles Miss Harlow played. When Lana arrived, with her mother along for moral support, she was obviously nervous, and the reading—from the Gable–Harlow *Red Dust*—was none too successful. Apart from her inexperience, a basic problem was the fact that Gable had always been Lana's favorite movie star and she was terribly in awe of him.

Here are Miss Turner's recollections on this, her first teaming with Gable: "I don't think I'll ever forget the day the studio told me I was going to make a picture with Clark. Experienced as I was by then I shook like a leaf at the very idea. Clark didn't exactly jump with joy either—he hadn't watched my career, never even went to the movies, as a matter of fact! When they told him his next leading lady was going to be Lana Turner, Clark still pictured that awkward, scared little school girl. 'Are you kidding?' he said."

"So, when we started *Honky Tonk*, he was the one person in the world I wanted to prove myself to. And I really put everything I had into our scenes that first morning. Then, later on in the afternoon, I found a box of flowers in my dressing room with a note. It read: 'I'm the world's worst talent scout! Clark.' I'd barely finished reading it when he poked his head through the door, wearing that well-known sheepish grin of his. Then he spoke the five words that made me prouder than any gold Oscar could.'Baby,' he said, 'you sure have learned a thing or two!'"

In *Honky Tonk*, Gable played "Candy" Johnson, a fast-talking con-man, eager to get his share of the rich pickings in the gold-mining town of Yellow Creek. Aided by Judge Cotton, a genial but unscrupulous promoter, Candy starts his own gambling place and makes himself a leader in social politics. He meets his match, however, when he tries his wiles on the Judge's daughter, Elizabeth. Romantic fireworks between the two reach a peak when she gets him drunk and he awakens to find himself married to her, and again when she locks him out of her room and orders him to begin a long courtship. With this, he promptly kicks down the door.

Later on in the story, the Judge is killed by an ally of Candy's and in the excitement Elizabeth falls out of a buggy. She loses the child she is carrying and this reforms Candy, who turns the town back to the aroused citizens. Quietly, he leaves town but Elizabeth follows him for a warm finish in a hotel room.

Honky Tonk caused such a stampede at the box office that trade papers were writing editorials about it. A sensational ad campaign pictured a hot clinch of Turner in Gable's arms with the somewhat prophetic tag-line, "Clark Gable kisses Lana Turner in *Honky Tonk*—and it's screen history."

The first of four co-starring vehicles for the team, *Honky Tonk* was reissued nationally by Metro in 1955 on a double bill with Robert Taylor's *Billy the Kid*. ★

With Marjorie Main and Claire Trevor

With Clark Gable

JOHNNY EAGER

A METRO·GOLDWYN·MAYER PICTURE
1942

A publicity photo showing the major cast members of JOHNNY EAGER. *Standing:*
Diana Lewis, Van Heflin, Patricia Dane and Robert Sterling. Seated: Robert Taylor,
Lana and Edward Arnold

CAST

ROBERT TAYLOR, *Johnny Eager;* LANA TURNER, *Lisbeth Bard;* EDWARD ARNOLD, *John Benson Farrell;* VAN HEFLIN, *Jeff Hartnett;* ROBERT STERLING, *Jimmy Courtney;* PATRICIA DANE, *Garnet;* GLENDA FARRELL, *Mae Blythe;* HENRY O'NEILL, *Mr. Verne;* DIANA LEWIS, *Judy Sanford;* BARRY NELSON, *Lew Rankin;* CHARLES DINGLE, *Marco;* PAUL STEWART, *Julio;* CY KENDALL, *Halligan;* DON COSTELLO, *Billiken;* LOU LUBIN, *Benjy;* JOSEPH DOWNING, *Ryan;* CONNIE GILCHRIST, *Peg Fowler;* ROBIN RAYMOND, *Matilda Fowler;* LEONA MARICLE, *Miss Mines;* BYRON SHORES, *Officer No. 711;* BERYL WALLACE, *Mabel;* ANTHONY WARDE, *Guard.*

CREDITS

Director, MERVYN LEROY; Producer, JOHN W. CONSIDINE, JR.; Screenplay, JOHN LEE MAHIN and JAMES EDWARD GRANT; Photography, HAROLD ROSSON; Art Direction, CEDRIC GIBBONS with STAN ROGERS; Set Decorations, EDWIN B. WILLIS; Music, BRONISLAU KAPER; Editor, ALBERT AKST; Sound, DOUGLAS SHEARER; Gowns, KALLOCH; Running time, 107 minutes.

With Robert Taylor in one of the film's many high-powered love scenes

NOTES ABOUT THE FILM

Having held her own with Clark Gable, Lana was next paired romantically with Robert Taylor, another of the studio's major male screen idols. The occasion for this event was *Johnny Eager*, an original screenplay by John Lee Mahin and Edward Grant. It was the first film in which Mervyn LeRoy directed Lana under the MGM aegis, and it's a particular favorite among Turner fans since it so beautifully displays her at the peak of her young loveliness (Hal Rosson was on the camera).

Not far behind in the looks department was co-star Robert Taylor, here cast as a cold-blooded gangster in another effort on Metro's part to toughen up his screen personality. Some of his recent character portraits had included roles as a track star (*A Yank at Oxford*), a boxing champion (*The Crowd Roars*), a mule skinner (*Stand Up and Fight*), and a western outlaw (*Billy the Kid*). Although Taylor's performance in *Johnny Eager* was an effective one and his character as unregenerate a killer as ever Cagney, Raft or Robinson created for the screen, it still didn't squelch his pretty-boy image—at least not with distaff critics. Wrote Wanda Hale in the New York *Daily News*: "Taylor makes as handsome a gangster as you'd find if you'd go through the underworld with a fine-tooth comb."

The script portrayed Johnny Eager as a mobster who covers his crooked dealings by reporting regularly to his parole officer and, on the surface, living respectably as a taxi driver. Beneath that front, however, he is a conscienceless killer, utterly incapable of understanding man's better nature until he meets Lisbeth Bard, a society girl and the daughter of the district attorney.

When Lisbeth falls in love with him, Johnny frames her into believing she has murdered a man. He then proceeds to use her as a tool against her father who had intended to send him back to prison. Eventually, Johnny reforms to the point of proving to Lisbeth that she was innocent of murder by producing in person the man she thought she killed. He sends her away with her fiance, and having accomplished the one unselfish act of his life, Johnny is killed by an honest cop in an ironic twist ending.

One of *Johnny Eager*'s most exploitable assets was its "sock" ending, which had Taylor planting a solid right cross on Turner's chin. To be sure, the always reliable

MGM ad men came up with another winning campaign. "T-N-T" (for Taylor 'n Turner) read the ads, inspired by some not too subtle love scenes, one of which consisted of some lengthy business on a couch. Highlights of the latter episode, incidentally, were reused by MGM nine years later in *Watch the Birdie* (1951), for a scene where Red Skelton studies the love techniques of famous stars by running off old films.

Robert Taylor and Lana Turner did, of course, make one of the most striking couples ever to grace the screen. Although the obligatory man-woman skirmishes had less sexual tension to them than that produced by the Gable–Turner combination, Taylor and Turner nonetheless possessed a unique sort of chemistry that ignited every romantic scene they shared.* Since audiences were evidently enthusiastic for more of the same, it's odd that Metro never reteamed them, although throughout the years several efforts were made along those lines. For instance, Taylor was to have been one of *The Three Musketeers* (1948), which starred Miss Turner. Then, in 1955, the studio's original intentions for *The Cobweb* were to star Taylor and Turner, along with Grace Kelly, in the roles eventually played by Richard Widmark, Gloria Grahame and Lauren Bacall. Five years later, when both were free of their MGM contracts and *By Love Possessed* (1961) was about to go into production, Taylor had been the top contender for the male lead opposite Miss Turner. However, he was committed to his *Detectives* TV series, and the role was taken by Efrem Zimbalist, Jr.

Also in the cast of *Johnny Eager* was Van Heflin, and although his star presence was far less overwhelming than that of his lustrous co-stars, he was in his own way just as attention-getting. Heflin's role as the alcoholic idealist who is Johnny's only friend was done to such perfection that he was given the Academy Award as 1942's Best Supporting Actor, and he deserved it. Glenda Farrell was present as well, distinguishing one quietly effective scene she consented to do as a favor to Mervyn LeRoy who directed her in her first film.

The reviewer for *Photoplay* had this to say about *Johnny Eager*: "Everyone in the cast shines in his role and, while the theme is repellently real, it's a tremendous picture . . . Frankly, we like Lana better in 'slitchy' roles; but, even so, her performance here is proof La Turner can act."

Less enthusiastic about the film, the critic for the *New York Morning Telegraph* suggested that the film's entire *raison d'être* was to show off its high-powered players: "Here is the star system in all its glory, with plot, action, situation and dialogue all subordinated to the idea of showing the principal players off to their best advantage. Here is a routine business in which nothing counts so much as the circumstance that it is Robert Taylor and Lana Turner who play the leading roles . . . it's the stars alone that the public will come to see in the end. And that this system pays off very handsomely may be discerned in the annual financial statement of MGM."

The "system" *did* pay off, needless to say. In fact, business was so good that, like *Honky Tonk* and *Dr. Jekyll and Mr. Hyde*, *Johnny Eager* warranted a national reissue by MGM—in 1949.★

---

*In a recent interview, when asked to name the sexiest woman in the world, producer Norman (TV's *All in the Family*) Lear replied: "Lana Turner, as she was held in the arms of Robert Taylor on the terrace in *Johnny Eager*."

With Robert Taylor

Above and below: with Robert Taylor

A METRO·GOLDWYN·MAYER PICTURE
1942

CAST

CLARK GABLE, *Jonny Davis;* LANA TURNER, *Paula Lane;* ROBERT STERLING, *Kirk Davis;* PATRICIA DANE, *Crystal McReagan;* REGINALD OWEN, *Willie;* LEE PATRICK, *Eve;* CHARLES DINGLE, *George L. Stafford;* TAMARA SHAYNE, *Mama Lugovska;* LEONID KINSKEY, *Dorloff;* MOLLY LAMONT, *Nurse Winifred;* SARA HADEN, *Miss Coulter;* "RAGS" RAGLAND, *Charlie;* GRADY SUTTON, *Boy;* DOROTHY MORRIS, *Girl;* LUKE CHAN, *Jap Soldier;* KEYE LUKE, *Thomas Chang;* MILES MANDER, *Floyd Kirsten;* DOUGLAS FOWLEY, *Captain;* VAN JOHNSON, *Lt. Wayne Halls;* KEENAN WYNN, *Sgt. Tom Purdy;* FRANK FAYLEN, *Slim.*

CREDITS

Director, WESLEY RUGGLES; Producer, PANDRO S. BERMAN; Screenplay, MARGUERITE ROBERTS; Adaptation by WALTER REISCH; Based upon a Story by CHARLES HOFFMAN; Photography, HAROLD ROSSON; Art Direction, CEDRIC GIBBONS with MALCOLM BROWN; Set Decorations, EDWIN B. WILLIS with HUGH HUNT; Editor, FRANK E. HULL; Sound, DOUGLAS SHEARER; Music, BRONISLAU KAPER; Gowns, KALLOCH; Hair Stylist, SYDNEY GUILAROFF; Running Time, 108 minutes.

NOTES ABOUT THE FILM

After the impressive box-office strength of *Honky Tonk,* it was inevitable that Metro would reteam Gable and Turner, whom one critic labelled "MGM's substitutes for boy scouts and matches." *Somewhere I'll Find You* was the vehicle, and it contained all the necessary elements for similar money-in-the-bank results. The picture was a highly pre-sold one, having been based on a popular 1940 *Cosmopolitan* serial with its script updated to include a rousing final sequence on Bataan, thrillingly staged by director Wesley Ruggles. Marguerite Roberts did the scenario, the dialogue of which was peppered with some of the frankest, sexiest innuendos yet heard on the screen.

Filming began in mid-January 1942 (under the title *Red Light*), and was halted after it had been in work three days when Gable's wife, Carole Lombard, was killed in an airplane crash while on a bond tour. With Gable in mourning, studio scuttlebutt had it that Metro would strike the production off the books and absorb the cost of a few months research and three days of actual filming. But less than four weeks after Miss Lombard's death, Gable strode onto the lot and, with quiet professionalism, finished the job he'd begun. When the film was finally in the can, he left to join the Armed Forces (it was during the making of *Somewhere I'll Find You* that, as a favor to "The King," Lana took over a radio spot to which Miss Lombard had been committed, a CBS

With Clark Gable

Screen Guild adaptation of Lombard's film, *Mr. and Mrs. Smith,* co-starring Errol Flynn).

But not all the publicity attendant with the making of *Somewhere I'll Find You* had tragic overtones. On the much lighter side: MGM's press department, possibly as an answer to Paramount's Veronica Lake publicity, made certain the wire services were on hand when Sydney Guilaroff created a new look for Lana's newspaper reporter role by cutting her hair into a shorter, more sensible bob. Dubbed "The Victory Hairdo," the

With Patricia Dane

newspaper gal he stood up three years before, and when he kisses her, he remembers—but definitely. He also discovers that she's the girl Kirk is crazy about. Jonny tries to give her up, not realizing that she is really in love with him, and he with her.

When Paula is sent on an assignment in the Far East, she disappears and the brothers are reinstated on the paper and sent after her. They find her on Bataan where Kirk is eventually killed in action. The closing scene of the film is quite stirring, with Jonny and Paula sitting in a tent feverishly hammering out the news for their paper. "More to come" are the final words of their story.

Time's reviewer said: "*Somewhere I'll Find You* is a farewell piece for Clark Gable, now a corporal in the Army Air Forces at Miami Beach. If he lacked stomach for the job (since the death of Miss Lombard), he tries manfully to conceal the fact, and does more than his share in turning out a typical Gable show, loud, expert, witty, rough . . . Lana Turner is a superbly toothsome foil for Gable's masterful routines. She can so tilt her chin that, in any posture, she suggests that she is looking up from a pillow."

Variety's critic got Lana's "message" as well: "Miss Turner is the modern Jean Harlow of celluloid—a sexy, torchy, clinging blonde who shatters the inhibitions of the staidest male. Gable has seemingly always made the same impression on women. Tossing them both together, even if surrounding their clinches with but a specious story, provides an extremely potent antidote for ailing exhibitors."

Newsweek's theory about the picture was perhaps the best: "The civilized way to consider *Somewhere I'll Find You* is calmly and in the generous spirit in which it is offered. MGM evolved the formula for this film with the production of *Honky Tonk* last year. *Honky Tonk* was a horse opera without horses; an action film that provided action chiefly for those who thrilled when Clark Gable gathered Lana Turner into his insisting arms. As this business occurred at frequent intervals throughout the script, the film proved a box-office bonanza. Impressionable customers even wrote MGM asking for more

new style was, according to a studio release, ultra-practical and ideal for war work, since it wouldn't get caught in defense plant machinery. Metro got considerable mileage out of this gimmick—when news of the bob reached England, they were asked to send instructions for the coiffure to the women of the British Isles as quickly as possible.

The plot of *Somewhere I'll Find You* had to do with two crack foreign correspondents, Jonny Davis and his younger brother, Kirk. Fired by his paper, Jonny returns to his Greenwich Village apartment and finds Paula Lane in his shower. Paula reminds him that she is the

With Robert Sterling and Clark Gable

With Clark Gable

With Clark Gable

of the same. And that is the best explanation for the co-stars' current command performance. *Somewhere I'll Find You* is more of the same—with variations . . . You can be sure MGM wouldn't have made this film if there weren't millions of people who would appreciate it.''

Predictably, millions of people did appreciate *Somewhere I'll Find You*. By September 1942, Metro sales executives were announcing that its domestic return alone would be $3,500,000—indicating that there would indeed be ''more to come'' for the team of Gable and Turner.

Note: A clip from *Somewhere I'll Find You* was used in *The Stratton Story* (1949), for a scene that shows James Stewart romancing June Allyson in a movie theatre as Gable and Turner make love on-screen. ''Hey,'' says the annoyed patron in back of them. ''You're good, but *they're* better.'' ★

SLIGHTLY DANGEROUS

A METRO·GOLDWYN·MAYER PICTURE
1943

CAST

LANA TURNER, *Peggy Evans*; ROBERT YOUNG, *Bob Stuart*; WALTER BRENNAN, *Cornelius Burden*; DAME MAE WHITTY, *Baba*; EUGENE PALLETTE, *Durstin*; ALAN MOWBRAY, *English Gentleman*; FLORENCE BATES, *Mrs. Roanoke-Brooke*; HOWARD FREEMAN, *Mr. Quill*; MILLARD MITCHELL, *Baldwin*; WARD BOND, *Jimmy*; PAMELA BLAKE, *Mitzi*; RAY COLLINS, *Snodgrass*; PAUL STANTON, *Stanhope*; ROBIN RAYMOND, *Girl*; KAY MEDFORD, *Girl Getting Off Bus*; GRACE HAYLE, *Lady Customer*; ANN DORAN, CATHERINE LEWIS, *Salesgirls*; ALMIRA SESSIONS, *Landlady*; EDWARD EARLE, *Employee*; EDDIE ACUFF, *Sailor*; FRANK FAYLEN, *Gateman*; NORMA VARDEN, *Opera Singer*; MANTAN MORELAND, *Negro Waiter*; CLIFF CLARK, *Detective*; HARRY HAYDEN, *Doctor*; MIMI DOYLE, *Miss Kingsway*; JOE DEVLIN, *Painter*; BOBBY BLAKE, *Boy on Porch*; ROBERT EMMET O'CONNOR, *Reporter*; MARY ELLIOTT, *Operator*; RAY TEAL, *Pedestrian*; MARJORIE "BABE" KANE, *Customer*.

Across the page: one of the super-sexy photos used in the ad campaign for SLIGHTLY DANGEROUS

CREDITS

Director, WESLEY RUGGLES; Producer, PANDRO S. BERMAN; Screenplay, CHARLES LEDERER and GEORGE OPPENHEIMER; Story by IAN MCLELLAN HUNTER and AILEEN HAMILTON; Photography, HAROLD ROSSON; Art Direction, CEDRIC GIBBONS with MALCOLM BROWN; Set Decorations, EDWIN B. WILLIS with MILDRED GRIFFITHS; Editor, FRANK E. HULL; Sound, DOUGLAS SHEARER; Music, BRONISLAU KAPER; Costumes, IRENE; Running time, 94 minutes. (Note: *Slightly Dangerous* is one of several late '30s/early '40s MGM features to boast the uncredited participation of BUSTER KEATON as a gag consultant.)

NOTES ABOUT THE FILM

Slightly Dangerous is typical Metro fluff of the period —attractively produced, briskly paced, and pointlessly entertaining. Its major function was to give Lana a chance to step out on her own—without the presence of a Gable or a Tracy or a Taylor for box-office assistance.

It was the first Grade-A production the studio built solely around her and tailored to her personality. This time, it was Lana who initiated all the plot intricacies and her co-star who was limited to providing the cus-

Lana had two different looks in SLIGHTLY DANGEROUS. *Left, as brunette Peggy Evans; right, as blonde Carol Burden*

119

tomary romantic foil (Robert Young, whom Lana had supported just five years earlier in *Rich Man, Poor Girl*, was the leading man).

Slightly Dangerous cast Lana as a rather militant Cinderella, and during the course of the film she appeared as both blonde and brunette. Charles Lederer and George Oppenheimer wrote the script which MGM had acquired as an original property in October 1941. Shooting began in September 1942, and during production the film had two working titles—*Nothing Ventured*, and the more pertinent *Careless Cinderella*.

The opening of the story placed Lana on familiar ground—at a soda fountain. However, this time she was on the other side of the counter. As Peggy Evans, a young and beautiful soda clerk in a small-town department store, her life is so monotonous that she resorts to making banana splits blindfolded. The customers get a kick out of this method but the store manager, Bob Stuart, doesn't. When he calls her into his office to reprimand her, Peggy becomes hysterical, rushes out, and in the excitement the girls think Bob has made unwelcome advances. When Peggy suddenly departs town, leaving a suicide note behind, Bob gets all the blame and even loses his job.

In New York, Peggy gets herself some new clothes and a new personality with her last dollar. She also gets hit on the head by a bucket of red paint at the entrance to a newspaper office. She pretends to have amnesia, and convinces the publisher of the paper that she is the long-lost daughter of Cornelius Burden, an industrial tycoon. And with a little luck and much subterfuge, Peggy even convinces the irascible Burden that she is his daughter, Carol.

Eventually, Bob sees her picture in the paper and swears to bring her back to town to clear his reputation. When he catches up with her, he confronts her with a phony marriage certificate and insists that she married him. With Peggy claiming amnesia, she has no choice but to go with him.

Burden, meanwhile, in checking Bob and the alleged marriage, discovers that Peggy is not his daughter, but by the film's end he doesn't even care. He is now so fond of her that he wants her for a daughter whether she's bona fide or not. To make the picture complete, Peggy and Bob have fallen in love.

Wesley Ruggles, who directed *Somewhere I'll Find You*, was also at the helm of *Slightly Dangerous*. A former Keystone Kop who had worked with Buster Keaton in silents, Ruggles did not hesitate to spark the film with several slapstick sequences, one of which called for Robert Young to topple over the balcony of a concert hall while a performance was in progress.

Turner and Ruggles worked well together, and *Slightly Dangerous* contains one of the best performances of Lana's early stardom. Her most effective moment in the film occurs in the scene where she moves with an unhappy desperation through a room full of toys, trying to recognize the one that will establish her identity as the long-lost daughter of a millionaire.

In the New York *Daily Mirror*, Lee Mortimer

In one hilarious sequence in SLIGHTLY DANGEROUS, *Lana is hit with a bucket of red paint. Above, with Eugene Pallette*

With Grace Hayle, Robert Young and Pamela Blake

thought the picture was "thin on material, but Ruggles'
directorial pacing and the cast's acting ability help
overcome plot handicaps; and when they falter, the
Turner chassis does the rest."

The reviewer for *The Family Circle* magazine had this
to say: "This new builder-upper for its No. 1 glamour
girl should do just that for both MGM and Lana, if
slightly less for audiences in general. The picture affords
the cash customers an opportunity to view Lana in
repose and in hysterics, in love and out, dark-haired and
blonde, dressed and not dressed. And despite certain
distractions, it must be conceded that the girl has the
beginnings of the makings of a trouper."

Slightly Dangerous' supporting cast should not go
unmentioned since it contained a veritable Who's Who
of the then-most-popular character actors in films. In
addition to Walter Brennan who played the millionaire,
there was Dame May Whitty, Eugene Pallette, Alan
Mowbray, Florence Bates, Ward Bond, Millard Mitchell
and Ray Collins.

Also worthy of note is the effective advertising
strategy used for the picture. The poster art consisted of
a series of cheesecake shots specially taken by MGM's
ace portrait artist, Eric Carpenter. Designed to perk up
the ad campaign, the *Slightly Dangerous* posters
showcased Lana in a sexy, black sequinned gown,
offering a come-hither look and a moist-lipped, pouty
invitation. It was one of the most provocative photo
sessions she ever posed for, and during World War II
these pictures were the Turner pin-ups most frequently
requested by her G.I. fans.★

With Walter Brennan and Dame Mae Whitty

With Robert Young and Walter Brennan

THE YOUNGEST PROFESSION

A METRO·GOLDWYN·MAYER PICTURE

1943

A 1943 publicity portrait used to promote Lana's appearance in THE YOUNGEST PROFESSION

CAST

VIRGINIA WEIDLER, *Joan Lyons;* EDWARD ARNOLD, *Burton V. Lyons;* JOHN CARROLL, *Dr. Hercules;* ANN AYARS, *Susan Thayer;* MARTA LINDEN, *Edith Lyons;* DICK SIMMONS, *Douglas Sutton;* AGNES MOOREHEAD, *Miss Featherstone;* JEAN PORTER, *Patricia Drew;* RAYMOND ROE, *Schuyler;* DOROTHY MORRIS, *Secretary;* SCOTTY BECKETT, *Junior Lyons;* MARCIA MAE JONES, *Vera Bailey;* SARA HADEN, *Sister Lassie;* BEVERLY JEAN SAUL (BEVERLY TYLER), *Thyra Winter;* JESSIE GRAYSON, *Lilybud;* MARJORIE GATESON, *Mrs. Drew;* THURSTON HALL, *Mr. Drew;* AILEEN PRINGLE, *Miss Farwood;* DOROTHY CHRISTY, *Sally;* MARK DANIELS, *Les Peterson;* ANN CODEE, *Sandra's Maid;* EDWARD BUZZELL, *Man in Theatre;* and LANA TURNER, GREER GARSON, WALTER PIDGEON, ROBERT TAYLOR, WILLIAM POWELL, *Themselves.*

CREDITS

Director, EDWARD BUZZELL; Producer, B. F. ZEIDMAN; Screenplay, GEORGE OPPENHEIMER, CHARLES LEDERER and LEONARD SPIGELGASS; Based on a book by LILLIAN DAY; Art Direction, CEDRIC GIBBONS with EDWARD CARFAGNO; Set Decorations, EDWIN B. WILLIS with HELEN CONWAY; Photography, CHARLES LAWTON; Music, DAVID SNELL; Costumes, IRENE and SHOUP; Editor, RALPH WINTERS; Sound, DOUGLAS SHEARER; Assistant Director, JULIAN SILBERSTEIN; Running time, 81 minutes.

NOTES ABOUT THE FILM

The Youngest Profession, according to Lillian Day's novel, was the collecting of movie star autographs. Metro's screen version was adapted as a vehicle for their young ingenue, Virginia Weidler, newly emerged from her pigtailed brat roles.

Miss Weidler played the part of Joan Lyons, the nation's most avid movie fan and president of the "Guiding Stars," a teen-age club bent on securing celebrity signatures at any cost. Every girl belonging has to gather at least four top names each month. The plot of the story develops some hilarious tangles as Joan leads the club members into scrape after scrape in her slavish devotion to the cause. A romantic sub-plot is thrown in: Joan, who has seen far too many movies, mistakenly decides that her father has fallen for his secretary. She sells one of her precious autograph books in order to pay a gigolo to lavish attentions on her bewildered mother, in hopes that her father will become jealous. When the hoax is eventually confessed, Joan runs away to join the Salvation Army. But her parents finally locate her and take her home for the traditional happy ending.

The Youngest Profession was geared for the small-town family trade but the presence of several important guest stars assured its reception in any house, including New York's vast Radio City Music Hall. Interspersed into the plot for obvious box-office reasons were fleeting appearances by such Metro luminaries as Lana Turner, Greer Garson, Walter Pidgeon, Robert Taylor and William Powell, all appearing as themselves.

Lana begins the parade of stars, knee-deep in fan mail in her studio dressing room; Miss Garson comes on

"NOTHING *absolutely* NOTHING can stop me from getting *Lana Turner's* autograph"

next, as the "Guiding Stars" trail her from Grand Central Station to her hotel suite where Walter Pidgeon is introduced as a visitor; Robert Taylor occupies the suite across the hall from the Lyons family (enabling him to hear a neophyte fan remarking, "Is Robert Taylor anybody?"); and William Powell closes the film, materializing in an elevator at the same time Joan is having daydreams about him.

Nepotism ran rampant during the proceedings as virtually every top Metro star received the name-dropping treatment. Only once—to Warners' Bette Davis—did the script bow to a player from a rival studio. Seen today, *The Youngest Profession* can be a lot of fun for the movie-oriented set, particularly when the dialogue is peppered with lines like: "I swear it on a stack of *Photoplays*!".★

123

DU BARRY WAS A LADY

A METRO·GOLDWYN·MAYER PICTURE
1943

A publicity photo of Lana in the gown she wears in DU BARRY WAS A LADY

CAST

RED SKELTON, *Louis Blore/King Louis;* LUCILLE BALL, *May Daly/Mme. Du Barry;* GENE KELLY, *Alec Howe/Black Arrow;* VIRGINIA O'BRIEN, *Ginny;* RAGS RAGLAND, *Charlie/The Dauphin;* ZERO MOSTEL, *Rami, the Swami/Taliostra;* DONALD MEEK, *Mr. Jones/Duc de Choiseul;* DOUGLAS DUMBRILLE, *Willie/Duc de Rigor;* GEORGE GIVOT, *Cheezy/Count de Roquefort;* LOUISE BEAVERS, *Niagara;* TOMMY DORSEY AND HIS ORCHESTRA, *Themselves;* CECIL CUNNINGHAM, *Wife;* HARRY HAYDEN, *Husband;* CLARA BLANDICK, *Old Lady;* MARIE BLAKE, *Woman;* PIERRE WATKIN, *Rich Patron;* DON WILSON,

Announcer's Voice; SIG ARNO, *Nick;* HUGH BEAUMONT, *Footman;* CHESTER CLUTE, *Doctor;* KAY ALDRIDGE, HAZEL BROOKS, GEORGIA CARROLL, INEZ COOPER, NATALIE DRAPER, MARILYN MAXWELL, EVE WHITNEY, KAY WILLIAMS, *Showgirl;* DICK HAYMES, JO STAFFORD, *Vocalists;* LANA TURNER, *Herself (Unbilled Guest Appearance).*

CREDITS

Director, ROY DEL RUTH; Producer, ARTHUR FREED; Screenplay, IRVING BRECHER; Adaptation, NANCY HAMILTON; Additional Dialogue, WILKIE MAHONEY; Based on a Play Produced by B. G. DeSYLVA and Written by HERBERT FIELDS and B. G. DeSYLVA; Music, COLE PORTER; Additional Songs, LEW BROWN, RALPH FREED, BURTON LANE, ROGER EDENS, E. Y. HARBURG; Musical Direction, GEORGIE STOLL; Orchestrations, GEORGE BASSMAN, LEO ARNAUD, AXEL STORDAHL, SY OLIVER; Musical Presentation, MERRILL PYE; Dance Direction, CHARLES WALTERS; Photography (Technicolor), KARL FREUND; Technicolor Color Direction, NATALIE KALMUS and HENRI JAFFA; Costumes, IRENE, SHOUP and GILE STEELE; Editor, BLANCHE SEWELL; Sound, DOUGLAS SHEARER; Art Direction, CEDRIC GIBBONS; Set Decorations, EDWIN B. WILLIS and HENRY GRACE; Songs: "I Love an Esquire Girl," "Madame, I Like Your Crepes Suzettes," "Friendship," "Salome," "Do I Love You," "Du Barry Was a Lady," "Katie Went to Haiti," "Ladies of the Bath," "Rise, Rise." Running time, 101 minutes.

NOTES ABOUT THE FILM

Like *The Youngest Profession,* *Du Barry* was another guest spot, only briefer (less than fifteen seconds of screen time, to be exact). This one was more on the order of a surprise appearance—minus screen credit— and was brief enough so that it could be filmed on one of Lana's free moments from *Slightly Dangerous,* which was shooting at the same time.

Du Barry was Metro's almost totally rewritten (for the Hays office) film version of the racy Herbert Fields–Buddy DeSylva stage hit which first debuted in New Haven, Connecticut on November 9, 1939, before a Broadway run that lasted almost a year. Red Skelton and Lucille Ball filled the spots held on the stage by Bert Lahr and Ethel Merman, and Gene Kelly and Virginia O'Brien were the film replacements for Ronald Graham and Betty Grable.

Du Barry's stage-to-screen launderization was so thorough it began with the occupation of its chief protagonist, a character named Louie Blore. As played on the stage by Lahr, he was a men's-room attendant (a situation that prompted some of the musical's bawdiest lyrics). For the film, however, Louie was yanked from the john and transformed into a nightclub coatroom clerk. Here, his fervent but futile devotion to the club's top singer, May Daly, is getting him nowhere fast since she's in love with dancer Alec Howe. When Louie becomes rich through a sweepstakes ticket and dubbed "King Louie" by the newspapers, May suddenly becomes very interested in him.

During a celebration party at the club, Louie is accidentally administered a potent Mickey Finn that transports him into dreamland. In the dream, he envisions himself to be Louis XV, King of France, with May Daly as his mistress, the celebrated Madame Du Barry. But even here he's burdened by the competition of his rival, Alec Howe, who appears in the form of the Black Arrow, a mysterious plotter against the throne.

In the midst of a French revolution, Louis wakes up back at the club where the plot's romantic complications untangle as May announces her engagement to Alec, and Louie winds up with Ginny, the cigarette girl, who has long loved him from afar.

Without the spicy qualities of the stage original, *Variety* thought *Du Barry* was *"too much* of a lady now . . .* As if to compensate, Metro has given the picture a topnotch production and a Technicolor setting. Sets and costumes are as lavish as a state dinner, and there's enough cheesecake for all the calendars in the world for the next twenty years."

On the subject of cheesecake, Lana's brief moment came in the dazzling "I Love an Esquire Girl" production number. Except for the title tune and "Friendship" finale, many of the original Cole Porter lyrics were given a complete reworking to include contemporary names and topics. A perfect example of this is the "Esquire Girl" verse which name-dropped everyone from photographer George Hurrell to the Frankenstein monster. Red Skelton performed the number, as an Esquire calendar came to life in the form of twelve of Metro's loveliest starlets. At the end of the number, Skelton's lyric concludes with the line: ". . . and if Lana Turner doesn't set you in a whirl, then you don't love a lovely girl." At this point, Lana materializes from out of nowhere, in a form-fitting white lace gown, to take her place alongside him. Skelton turns and looks at her, does a double-take and passes out. On this note, Lana moves in for a full close-up and winks into the camera as the number ends and the scene fades.

Discounting her barely visible appearance as an extra in *A Star Is Born*, *Du Barry* marked the first time movie audiences had the opportunity to see what Lana looked like in Technicolor. But they really had to look fast! ★

With Red Skelton

MARRIAGE IS A PRIVATE AFFAIR

A METRO·GOLDWYN·MAYER PICTURE
1944

CAST

LANA TURNER, *Theo Scofield West;* JAMES CRAIG, *Capt. Miles Lancing;* JOHN HODIAK, *Lieut. Tom West;* FRANCES GIFFORD, *Sissy Mortimer;* HUGH MARLOWE, *Joseph I. Murdock;* NATALIE SCHAFER, *Mrs. Selworth;* KEENAN WYNN, *Major Bob Wilton;* HERBERT RUDLEY, *Ted Mortimer;* PAUL CAVANAGH, *Mr. Selworth;* MORRIS ANKRUM, *Ed Scofield;* JANE GREEN, *Martha;* TOM DRAKE, *Bill Rice;* BYRON FOULGER, *Ned Boulton;* SHIRLEY PATTERSON, *Mary Saunders;* NANA BRYANT, *Nurse;* ALEXANDER D'ARCY, *Mr. Garby;* CECILIA CALLEJO, *Señora Guizman;* VIRGINIA BRISSAC, *Mrs. Courtland West;* EVE WHITNEY, *Maid of Honor;* HAZEL BROOKS, *Bridesmaid;* KATHERINE (KARIN) BOOTH, *Girl with Miles;* KAY WILLIAMS, *Pretty Girl;* JODY GILBERT, *Girl Taxi Driver;* BRUCE KELLOGG, *Young Lieutenant.*

CREDITS

Director, ROBERT Z. LEONARD; Producer, PANDRO S. BERMAN; Screenplay, DAVID HERTZ and LENORE COFFEE; Based on the Novel by JUDITH KELLY; Photography, RAY JUNE; Art Direction, CEDRIC GIBBONS and HUBERT B. HOBSON; Set Decoration, EDWIN B. WILLIS with RICHARD PEFFERLE; Music, BRONISLAU KAPER; Editor, GEORGE WHITE; Sound, DOUGLAS SHEARER; Costume Supervision, IRENE; Costume Associate, MARION HERWOOD; Makeup, JACK DAWN; Assistant Director, WILLIAM LEWIS; Running time, 116 minutes.

NOTES ABOUT THE FILM

Although hardly embraced by critics in 1944, *Marriage Is a Private Affair* has in recent years attained "cult" status among diehard Turner fans. This was the film that brought Lana back to the screen after an eighteen-month absence during which time she gave birth to her daughter Cheryl. Accordingly, Metro made up for her absence in a big way—not only was she on screen for virtually all of the film's 116 minutes, but it was the first picture to give her solo star billing. As further bonuses, it permitted her to wear a succession of dazzling Irene gowns, sport an equal amount of Sydney Guilaroff hair styles, and receive the most loving photographic attention of her career to date. An endless glamour display, *Marriage Is a Private Affair,* more than anything else, was—and still is—a valentine to her fans.

Robert Z. Leonard, who directed *Ziegfeld Girl,* was at the helm of the film which stemmed from the Judith Kelly best-seller about matrimonial discord and which required the star to make the transition from frivolous society girl to wartime bride and mother. Lana played Theo Scofield, a New York playgirl, who "spends her winters in Miami and her summers in Reno," the latter while waiting for the next divorce of her much-married

With John Hodiak

With Fred Beckner

reconciliations follow, and threaded through it all is a romantic triangle that involves Tom's three best friends and only adds to Theo's problems. In the final scene, Theo, contemplating a divorce, has a change of heart, and makes up with Tom via an Army radio hookup between their home and his New Guinea flying base.

In her *New York Sun* review, Eileen Creelman described *Marriage Is a Private Affair* as a "pin-up girl picture." Appropriately enough, Metro concocted one of its most unusual "gimmick" premieres for the film, inspired by a fan letter received from a bomber group overseas. They called themselves the "Lana Turner Squadron" and wrote that they hoped they'd be among the first to see her next movie. A screening was arranged, which in true MGM fashion, grew to colossal proportions. The studio readied not one, but ninety-eight prints of *Marriage*, and designated a date late in September 1944 for a huge world premiere in all theaters of

With Frances Gifford

With John Hodiak

mother who tells her daughter "the first marriage, at least, should be romantic." On this theory, Theo marries Tom West, a fighter pilot on furlough, who is later grounded to handle an important war job in a laboratory.

After their baby is born, Theo devotes herself conscientiously to being a model wife and mother. She tries hard at first, but has little faith in her ability to make a good wife. She misses her carefree youth, her string of boyfriends, the glitter and glamour of being loved by a lot of men instead of just one. When she runs into Miles Lancing, an ex-beau, Theo is annoyed because he doesn't act as romantic as he once did. So she dons a sexy gown and heads for the Officers' Club to find him and recapture his attention.

But when she returns home that night she finds Tom angry because this was the night they were to celebrate their baby's first birthday. More misunderstandings and

With John Hodiak

With James Craig

one scene in which the newlyweds are shown sound asleep in twin beds the morning after the wedding drew some strange noises from the audience . . ."

When the U.S. release occurred one month later, the *Los Angeles Times* said: " . . . the picture is unimportant except as a vehicle for Miss Turner but it is effective as such, and it demonstrates her ability to act, to project a soft and appealing femininity, with, of course, that pronounced loveliness which has always been hers."

Despite the manpower shortage at the time, this Turner vehicle spotlighted not one, but two, handsome new studio contract players, James Craig and John Hodiak (replacing Gene Kelly). A good supporting cast included Frances Gifford, Hugh Marlowe, Keenan Wynn and Natalie Schafer, in her film debut as Lana's frivolous mother (Miss Schafer repeated her role as Lana's mother approximately twenty-five years later in the TV series, *The Survivors*). ★

war. As icing on the cake, they filmed a special prologue that shows Lana greeting the GI audience from the screen with this typically wartime "chin-up" message:

"Well . . . here we are, having a world premiere of our picture for the armed forces overseas. And if you think that isn't pretty important, boys, you've got another think coming. But . . . seriously . . . you should see all the best pictures, and you should see them first because . . . well, because you're you. Because you're first in our hearts, our hopes and our thoughts. Thanks for coming to the show. I hope you like it. So long and good luck."

The first screening took place as planned before the Lana Turner Squadron at the Teatro delle Palme in Naples, Italy on September 23, 1944 and a reporter covering the event for an Army newspaper noted: "Miss Turner's fine points are revealed to advantage in a few idyllic sequences which suit the GI appetite. However,

KEEP YOUR POWDER DRY

A METRO·GOLDWYN·MAYER PICTURE
1945

With Susan Peters and Laraine Day

CAST

LANA TURNER, *Valerie Parks;* LARAINE DAY, *Leigh Rand;* SUSAN PETERS, *Ann Darrison;* AGNES MOOREHEAD, *Lt. Col. Spottiswoode;* BILL JOHNSON, *Capt. Bill Barclay;* NATALIE SCHAFER, *Harriet Corwin;* LEE PATRICK, *Gladys Hopkins;* JESS BARKER, *Junior Vanderheusen;* JUNE LOCKHART, *Sarah Swanson;* MARTA LINDEN, *Capt. Sanders;* TIM MURDOCK, *Capt. Joseph Mannering;* MICHAEL KIRBY, *Capt. John Darrison;* HENRY O'NEILL, *Brig. Gen. Rand;* PIERRE WATKIN, *Mr. Lorrison;* SHIRLEY PATTERSON, *WAC Brooks;* BARBARA SEARS (BOBO ROCKEFELLER), *WAC McBride;* MARIE BLAKE, *WAC Corporal;* CLAIRE ROCHELLE, *WAC Corporal;* ELIZABETH RUSSELL, *WAC Sergeant;* GERALDINE WALL, *Judo Instructor;* RAY TEAL, *Army Captain.*

CREDITS

Director, EDWARD BUZZELL; Producer, GEORGE HAIGHT; Screenplay, MARY C. MCCALL, JR. and GEORGE BRUCE; Photography, RAY JUNE; Art Direction, CEDRIC GIBBONS and LEONID VASIAN; Set Decorations, EDWIN B. WILLIS

with RALPH S. HURST; Editor, FRANK E. HULL; Sound, DOUGLAS SHEARER; Music, DAVID SNELL; Costume Supervision, IRENE; Costume Associate, MARION HERWOOD KEYES; Technical Advisor, 1ST LT. LOUISE V. WHITE; Assistant Director, HORACE HOUGH; Running time, 93 minutes.

NOTES ABOUT THE FILM

Here was a distinct novelty: a Lana Turner feature in which the romantic element was virtually nonexistent.

An original story by Mary McCall, Jr. and George Bruce, *Keep Your Powder Dry* was largely propaganda for the WACs, and a feminine prototype of the countless servicemen films that engulfed the market during the war years. Unlike the heavy dramatics of previous films dedicated to the women's military (Paramount's *So Proudly We Hail*, Universal's *Ladies Courageous* and Metro's own *Cry Havoc*), its treatment was nonserious although not quite as light as its flip title suggests.

The story centered on three new WAC recruits. Valerie Parks, a New York playgirl, enlists in the WACs so she can capture the sympathy of the bank trustees empowered to turn over to her a fortune, if she is

With Natalie Schafer

As Valerie Parks

With Laraine Day

deserving of it. Once she gets her money, she plans to flunk out of the service and return to her wild nightclub existence.

Born and reared in the Army, Leigh Rand goes into the WACs simply because it's the natural thing for her to do. As an Army brat, she continuously flaunts her superior knowledge of the military life, which proves to be a nuisance to the other girls in the barracks—particularly Valerie. The plot development hinges on the feud between Leigh, officious and patronizing, and Valerie, determined to prove she is the better soldier.

Ann Darrison, the third "musketeer" of the group, who has joined the WACs because she wants to be near her soldier husband, is the leveling influence between the two other girls. But when Leigh gets to be cadet company commander, the old dislike springs up again.

With Susan Peters

Finally, on the drill field, Leigh proceeds to bully Valerie so much that Val, who has been keeping her temper admirably, can stand no more and slaps Leigh in front of the other recruits.

This precipitates the showdown in which, at the official inquiry, Leigh is shocked to learn that few of her confreres consider her officer material.

Ann, meanwhile, is notified that her husband has been killed in action. In an effort to patch up the differences between her two friends, however, she hides her grief within herself. Then, by accident, Val and Leigh learn of Ann's tragedy. Thoroughly ashamed of themselves, they resolve their problems and by the film's end, Val has even decided to remain in the Corps with the other two girls.

Wrote critic Philip K. Scheuer in the *Los Angeles Times*: "Even when it turns to the severities of military discipline, Metro-Goldwyn-Mayer manages to pour on the glamour. Intended as an animated recruiting poster for the Women's Army Corps, *Keep Your Powder Dry* somehow emerges as a high-powered vehicle for the studio's stable of beauties . . . For all I know, it may still cause the more impulsive among you girls to rush right out and join. Certainly our three heroines succeed in looking remarkably well groomed through it all—the basic training, the drills, the staging and all the rest . . . through their personal relations, however, there runs a strain of acrimony—a 'feud,' as it's called in the movies —which also suggests that the life of a soldier in skirts may not altogether be a bed of roses."

Despite the all too obvious MGM glamour which made it hardly an exact picture of "life in the Women's Army Corps," as the advertisements said, *Keep Your Powder Dry* was produced through the cooperation of that uniformed body and even had a WAC—1st Lt. Louise V. White—as technical advisor.

"You'll be fascinated with the way the inner workings of the WAC are shown in this picture," wrote Virginia Wilson in *Modern Screen*. "And when you see Lana in her uniform, you'll probably rush right out and join up yourself."

Which may have been the reason why MGM and the Women's Army Corps joined forces to make this film in the first place. When *Keep Your Powder Dry* premiered at the Capitol Theatre in Washington, D.C. on March 8, 1945, it opened as part of a WAC recruiting campaign. Miss Turner was present in one of a series of personal appearances she made on behalf of the film. How many recruits she inspired hasn't been recorded. But one thing is certain—none of them could possibly have looked as good as she did in khaki.★

WEEK-END AT THE WALDORF

A METRO·GOLDWYN·MAYER PICTURE

1945

A publicity photo showing the stars of the film: Van Johnson, Lana, Ginger Rogers and Walter Pidgeon

CAST

GINGER ROGERS, *Irene Malvern;* LANA TURNER, *Bunny Smith;* WALTER PIDGEON, *Chip Collyer;* VAN JOHNSON, *Capt. James Hollis;* EDWARD ARNOLD, *Martin X. Edley;* PHYLLIS THAXTER, *Cynthia Drew;* KEENAN WYNN, *Oliver Webson;* ROBERT BENCHLEY, *Randy Morton;* LEON AMES, *Henry Burton;* LINA ROMAY, *Juanita;* SAMUEL S. HINDS, *Mr. Jessup;* XAVIER CUGAT AND HIS ORCHESTRA, *Themselves;* WARNER ANDERSON, *Dr. Campbell;* PORTER HALL, *Stevens;* GEORGE ZUCCO, *Bey of Aribajan;* BOB GRAHAM, *Singer;* MICHAEL KIRBY, *Lt. John Rand;* CORA SUE COLLINS, *Jane Rand;* JACQUELINE DE WIT, *Kate Douglas;* FRANK PUGLIA, *Emile;* CHARLES WILSON, *Hi Johns;* IRVING BACON, *Sam Skelly;* MILES MANDER, *British Secretary;* NANA BRYANT, *Mrs. H. Davenport Drew;* RUSSELL HICKS, *McPherson;* MORONI OLSEN, *House Detective Blake;* BYRON FOULGER, *Barber;* BESS FLOWERS, *Guest.*

CREDITS

Director, ROBERT Z. LEONARD; Producer, ARTHUR HORNBLOW, JR.; Screenplay, SAM and BELLA SPEWACK; Adaptation by GUY BOLTON; Suggested by the Play *Grand Hotel* by VICKI BAUM; Photography, ROBERT PLANCK; Art Direction, CEDRIC GIBBONS and DANIEL B. CATHCART; Set Decorations, EDWIN B. WILLIS with JACK BONAR; Editor, ROBERT J. KERN; Sound, DOUGLAS SHEARER; Music, JOHNNY GREEN; Orchestrations, TED DUNCAN; Choral Arrangement, KAY THOMPSON; Dance Direction, CHARLES WALTERS; Costume Supervision, IRENE; Costume Associate, MARION HERWOOD KEYES; Hair Stylist, SYDNEY GUILAROFF; Technical Advisor, TED SAUCIER; Special Effects, WARREN NEWCOMBE; Assistant Director, WILLIAM LEWIS; Songs: "And There You Are" by SAMMY FAIN and TED KOEHLER, "Guadalajara" by PEPE GUIZAR; Running Time, 130 minutes.

NOTES ABOUT THE FILM

This considerably refurbished variation on *Grand Hotel,* Vicki Baum's inspiration for jamming a crowd of picturesque and melodramatic characters together under one roof, may not have reached the classic proportions of its lofty predecessor, but it did bring a lot of pleasure to escapist movie audiences of 1945, not to mention Metro-Goldwyn-Mayer stockholders.

Lavishly produced, carefully written and directed, and studded with some of the most attractive stars of the period, *Week-End at the Waldorf* was an extremely powerful box-office entrant in what appeared to be a then-current film cycle dedicated to the glorification of New York landmarks (*The Stork Club* and *Billy Rose's Diamond Horseshoe* had been released earlier in the year).* Not only did *Waldorf* enjoy a record-breaking nine-week run at Radio City Music Hall but its special look into the inner workings of the world's most famous hotel had non-New Yorkers flocking to it as well and it was the sixth largest grossing film of 1945.

A good deal of its success must be attributed to the ingenuity of the screenplay authors, Sam and Bella Spewack, and the film's adapter, Guy Bolton, in creating a modern American picture plot out of Miss Baum's European stage drama of 1930 and of its picturization which followed two years later. In transforming the Grand Hotel of pre-Hitler Berlin into the Waldorf-Astoria of New York City in the '40s, only the general pattern of Miss Baum's original was retained, along with a few reminiscent characters. Although the story was still episodic, its treatment was light with the accent on glamour. Accordingly, the film was peopled with a more Hollywood variety, an easy-to-live-with group bearing little evidence of the world-weariness that characterized

With Edward Arnold

*According to *Newsweek*, Billy Rose charged 20th Century-Fox $76,000 for the right to fashion a Betty Grable musical around his Diamond Horseshoe nightclub. For a similar claim on his Stork Club, Sherman Billingsley asked Paramount for a reputed $100,000. Lucius Boomer of the Waldorf, on the other hand, was so pleased with the grand treatment MGM accorded his hostelry, that he settled with the studio for nothing more than the free advertising involved. "In this case," said *Newsweek*, "the publicity is more than worth its weight in royalties."

their 1932 counterparts. The roles that Greta Garbo, Joan Crawford, John Barrymore and Lionel Barrymore first played on the screen* were divertingly recreated by Ginger Rogers, Lana Turner, Walter Pidgeon and Van Johnson, but with markedly Americanized, up-to-date alterations.

Garbo's bored ballerina Grusinskaya became Miss Rogers' Irene Malvern, a famous but lonely Hollywood star; her light-fingered lover, the Baron, done earlier by John Barrymore, was transformed into Walter Pidgeon's Chip Collyer, a debonair news correspondent who, in this version, is merely *suspected* of being a jewel thief; Miss Crawford's amoral stenographer, Flaemmchen, became Lana's Bunny Smith, the luscious Waldorf hotel typist; and the bull-headed Preysing (Wallace Beery in the '32 film) reappeared in the form of Edward Arnold as Martin X. Edley, the pompous promoter who, like his earlier facsimile, had quite an eye for the ladies. But it was the pathetic figure of Lionel Barrymore's aging Kringelein, out for a last fling at life, who underwent *Waldorf's* biggest transformation job. An apparent bow to the almost obligatory '40s element of young romance, Kringelein became the boyishly appealing Captain Jimmy Hollis (Van Johnson), a lonely soldier with a fifty-fifty chance of survival from a war injury.

A number of fresh secondary plots were also introduced in the film, the action of which took place over a period of nearly three days as opposed to the thirty-six hours of *Grand Hotel*. The story opens on a Friday, and closes on a Monday morning with much of the action focusing on Irene Malvern, a glamorous film star whose fame and fortune have brought her nothing but loneliness. In New York for the premiere of her latest film, Irene mistakes Chip Collyer, a war correspondent, for a thief when he enters her room in error. As a result of this encounter, they fall in love—although neither will admit it.

On another floor, Bunny Smith, the beautiful hotel stenographer, is having her own romantic problems. Martin X. Edley, a crooked financier, for whom she is working in the hotel, promises her a Park Avenue penthouse in exchange for a life which doesn't include a wedding ring. It's a tempting offer until Bunny meets Captain Jimmy Hollis, a lonely war hero desperate for a good time at the Waldorf before facing an operation which may be fatal. To prevent Bunny's throwing herself away on a man like Edley, Jimmy signs over his insurance to her. When she learns what he has done, Bunny rejects Edley's back street affair in favor of a life with Jimmy, who feels certain that Bunny's love will give him the courage he needs for a successful operation.

Before the weekend is over, Irene, too, has come to the realization that her life is empty without romance, and in the film's final reel, she and Chip make a date to meet in London where he has been assigned to a job.

Other guests involved in the hotel's ceaseless activity were either new script additions or reworkings of old characters: a junior reporter, hot on the trail of the crooked promoter; a maid who's become involved in the shady affairs of a thief; the hotel doctor and his bride; a multi-millionaire who lends his suite to a young naval lieutenant on his honeymoon; and a newspaper columnist whose pampered Scottie has pups in the final reel. *Week-End at the Waldorf* had, in fact, so many extraneous subplots that one filmed episode involving character actress Constance Collier as Madame Jaleska, an

*On the Broadway stage, these parts were held by Eugenie Leontovich, Hortense Alden, Henry Hull and Sam Jaffe.

As Bunny Smith, the girl who "travels from 10th Avenue to Park—on curves!"

ex-diva doomed to an old folks' home, wound up on the cutting-room floor.

In its review, *Cue* said: ". . . authors Sam and Bella Spewack have whipped together a bright, amusing and elaborately frothy three-corner comedy drama. Enhanced by a million-dollar production and luxurious Waldorf sets, *Week-End* may be no great drama but it is first-rate entertainment. There's plenty of color and comedy as the mosaic of life in a great hotel falls into a neat kaleidoscope of lively plot and counterplot, mixing drawing room comedy, a touch of slapstick, and a bit of soulful romance . . . Most interesting aspect of the picture, and almost as entertaining as the stories, is the astonishing realism of the Waldorf sets, as recreated by MGM's set designer Cedric Gibbons and staff."

Like Garbo and Crawford, their *Grand Hotel* counterparts, Rogers and Turner never had any scenes together in the 191 pages of *Waldorf's* script. Although largely saddled with the conservative garb of a working girl, Lana can easily go on record as having been the most resplendent hotel stenographer in film history. William Hanna and Joseph Barbera, the artists responsible for the popular Tom and Jerry cartoons, did in fact, use Lana's character of Bunny Smith as the model for Toodles, a new cast addition to their series. Toodles, very much on the resplendent side herself, made her debut later in 1945 in the MGM cartoon, *Springtime for Thomas.* ★

Bunny and Toodles

THE POSTMAN ALWAYS RINGS TWICE

A METRO·GOLDWYN·MAYER PICTURE
1946

CAST

LANA TURNER, *Cora Smith;* JOHN GARFIELD, *Frank Chambers;* CECIL KELLAWAY, *Nick Smith;* HUME CRONYN, *Arthur Keats;* LEON AMES, *Kyle Sackett;* AUDREY TOTTER, *Madge Gorland;* ALAN REED, *Ezra Liam Kennedy;* JEFF YORK, *Blair;* CHARLES WILLIAMS, *Doctor;* CAMERON GRANT, *Willie;* WALLY CASSELL, *Ben;* WILLIAM HALLIGAN, *Judge;* MORRIS ANKRUM, *Judge;* EDWARD EARLE, *Doctor;* BYRON FOULGER, *Picnic Manager;* BETTY BLYTHE, *Customer.*

CREDITS

Director, TAY GARNETT; Producer, CAREY WILSON; Screenplay, HARRY RUSKIN and NIVEN BUSCH; Based on the Novel by JAMES M. CAIN; Photography, SIDNEY WAGNER; Art Direction, CEDRIC GIBBONS and RANDALL DUELL; Set Decorations, EDWIN B. WILLIS; Editor, GEORGE WHITE; Sound, DOUGLAS SHEARER; Music, GEORGE BASSMAN; Orchestrations, TED DUNCAN; Costume Supervision, IRENE; Costume Associate, MARION HER-WOOD KEYES: Makeup, JACK DAWN: Assistant Director, WILLIAM LEWIS; Song: "She's Funny That Way," Music by NEIL MORET and Lyrics by RICHARD A. WHITING; Running time, 113 minutes.

NOTES ABOUT THE FILM

The Postman Always Rings Twice was Lana's only screen appearance in 1946 and it is the picture she is probably best remembered for today. Some think she gave her finest performance in it; others feel she has never been more beautiful; for many, the film contains both of these elements. Undoubtedly, if Turner fans had to make a choice, *Postman* is the movie they would most elect to have time-capsuled.

The Postman Always Rings Twice was the screen version of James M. Cain's controversial first novel. MGM acquired the movie rights shortly after its publication in 1934 but the then all-powerful Hays office insisted the story couldn't be filmed in its original form and, despite countless tries, no one at Metro seemed able to develop an acceptable screenplay. The result: *Postman* was shelved for more than ten years.

With Cecil Kellaway and John Garfield

In the interim, the novel was dramatized by its author and brought to the New York stage in 1936 with Richard Barthelmess, Mary Philips and Joseph Greenwald in the leading roles; in 1939, a French film adaptation was produced, titled *Le Dernier Tournant*, with Fernand Gravet, Michel Simon and Corinne Luchaire; and in 1942, Luchino Visconti offered his Italian neo-realist version, *Ossessione,* which starred Massimo Girotti, Clara Calamai and Elio Marcuzzo.*

In the changing moral climate of the 1940s, Hollywood began to bend the Code and after several quiet attempts, Carey Wilson, the writer-producer whose film credits included such sugar-coated preachments as the

*Visconti's *Ossessione* has been described by critic Arthur Knight as a "true masterpiece." Although uncredited to James M. Cain's novel, it is clearly an adaptation of *The Postman Always Rings Twice.* Says Knight: "Not only was Visconti's film a fairly flagrant violation of copyright, but the film rights to Cain's novel already belonged to MGM . . . MGM has been adamant in refusing prints of *Ossessione* to enter the United States."

With John Garfield

With Leon Ames

Hardy Family and Dr. Gillespie pictures, managed to wrest a censor-proof script from Cain's novel without disfiguring its theme.

The Postman Always Rings Twice, MGM's "unfilmable" property, finally went before the cameras in May 1945. By this time, James M. Cain had become one of the most successful novelists in Hollywood. The film version of his *Double Indemnity* (1944) had just struck box-office gold; *Mildred Pierce* was being readied for release; and even when watered down for the censors, Cain's stories possessed a brutal sexiness.

Postman's male protagonist is Frank Chambers, a young wanderer with itchy feet and no ethics. As the film opens, he has stopped at the roadside cafe owned by affable, middle-aged Nick Smith. When Frank catches a glimpse of Nick's beautiful young wife, Cora, he decides to accept the handyman job offered him. Without too much difficulty, Frank eventually breaks down Cora's resistance and the two become lovers.

At first they decide to run away together but Cora is loath to leave the security afforded her at the diner. The

With John Garfield

With Hume Cronyn

With John Garfield

only solution is to get rid of Nick, and it is Cora who puts the idea of murder into Frank's head. A clumsy first attempt fails, but the pair become suspect and after their next attempt, which is successful (Nick is hit over the head with a wine bottle and pushed over a cliff in his car), the lovers are booked for murder. Clever courtroom maneuvers by Cora's lawyer get them off with a suspended sentence and they return to pick up their romance, only to find it riddled with mistrust. The roadside diner prospers, meanwhile, and Frank and Cora are advised by her lawyer to marry for appearance's sake.

When she discovers she is pregnant, Cora becomes a changed woman, determined to make a success of her marriage. Finally, worn out by fear and suspicion, she and Frank return to the moonswept beach where they first succumbed to one another, and resolve to forget the past and begin anew. Just before they reach home the car crashes and Cora is killed. Ironically, although it was an accident, Frank is convicted of her murder. The suspected motive: Nick's insurance policy. In the end, Frank accepts his fate and goes to the gas chamber with one prayer—that Cora, wherever she is, will know it really was an accident.

The Postman Always Rings Twice opened at New York's Capitol Theatre on May 2, 1946 and it was enthusiastically received by the critics. In a special piece on the film, Bosley Crowther told his *New York Times* readers: "It is pleasing to see a story that was held at arm's length for ten years finally come in as a picture which is not only 'moral' but brilliant to boot . . . The lesson is, we would proffer, that a film need not be obscene in order to give a comprehension of a carnal and

Lana in the famous white bathing suit she wears in the film

sordid side of life. Mr. Cain's novel and the picture now on the Capitol's screen, tell as mean and indelicate a story as a tabloid would dare to repeat . . . It is also a human one and it has in it elements of pathos which are prevalent in modern life. Apart from its melodramatic highlights, which are vividly pictured in the film, it has in it a great deal of insight into the natures of wretched characters. Passion and greed quite obviously drive the two conspirators to their deed, but the frustrations of their social milieu are partly responsible for their acts."

In the *New York World-Telegram*, Alton Cook praised the screenplay which he thought "preserved every iota of Cain's superb gift of storytelling. Harry Ruskin and Niven Busch, the scenarists, had a minimum of tinkering to do with this story. They turned it into terse, rough dialogue, one of the season's really great achievements in screenplay-writing . . . One of the astonishing excellences of this picture is the performance to which Lana Turner has been inspired."

Archer Winsten in the *New York Post* wrote that Lana "was holding up much better than in the past when all she had in front of a camera was looks—which was plenty. This time she gives a performance, too, and if it is possible not to be dazzled by that baby beauty and pile of taffy hair, you may agree that she is now beginning to roll in the annual actresses' sweepstakes."

Postman also contains one of John Garfield's best performances. He had been borrowed from Warners for the role of Frank and, under Tay Garnett's expert direction, Garfield and Turner worked surprisingly well together. Her blonde, angel-faced sexuality contrasted brilliantly with his dark, brooding features and they created one of the most exciting star combinations of the year.

Critics Arthur Knight and Hollis Alpert have described Lana's Cora Smith as "the quintessential sex object—the woman to be had at *any* cost." Much, of course, has been written about the "all-white look" Lana affected to play Cora. Indeed, at the time of *Postman*'s release, it was as controversial a subject as the movie itself. As Cora, Lana was costumed throughout in a stark white wardrobe.* Her hair was a snowy white as well, and against a deep suntan she acquired for the role, the effect was startling. At the time, *Life* predicted Lana's all-white wardrobe would "become historic." More recently, director Garnett recalled the incentive for this striking conversation piece: "The white clothing was something that Carey (Wilson) and I thought of. At that time there was a great problem of getting a story with that much sex past the censors. We figured that dressing Lana in white somehow made everything she did seem less sensuous. It was also attractive as hell. And it somehow took a little of the stigma off everything that she did. They didn't have 'hot pants' then, but you couldn't tell it by looking at hers."

The "hot pants" referred to by Garnett was actually a two-piece playsuit designed by MGM's Irene and her associate, Marion Herwood Keyes. It was so effective at the time that it helped popularize the vogue for women's shorts. This is the outfit that Cora is wearing when she makes her first breathtaking entrance into the film. The scene begins as a lipstick rolls across the floor. Frank Chambers (Garfield) stoops to retrieve it and his eyes

---

*The wardrobe was totally white except for two brief instances necessitated by the script. As a dramatic means of conveying mood, Cora is attired in a solid black robe for an early scene where she contemplates suicide with a kitchen knife. Later on in the film, she wears black a second time to attend her mother's funeral.

A wardrobe test shot of Lana (taken before her hair was shortened for the role of Cora)

hit upon a figure in the doorway. At first glance, it appears to be an apparition. The camera slowly scans the figure from her white high heels, up her slim naked legs, to her white form-fitting shorts and well-filled blouse. Finally, it settles on her face and her lush, platinumed hair, so perfectly encased in a white turban. Here, we see Cora for the first time and simultaneously witness one of the screen's most memorable man-woman encounters.

Cora's exit is also cued by the roll of a lipstick—and it is just as spellbinding as her entrance: just moments after the climactic car crash, we see only her lifeless hand sliding across the death seat. Slowly, it releases a lipstick which falls to the dashboard, caught in an endless rolling motion.

Tay Garnett's strong directorial touch is evident throughout *Postman* and there are many who feel it is his best film. "Yeah, I was rather pleased with it," says Garnett. "There was great chemistry in the combination of Lana Turner and John Garfield. We almost didn't get

Fun between scenes as director Tay Garnett coaches Turner and Garfield for the love scene below

Garfield. He went into the Army, and we tested Cameron Mitchell. He did a great test, then Garfield was invalided out of the service—he had a bad ticker even then. It was a real chore to do *Postman* under the Breen Office, but I think I managed to get the sex across. I think I like doing it better that way. I'm not a voyeur, and I don't like all the body display that you get in pictures nowadays. I think that's just a crutch for untalented directors and writers."

In 1952, when Lana Turner was asked to select her favorite role for the readers of *The Saturday Evening Post*, she chose *Postman*'s Cora and gave these reasons: "It may seem strange that I should choose the part of a completely bad woman as my favorite. The fact is, playing a 'wicked woman' makes the audience more aware of you as an actress. This role gave me something to work with. Cora was not the usual heroine . . . I thought I understood the odd, twisted reasoning that made her yearn for a small piece of property out in the hills—for what she considered respectability and security —and yet, at the same time, led her to do things which ruined her chance of getting what she wanted.

"I liked the all-white wardrobe Cora wore and the way she did her hair. But the high point in my enjoyment of this role came after the film was completed. Then James Cain presented me with a leatherbound first edition of *The Postman Always Rings Twice*, bearing the message, 'For my dear Lana, thank you for giving a performance that was even finer than I expected.' "★

GREEN DOLPHIN STREET

A METRO·GOLDWYN·MAYER PICTURE
1947

As Marianne Patourel

CAST

LANA TURNER, *Marianne Patourel;* VAN HEFLIN, *Timothy Haslam;* DONNA REED, *Marguerite Patourel;* RICHARD HART, *William Ozanne;* FRANK MORGAN, *Dr. Edmond Ozanne;* EDMUND GWENN, *Octavius Patourel;* DAME MAY WHITTY, *Mother Superior;* REGINALD OWEN, *Captain O'Hara;* GLADYS COOPER, *Sophie Patourel;* MOYNA MACGILL, *Mrs. Metivier;* LINDA CHRISTIAN, *Hine-Moa;* BERNIE GOZIER, *Jacky-Pato;* PAT AHERNE, *Kapua-Manga;* AL KIKUME, *A Maori;* EDITH LESLIE, *Sister Angelique;* GIGI PERREAU, *Veronica (4 years);* DOUGLAS WALTON, *Sir Charles Maloney;* LESLIE DENNISON, *Captain Hartley;* LUMSDEN HARE, *Anderson;* WILLIAM FAWCETT, *Nat;* PEDRO DeCORDOBA, *Priest;* LILA LEEDS, *Eurasian Girl;* MICHAEL KIRBY, *Brown;* CAROL NUGENT, *Veronica (7 years).*

CREDITS

Director, VICTOR SAVILLE; Producer, CAREY WILSON; Screenplay, SAMSON RAPHAELSON; Based on the Novel by ELIZABETH GOUDGE; Photography, GEORGE FOLSEY; Art Direction, CEDRIC GIBBONS and MALCOLM BROWN; Set Decorations, EDWIN B. WILLIS; Editor, GEORGE WHITE; Sound, DOUGLAS SHEARER; Music, BRONISLAU KAPER; Special Effects, WARREN NEWCOMBE and A. ARNOLD GIL-LESPIE with DONALD JAHRAUS; Costume Supervision, IRENE; Women's Costumes, WALTER PLUNKETT; Men's Costumes, VALLES; Hair Stylist, SYDNEY GUILAROFF; Makeup, JACK DAWN; Assistant Director, NORMAN ELZER; Running time, 141 minutes.

NOTES ABOUT THE FILM

In the Fall of 1943, MGM instituted an annual award that was offered to novelists as a stimulus to creative writing. The winning author was guaranteed at least $150,000 and awarded the opportunity of seeing his work developed into a film. In 1944, the first prize was won by Elizabeth Goudge for *Green Dolphin Street,* a romantic novel of wide popularity that had sales of nearly a million and a half copies*.

Since Miss Goudge's story could suggest no other production form than the epic, that was precisely the treatment lavished upon the screen version of her novel. Into *Green Dolphin Street,* MGM crammed all the formula-tested ingredients: thousands of extras; tremendous sets; and spectacular scenes set in the Channel Islands, China and New Zealand. They created giant clipper ships, terrifying tidal waves and, most noteworthy, a hair-raising earthquake sequence set in the back country of New Zealand in the 1840s that is one of the most frighteningly realistic movie-made cataclysms ever photographed, and which can stand as a monument to the mechanical genius of Hollywood's special effects technicians.

Judging that Lana was ready for more heavy dramatic projects after her work in *The Postman Always Rings Twice,* the powers at MGM next cast her as *Green Dolphin Street*'s spirited heroine, Marianne Patourel. It was a role that Katharine Hepburn had at one time been mentioned for. Essentially a modern, Lana was in costume again for the first time in six years and the characterization required her to become a brunette as well.

The story takes place in 1840, and tells of two young and beautiful sisters, Marianne and Marguerite Patourel, daughters of an aristocratic family residing in the Channel Island seaport of St. Pierre.

When William Ozanne comes to the island, both girls fall in love with him, although William prefers the gentle Marguerite to her headstrong sister. Marianne's ambitions, however, forestall the budding romance between William and Marguerite, and she eventually makes it possible for William to realize his ambition of joining the Royal Navy. But in China, during a cruise the following year, William misses his ship. Fearing a charge of desertion, he meets another fugitive from England named Timothy Haslam and joins him in his lumber business in the New Zealand wilderness. There, in a drunken moment, William writes to Marguerite requesting that she join him as his bride, but in his fogged condition he errs and writes the name of Marianne.

After a long and arduous voyage, an ecstatic Marianne arrives in Wellington, where William is goaded into keeping his mistake a secret by Timothy, who himself has been secretly in love with her since he was a boy in St. Pierre. Although Marianne senses there is something missing in her marriage to William, her business acumen makes them prosper until a violent

---

*MGM's annual novel award was discontinued in 1948. In addition to *Green Dolphin Street,* there were four more winners, only one of which—*Raintree County*—was eventually made into a film.

With Donna Reed

With Gladys Cooper, Donna Reed and Edmund Gwenn

With Moyna MacGill, Richard Hart and Frank Morgan

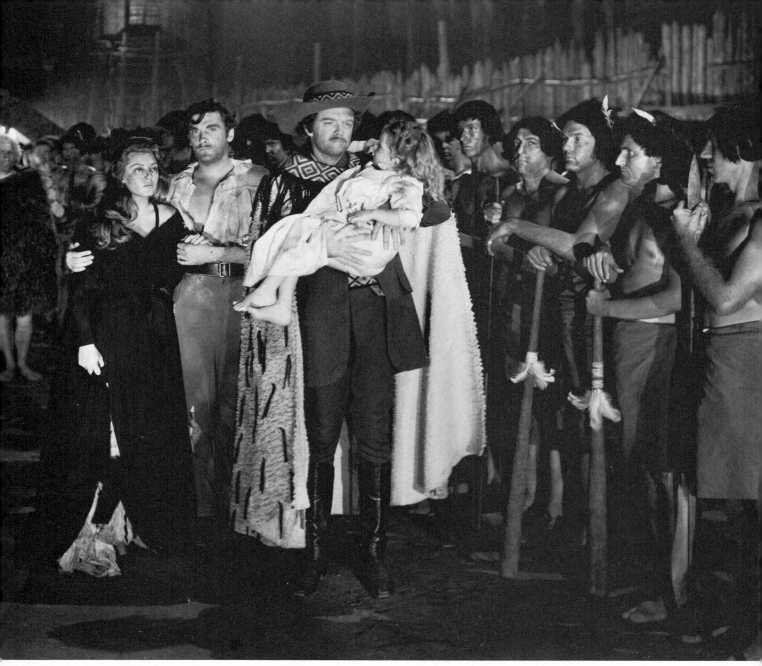

With Richard Hart, Van Heflin, Gigi Perreau and extras in the native uprising sequence

earthquake devastates their investment. In the midst of it, Marianne's baby is born. The earthquake is followed by a Maori uprising against the white settlers, but Timothy is able to arrange for Marianne and William's escape to a neighboring island, where they find new prosperity.

Returning to St. Pierre, Marianne learns of the mistake that made her William's wife. She offers him his freedom, but by now William's love for her is stronger than the adolescent affection he once had for her sister, and in time he convinces her of his feelings. Marguerite, meanwhile, has found happiness in religion and the film ends with Marianne and William present as she is about to be ordained a nun.

A brilliant technical achievement, *Green Dolphin Street* was MGM's largest-grossing release of 1947 and was nominated for two Academy Awards—for Best Sound Recording and for Best Special Effects (in the latter category, the film won the award). Ironically, one of its most spectacular moments—the wrecking of the *Green Dolphin*, a sailing clipper constructed for the film which dwarfed any ship ever built for movies—was deleted from the final print. *Life* ran an article at the time, illustrating this scene which, because of the picture's excessive length, wound up on the cutting-room floor.

Although it was a huge hit with the public, Leo Mishkin's review in the *New York Morning Telegraph* is typical of the film's critical reception: "The reports are that the lady who wrote *Green Dolphin Street* as a prize novel received some $200,000 for her effort . . . not a penny of it has been wasted. As it stands now, *Green Dolphin Street* is probably worth even a good deal more than the two hundred grand, what with Lana Turner in the leading role, what with a tremendous earthquake scene staged to scare the daylights out of you, what with two and a half hours of running time filled with costumes, sets, extras, and even a plot. Yes indeed, the MGM studios have a very wise investment for their two hundred grand. They've got themselves an eye-popping picture. It would be most impolite, of course, to ask at this point whether *Green Dolphin Street* is a good picture. Good pictures, after all, are not produced in direct ratio to the price of the original book. *Green Dolphin Street*, as has been indicated, is a big picture. It is big in the names of its stars, it is big in its ponderous, elephantine approach and treatment, it is big in a number of its individual scenes. When you emerge from such an affair as this, the feeling you have is not so much the exaltation that comes from seeing a good picture, as it is a sort of stupefied wonder that so much has taken place on the screen. This thing is impressive by sheer weight more than anything else."

June Allyson had been originally announced for the role of Marguerite, which was ultimately played by Donna Reed who turned blonde for the part. Reviewing the film for the *Los Angeles Times*, Edwin Schallert noted that both of *Green Dolphin Street*'s leading ladies "bring beauty of a rare order to this costumed event." Their elaborate period costumes (which, incidentally, screamed for Technicolor instead of the black-and-white treatment accorded the film) were the work of Walter Plunkett, who in designing his gowns for the ladies accentuated the contrast of their characters by choosing bright tones, stripes and daring lines to bring out the ruthlessness of Marianne, and soft shades and frills to reflect the gentle loveliness of Marguerite.

In *PM*, Cecilia Ager wrote: ". . . no matter what the

One of GREEN DOLPHIN STREET'S *most exciting moments: the spectacular earthquake scene during which Lana gives birth to a baby*

With Van Heflin

With Linda Christian

With Donna Reed

century Miss Turner's consigned to, she brings to it her own firm-fleshed, contemporary glamour. Wherever she is, she stands out as Lana Turner, unquestionably pho-togenic, one of Metro's most glittering productions all by herself. In a movie dedicated to production values, Miss Turner right or wrong is most eminently right."★

CASS TIMBERLANE

A METRO·GOLDWYN·MAYER PICTURE
1947

CAST

SPENCER TRACY, *Cass Timberlane;* LANA TURNER, *Virginia Marshland;* ZACHARY SCOTT, *Bradd Criley;* TOM DRAKE, *Jamie Wargate;* MARY ASTOR, *Queenie Havock;* ALBERT DEKKER, *Boone Havock;* MARGARET LINDSAY, *Chris Grau;* ROSE HOBART, *Diantha Marl;* JOHN LITEL, *Webb Wargate;* MONA BARRIE, *Avis Elderman;* JOSEPHINE HUTCHINSON, *Lillian Drover;* SELENA ROYLE, *Louise Wargate;* FRANK WILCOX, *Gregg Marl;* RICHARD GAINES, *Dennis Thane;* JOHN ALEXANDER, *Dr. Roy Drover;* CAMERON MITCHELL, *Eino Roskinen;* HOWARD FREEMAN, *Hervey Plint;* JESSIE GRAYSON, *Mrs. Higbee;* GRIFF BARNETT, *Herman;* PAT CLARK, *Alice Wargate;* MILBURN STONE, *Nestor Purdwin;* ALMIRA SESSIONS, *Zilda Hatter;* BESS FLOWERS, *Mary Ann Milligan;* BETTY BLYTHE, *Nurse;* WALTER PIDGEON, *Himself (Unbilled Guest Appearance).*

CREDITS

Director, GEORGE SIDNEY; Producer, ARTHUR HORNBLOW, JR.; Screenplay, DONALD OGDEN STEWART; Adaptation, DONALD OGDEN STEWART and SONYA LEVIEN; Based on the Novel by SINCLAIR LEWIS; Photography, ROBERT PLANCK; Art Direction, CEDRIC GIBBONS and DANIEL B. CATHCART; Set Decorations, EDWIN B. WILLIS with RICHARD PEFFERLE; Editor, JOHN DUNNING; Sound, DOUGLAS

With Spencer Tracy

Pitching curves: a highlight of the film was the softball game sequence with Lana up at bat and umpire Tracy striking her out

SHEARER; Costumes, IRENE; Hair Stylist, SYDNEY GUILAR-OFF; Makeup, JACK DAWN; Assistant Director, GEORGE RYAN; Special Effects, WARREN NEWCOMBE and A. ARNOLD GILLESPIE; Music, ROY WEBB; Musical Director, CONSTANTIN BAKALEINIKOFF; Running time, 119 minutes.

NOTES ABOUT THE FILM

Cass Timberlane is Sinclair Lewis's novel of May–December love, marital readjustment, judicial integrity and country club hypocrisies in a midwestern town. Although not generally regarded as one of the author's best works, it was extremely successful and had a reading public of 17,000,000, presumably because of the Lewis name.

What the film version had in its favor, in addition to a pre-sold title, was a highly polished, entertaining screenplay; a strong romantic flavor; a chemically interesting star combination and an effective ad campaign—*two* distinct campaigns, to be exact. The first, rather unashamedly proclaimed: "No adjectives necessary": The second campaign featured a more commercial approach that reactivated the "T.N.T." slogan that had worked so well for *Johnny Eager* five years earlier (this time the reference was to *Tracy* 'n Turner).

Author Lewis's hero was an idealistic, middle-aged Minnesota judge who falls in love with a fierce young rebel from the wrong side of the tracks named Jinny Marshland, and marries her despite the tacit disapproval of his society friends. But Jinny, who adapts herself readily to her new life, soon becomes bored with the town, with Cass's friends and with the stuffy sameness of the country club routine. Only the flattering attentions of Bradd Criley, the local playboy, lighten her dull existence.

When Jinny loses a baby in childbirth, she persuades Cass to accept a job in a law office in New York. The

With Spencer Tracy

Of the film, *Boxoffice* magazine said: "Because of his understanding, earthy, yet exciting, word paintings of the middle-stratum American scene, novels by Sinclair Lewis (*Dodsworth, Arrowsmith,* etc.) have always been proven prime screen material. The celluloid version of what he considers his most successful book attains a new high of excellence for pictures based on the author's work . . . Producer Arthur Hornblow mounted the subject richly but in unusually good taste. Direction by George Sidney is masterful and replete with clever undertone touches to accent the locale and aura. And performances are virtually flawless throughout . . ."

Not all of *Cass Timberlane*'s reviews were as glowing, although the players were seldom faulted. Nonetheless, it was an extremely profitable venture for the studio and, like *Green Dolphin Street*, which was also released in the final months of 1947 (and had Lana competing with herself at the box office), *Cass Timberlane* is today on *Variety*'s list of all-time money-making films.

In the opening shots of the picture, director Sidney introduces the locale of the story in loving detail,

With Zachary Scott and Spencer Tracy

glamour of the city dazzles her, and when Cass refuses to remain there, they quarrel and separate. Jinny takes up with Bradd again but when she is injured in a car accident, Cass rushes to her bedside and, in due course, they are reconciled.

Metro was giving Lana some diverse roles during this period, moving her from *Postman*'s lethal, platinum-haired Cora to the dominating, brunette Marianne of *Green Dolphin Street*. *Cass Timberlane*'s young and headstrong Jinny was as noncharacteristic a part as anything she'd yet been assigned, and its very offbeat nature, perhaps, reaped her some of her best notices, including this one from *Variety*: "Miss Turner is the surprise of the picture via her top performance thespically. In a role that allows her the gamut from tomboy to the pangs of childbirth and from being another man's woman to remorseful wife, she seldom fails to acquit herself creditably. Tracy, as a matter of fact, is made to look wooden by comparison."

In the New York *Daily News*, Kate Cameron wrote: "There is no doubt about it, Lana Turner screens more beautifully than any other blonde in Hollywood. In *Cass Timberlane,* she literally illumines the Music Hall screen with a glow that is soft, warm and altogether feminine. . . . That she is able to hold the spotlight while Spencer Tracy is on the scene is a test of her ability as an actress and a charmer. Her vis-a-vis in the picture is a veteran of screen and stage who knows how to command attention when he wishes . . . He is always sure of himself, even when he gives way a bit to let the glamourous Lana have the spotlight."

giving us an *Our Town*-like glimpse of small-town Americana. This leads to a lively softball sequence that called for Lana to romp around the field in a pair of blue jeans (tailored in all the right places by MGM's Irene), and to pitch, brawl vigorously with umpire Tracy, and even make a two-base hit (for her role as pitcher of the team, Lana took about two hours of coaching from two professional members of the Monterey Blue Jays, an event that reaped Metro considerable press coverage).

Another vital aspect of the film was Sidney's precise strokes of satire in the scenes depicting the upper strata of Minnesota society. Some mention should be given to the supporting cast—Zachary Scott, Mary Astor, Albert Dekker, Margaret Lindsay, Rose Hobart, John Litel, Mona Barrie, Josephine Hutchinson, Tom Drake, Selena Royle, and Cameron Mitchell, among others. Each and every one of these players gave outstanding performances and, as if this impressive assemblage wasn't enough, Walter Pidgeon made a surprise guest appearance playing himself in a cocktail party scene. ★

HOMECOMING

A METRO·GOLDWYN·MAYER PICTURE
1948

CAST

CLARK GABLE, *Ulysses Delby Johnson*; LANA TURNER, *Lt. Jane "Snapshot" McCall*; ANNE BAXTER, *Penny Johnson*; JOHN HODIAK, *Dr. Robert Sunday*; RAY COLLINS, *Lt. Colonel Avery Silver*; GLADYS COOPER, *Mrs. Kirby*; CAMERON MITCHELL, *Monkevickz*; MARSHALL THOMPSON, *Sgt. McKeen*; LURENE TUTTLE, *Miss Stoker*; JESSIE GRAYSON, *Sarah*; J. LOUIS JOHNSON, *Sol*; ELOISE HARDT, *Nurse Aldine Bradford*; ART BAKER, *Williams*; JEFF COREY, *Cigarette Smoker*; GERALDINE WALL, *Head Nurse*; ALAN HALE, JR., *M.P.*; ARTHUR O'CONNELL, *Driver*; WALLY CASSELL, *Patient*; LISA GOLM, *Anna*; MICHAEL KIRBY, *Corpsman*; WILLIAM FORREST, DOROTHY CHRISTY, ANNE NAGEL, *Party Guests*.

CREDITS

Director, MERVYN LEROY; Producer, SIDNEY FRANKLIN (In Association with GOTTFRIED REINHARDT); Screenplay, PAUL OSBORN; Original Story, SIDNEY KINGSLEY; Adaptation, JAN LUSTIG; Music, BRONISLAU KAPER; Music Conductor, CHARLES PREVIN; Photography, HAROLD ROSSON; Art Direction, CEDRIC GIBBONS and RANDALL DUELL; Set Decorations EDWIN B. WILLIS with HENRY W. GRACE; Editor, JOHN DUNNING; Sound, DOUGLAS SHEARER; Miss Baxter's Gowns, HELEN ROSE; Hair Stylist, SYDNEY GUILAROFF; Makeup, JACK DAWN; Special Effects, WARREN NEWCOMBE and A. ARNOLD GILLESPIE; Assistant Director, NORMAN ELZER; Technical Adviser, PAUL LUND; Running time, 114 minutes.

NOTES ABOUT THE FILM

Throughout the years, much has been written about the Mervyn LeRoy–Lana Turner association. Less publicized but just as significant is the part that LeRoy played in aiding Clark Gable's career as well.

In 1930, Gable was playing a small role in *The Last Mile* at Los Angeles' Majestic Theater. Spotting the show, LeRoy felt he had film possibilities and arranged a screen test at Warners. None of the studio's powers-that-be were impressed with the results. But LeRoy didn't give up. He and Gable became close friends, and the director's dogged persistence inspired the actor to pursue a film career. Eventually, Gable landed a part in *The Painted Desert* at Pathé. After that 1931 Western, his film career steadily shot forward.

Although LeRoy had directed Lana in several pictures, *Homecoming*, oddly enough, marked the first time he had Gable under supervision. Its original story, titled *The Homecoming of Ulysses*, was written in 1944 expressly for Gable by Sidney Kingsley, the Pulitzer Prize–winning playwright, whose *Men in White* had served as the basis for one of the star's earlier film hits. Paul Osborn did the screenplay and under its final title, *Homecoming*, it went before the cameras as the first postwar Gable–Turner starrer.

What Kingsley conceived was the story of a midwestern surgeon whose coming of age is delayed—until the war and a love affair overseas wear through his veneer of sophistication. It's the only Gable–Turner love affair that ends on a tragic note, and although the stars didn't wind up in the traditional Big Clinch at the fadeout, there were enough heavy-breathing episodes within the film to satisfy their fans. Romantics found the going rough, however, since the scenario delayed their initial kiss for more than one full hour of screen time

As "Snapshot" McCall

*A romantic moment
for "The Team
That Generates Steam"*

and when their love is eventually consummated it occurs in a ruined barn amid, of all things, the roar of the Battle of the Bulge. Appropriately enough, the trumpeting for the movie on its release in April 1948 was equally clamorous. In what was one of the most effective publicity campaigns ever devised for a Gable–Turner starrer, the ads billed the popular duo as "the Team That Generates Steam!"

Homecoming presented as its leading character Dr. Ulysses Johnson, a self-centered physician just approaching middle age whose work thus far has lacked any real purpose. Ulysses is so caught up with his rich clients and the country club set life he leads with his attractive young wife, Penny, that he turns a deaf ear to a plea for aid in rehabilitating a neighboring malaria-ridden slum area. When war is declared, he joins the army because it's the fashionable thing to do.

Overseas, the doctor comes up against real problems for the first time in his life. But it is through the friendship and guidance of his nurse, Lt. Jane "Snapshot" McCall, that he learns idealism and unselfishness of purpose. When their friendship turns to love, Snapshot has herself transferred so that she and "Useless" (as she calls the doctor) will be separated. But they

meet again in Paris. On their way to the battle front, an air raid forces them to spend the night together in a bombed-out building where they confess their love for each other. Later, Snapshot is wounded and she dies shortly afterwards. When hostilities have ceased, Ulysses at last returns home, a changed man sobered by his experiences and more in need of his understanding wife than ever before.

Homecoming, in the words of Lee Mortimer, was "an exhibitor's dream and a patron's paradise."

Bosley Crowther, on the other hand, wrote in his *New York Times* review: "*Homecoming* is a picture which pretends to be serious about serious things—the war and medicine in particular—but it is really nothing more than a cheap, synthetic chunk of romance designed to exploit two gaudy stars." The critic for *PM* pegged the film as follows: "There were times at the Capitol yesterday when the war seemed to have happened solely to give Clark Gable and Lana Turner a new romantic background. For *Homecoming* is their love story from North Africa to the Battle of the Bulge. Since they are two glamorous people, theirs is a glamorous war—in battle, in bombings, in death, there is no real agony or ugliness or heartache. Even the mud in *Homecoming*

With Clark Gable

looks slick and unreal, like it passed an MGM screen test."

In the New York *Daily News,* Wanda Hale wrote: "Clark Gable and Lana Turner take up where they left off before the war, when as Metro-Goldwyn-Mayer's big money team their screen romances followed this routine —man and girl meet, they dislike each other on first sight, they fight, they hate each other and then they fall in love. All of which was, and still is, thrilling to those who rate such a love affair higher than the story . . . Gable and Turner are Gable and Turner and that's all their fans want."

Miss Hale, it would seem, proved herself the most astute critic of all for, on May 3, 1948, *The Hollywood Reporter* printed this business report: "*Homecoming* had the biggest opening of any MGM Capitol cinemattraction. Over the weekend, the Gable–Turner fan following was out in full force, thumbing their noses at the critics and pounding their palms for the stars."

Amidst the huzzahs for the reunion of this popular screen team, *Homecoming* offered a very fine performance by Anne Baxter in the role of the wife Gable has

With Clark Gable

With Clark Gable on the set of HOMECOMING

left back home, and to whom he ultimately returns. A fourth co-star was John Hodiak, Miss Baxter's then real-life husband, who played, ironically, a family friend who urges her to remain with Gable in the end.

The character of Snapshot is the most appealing of the "other woman" roles Lana Turner has played on the screen. Warm and good-natured, there's an air of knowing wisdom about the nurse and, stripped of her usual glamour accouterments, in *Homecoming* Lana's sex appeal comes from within. There's a particularly charming scene midway into the film with an eager Turner and an embarrassed Gable taking separate baths amidst some Roman ruins. But her most effective moment comes in the end and Mervyn LeRoy places her deathbed scene high on the list of the most sensitively played sequences he's ever directed. In September 1948, Adela Rogers St. Johns wrote: "I thought Lana Turner gave one of the greatest performances ever in *Homecoming* and was burned up because I didn't think she got enough credit. I remember a gal named Clara Bow who every once in a while used to turn in a heart-twisting job like that."★

With Clark Gable

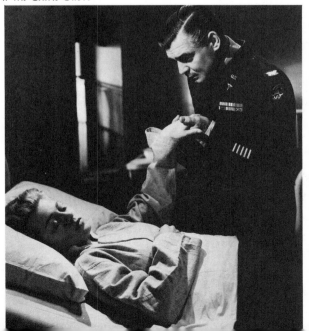

THE THREE MUSKETEERS

A METRO·GOLDWYN·MAYER PICTURE

1948

LANA TURNER! FIRST TIME IN TECHNICOLOR!
She's gorgeous but wicked in this all-star masterpiece of romance and adventure!

CAST

LANA TURNER, *Lady de Winter;* GENE KELLY, *D'Artagnan;* JUNE ALLYSON, *Constance;* VAN HEFLIN, *Athos;* ANGELA LANSBURY, *Queen Anne;* FRANK MORGAN, *King Louis XIII;* VINCENT PRICE, *Richelieu;* KEENAN WYNN, *Planchet;* JOHN SUTTON, *The Duke of Buckingham;* GIG YOUNG, *Porthos;* ROBERT COOTE, *Aramis;* REGINALD OWEN, *Treville;* IAN KEITH, *Rochefort;* PATRICIA MEDINA, *Kitty;* RICHARD STAPLEY, *Albert;* BYRON FOULGER, *Bonacieux;* SOL GORSS, *Jussac;* RICHARD SIMMONS, *Count de Wardes;* ROBERT WARWICK, *D'Artagnan, Sr.;* WILLIAM "BILL" PHILLIPS, *Grimaud;* MARIE WINDSOR, *Spy;* TOM TYLER, *1st Traveler;* KIRK ALYN, *1st Friend of Aramis;* FRANCIS McDONALD, *Fisherman.*

CREDITS

Director, GEORGE SIDNEY; Producer, PANDRO S. BERMAN; Screenplay, ROBERT ARDREY; From the Novel by ALEXANDRE DUMAS; Photography (Technicolor), ROBERT PLANCK; Technicolor Color Director, NATALIE KALMUS; Color Associate, HENRI JAFFA; Art Direction, CEDRIC GIBBONS and MALCOLM BROWN; Set Decorations, EDWIN B. WILLIS with HENRY W. GRACE; Editors, ROBERT J. KERN and GEORGE BOEMLER; Sound, DOUGLAS SHEARER; Costumes, WALTER PLUNKETT; Hair Stylists, SYDNEY GUILAROFF and LARRY GERMAIN; Makeup, JACK DAWN; Special Effects, WARREN NEWCOMBE; Music, HERBERT STOTHART; Themes by TSCHAIKOWSKY; Orchestral Collaboration, ALBERT SENDREY; Conducted by CHARLES PREVIN; Assistant Director, GEORGE RHEIN; Montage, PETER BALLBUSCH; Running time, 126 minutes.

NOTES ABOUT THE FILM

Undoubtedly one of the flashiest villainesses ever to strut her way through literature was Lady de Winter, the memorable menace of Alexandre Dumas' *The Three Musketeers.* Amidst the swordplay and romance, this lethal lady is rather a peripheral character but so forbidding a creature is she as she lies, steals and murders her way from France to England, from palace to boudoir, that she makes Lucretia Borgia look like Mary Poppins.

With Gene Kelly

Before her inevitable demise, Milady wreaks havoc on
one and all—including the novel's sainted heroine,
whom she coldbloodedly does away with in the plot's
climactic moments.

When, in 1948, MGM produced its elaborate
Technicolor version of the Dumas classic, the role of
Milady was assigned to Lana Turner. Miss Turner's last
five pictures had been among the studio's biggest
moneymakers, and as Leo the Lion's Golden Girl *par
excellence*, a perfect example of the gilt-edged star
treatment MGM consistently accorded her can be found
in the top billing she received in *Musketeers*—despite
her limited footage in the film and the fact that the
entire production was first and foremost a grandiose
showcase for the nonmusical acrobatic talents of Gene
Kelly, the film's D'Artagnan.

The Three Musketeers also marked Lana's long
overdue starring debut in a Technicolor feature. "For the
first time—Lana in Technicolor!" boasted the ad copy
and in MGM's advertising, at least, the musketeers had
to take a back seat to Dumas' wily arch-villainess.

The Three Musketeers has been filmed so often
(including innumerable European interpretations) that it
all but constitutes a genre in itself. This 1948 version
claimed distinction over its many predecessors by being
the first screen adaptation to utilize Dumas' entire plot,
with past versions (Douglas Fairbanks, 1921; Walter
Abel, 1935; and the Ritz Brothers, 1939; among the

With Vincent Price

162

With Gene Kelly

Kelly's D'Artagnan was just as Dumas portrayed him —a seventeenth-century country bumpkin who combines cockiness with courage, ingenuity and a fine gift of swordsmanship. His first meeting with the three musketeers, Athos, Porthos and Aramis; their consternation at finding that each is to fight a duel with the newcomer at almost the same hour; their sudden enduring friendship

With June Allyson

With Ian Keith

most prominent) having confined themselves to the episode of the diamond studs.*

*Dumas' characters first came to life on film in a 1903 French production directed by George Melies. The first U.S. adaptation most closely related to the novel, however, was Thomas A. Edison's 1911 treatment. In June, 1947, upon MGM's announcement of their upcoming production, it was simultaneously revealed that producer Edward Small had cancelled his plans to make a version for Columbia. At that time, MGM's initial press releases for the film indicated that Robert Taylor and Ricardo Montalban would play two of the musketeers and Sydney Greenstreet would appear in the role of Richelieu. But the most headline-making casting involved Lana Turner, who originally accepted a studio suspension in preference to playing Lady de Winter. Her complaint: she considered Milady a "secondary" character. Before she was convinced otherwise, MGM, in need of a fast replacement, had begun negotiations with David O. Selznick to borrow Alida Valli for the role.

Imprisoned for her treachery, Milady feigns illness to win the sympathy of her captors. Later, she coldly murders three of them

with the country lad; D'Artagnan's romance with Constance, the Queen's lady-in-waiting—all this leads into a rapid succession of adventures on land and sea, in tavern, court and boudoir, as they slash their way through a dozen ambushes to save the Queen's honor and to foil the scheming Prime Minister, Richelieu, and his evil accomplice, Lady de Winter, in their plot to dethrone the King.

Like the novel, the second half of the film plays heavily upon the amours and crimes of the beautiful Milady. Aware that she is a key figure in all of Richelieu's schemes, D'Artagnan has an affair with the woman. In time, however, she is revealed to be Athos' former wife, who left him soon after their marriage for another man and who later was branded for criminal acts.

Richelieu's climactic plot sends Milady to England to assassinate the Duke of Buckingham. But through the intervention of the musketeers, Buckingham is warned in

time. He has Milady arrested, and assigns Constance, now D'Artagnan's wife, as her jailer. When the musketeers discover this, they realize that Constance can never be a match for the wily Milady, but although they hurriedly carve their way to England, they are too late to prevent the murders of both the Duke and Constance.

In the final reel, Milady's perfidy comes to an end when she falls into the hands of the musketeers who turn her over to an executioner. She is beheaded for her crimes; Richelieu is exposed for his plots against the throne; and the musketeers are suitably rewarded by the King.

MGM released *The Three Musketeers* in October 1948. Some critics compared it to an elaborately staged operetta; a few carped about its not always successful attempt at balancing farce and tragedy; but, on the whole, the picture was very well received. It was a huge commercial success and eight years later it was put into theatres again, double-billed with another of the studio's big box-office winners, *The Stratton Story*.

Cue thought that *Musketeers* was "the best movie version of Dumas' novel to come out of Hollywood", while *Cosmopolitan* described this MGM adaptation as "one of Leo's longest and most successful house parties . . . Director George Sidney, acting as games-master, has wisely let everybody enjoy himself hugely, with the result that filmgoers are likely to have almost as good a time at this movie. Liberties have been taken with the 100-year-old novel, but Alexandre Dumas, who took a few liberties himself, is hardly the type to roll over in his grave. And he would certainly have approved Lana Turner as the lovely, lethal Milady, perhaps the only really inspired piece of casting in the picture."

As photographed by Robert Planck, Miss Turner's much-heralded color debut proved well worth waiting for and it's easy to see why MGM was prompted to play it up in the ad campaign. Cinematographer Planck's

With Van Heflin

method of accentuating Milady's predatory nature was to employ a series of overwhelming closeups and odd-angled facial studies of Miss Turner and, from her first dazzling appearance in the darkness of a coach to her final come-uppance at the hands of an executioner, all of Lana's footage screens like homage to her beauty. Planck's superlative work on *The Three Musketeers* won him an Oscar nomination and in a recent article on Natalie Kalmus, the film's noted color consultant, *Cahiers du Cinema* listed Planck's lensing of Miss Turner in *Musketeers* among "the most beautiful sequences in color of the American cinema."

Apart from the superb camera work accorded Lana, her appearance as Milady is noteworthy for another reason: it's the only scarlet woman she's every played who had absolutely no redeeming graces. Turner femme fatales were *always* allowed their big regeneration scene—but not Milady. Uncharacteristic of MGM's protective measures towards its players in those days, Milady was one of the few deep-dyed villainesses ever to escape the whitewashing treatment ordained by the studio to gain audience sympathy for a valuable star playing a "heavy." This favorite studio ruse did, of course, often sap the vitality from an otherwise potent character.

Milady, however, remained Evil Incarnate from first reel to last and the decision to sustain her satanic nature throughout was a great asset to the film and true to the spirit of the original Dumas delineation.

In other screen adaptations of the popular classic, Milday's special brand of bitchery has been interpreted by such actresses as Barbara La Marr (1921), Margot Grahame (1935), Binnie Barnes (1939), Mylene Demongeot (in a 1961 French production) and, most recently, by Faye Dunaway (in the two-part Richard Lester treatment of 1974–75).★

A never-before-published wardrobe test shot

Milady's execution. In the film this scene is shown in longshot only

A LIFE OF HER OWN

A METRO·GOLDWYN·MAYER PICTURE
1950

CAST

LANA TURNER, *Lily Brannel James;* RAY MILLAND, *Steve Harleigh;* TOM EWELL, *Tom Caraway;* LOUIS CALHERN, *Jim Leversoe;* ANN DVORAK, *Mary Ashlon;* BARRY SULLIVAN, *Lee Gorrance;* MARGARET PHILLIPS, *Nora Harleigh;* JEAN HAGEN, *Maggie Collins;* PHYLLIS KIRK, *Jerry;* SARA HADEN, *Smitty;* HERMES PAN, *Specialty Dancer;* TOM SEIDEL, *Bob Collins;* DOROTHY TREE, *Caraway's Secretary;* GERALDINE WALL, *Hosiery Woman;* PERCY HELTON, *Hamburger Proprietor;* SARAH PADDEN, *Overseer;* WHIT BISSELL, *Rental Agent;* HARRY BARRIS, *Piano Player;* KENNE DUNCAN, *Man Asking Invitation;* BEVERLY CAMPBELL (BEVERLY GARLAND), *Girl at Party;* FRANKIE DARRO, *Bellboy;* JOAN VALERIE, ARTHUR LOEW, JR., *Party Guests.*

CREDITS

Director, GEORGE CUKOR; Producer, VOLDEMAR VETLUGUIN; Screenplay, ISOBEL LENNART; Photography, GEORGE FOLSEY; Art Direction, CEDRIC GIBBONS and ARTHUR LONERGAN; Set Decorations, EDWIN B. WILLIS with HENRY W. GRACE; Editor, GEORGE WHITE; Sound, DOUGLAS SHEARER; Lana Turner's Gowns, HELEN ROSE; Hair Stylist, SYDNEY GUILAROFF; Makeup, WILLIAM TUTTLE; Music, BRONISLAU KAPER; Conducted by JOHNNY GREEN; Running time, 108 minutes.

NOTES ABOUT THE FILM

A Life of Her Own was Lana's much-publicized return to the screen after a two-year absence during which time she married millionaire Bob Topping and spent considerable time traveling abroad. In the film, she played a small-town girl named Lily James who goes to New York to embark on a modeling career. She settles at an agency and is befriended by a fading model named Mary Ashlon. Ashlon is beginning to lose jobs and men friends, and in her despondency, commits suicide by jumping from a window. Deeply affected by her death, Lily resolves not to make the same mistakes and sets to work with a will. Eventually she becomes the most photographed woman in the country, and one of its highest-paid models.

Through her lawyer, Lily meets and falls in love with Steve Harleigh, a Montana copper magnate. She becomes his mistress and he sets her up in a penthouse, but when he tells her about his crippled wife and that marriage for them is out of the question, she embarks on a life of wild parties and high living. In an effort to persuade the wife to set Steve free, Lily goes to the woman. But once she sees Mrs. Harleigh's utter dependence on her husband, Lily comes to her senses and ends the affair, resolved never to succumb to the same pitfalls as did her friend, Mary Ashlon.

A Life of Her Own was just one of several properties

With Ray Milland

With Hermes Pan in the party sequence

MGM had under consideration as Lana's return film. Everything from period drama (*Madame Bovary*) to comedy (*The Reformer and the Redhead*) had been announced before the studio finally decided on this modern love story which was inspired by a Rebecca West novel called *The Abiding Vision*.

Every apparent effort was made to insure the film's success. A top supporting cast was assembled, and to strengthen the film's strong feminine slant, the noted "woman's director," George Cukor, was signed to guide the drama. In a *New York Times* interview, Cukor expressed great enthusiasm for the film's potential, and told the paper's reporter that Miss Turner was "in fine

acting trim these days," and that he was "greatly impressed with her virtuosity."

With so much going for it before and behind the cameras, it's hard to pinpoint just why *A Life of Her Own* ultimately failed to live up to its initial great promise, although from the very beginning, this ambitious project was besieged with production problems. In Metro's determination to make this Turner vehicle a special one, there were certainly enough—possibly *too many*—fingers in the pie. The project started early in 1949, but censorship difficulties interfered with its adaptation for so long that little of Miss West's original story remained. Samson Raphaelson, Donald Ogden

Stewart and Isobel Lennart all worked on the scenario at various times, and although Miss West's basic situation, an adulterous love affair, still persisted, its final treatment was so lugubrious that director Cukor stated, "with this picture, we will probably succeed in ending adultery forever."

After many rewrites, *A Life of Her Own* finally went before the cameras in February 1950. James Mason, who had long been set for the male lead, backed out just prior to production with this explanation: "The part is so typically midwest American, one crisp British accept would throw the whole thing out of key." Wendell Corey was promptly borrowed from Paramount for the role until he, too, asked to be relieved because he felt he was "not right" for the part (other sources have intimated that the Turner-Corey on-screen chemistry didn't mix well.) MGM then acceded to Corey's request and engaged Ray Milland to replace him.

One of the picture's major script problems involved the ending. The original scenario had model Lily James winding up as a forty-five-year old hotel maid. In the script that was eventually filmed, Lily follows in the footsteps of Mary Ashlon and commits suicide at a relatively early age. This downbeat ending, however, drew such negative reactions at the sneak preview that a new ending was substituted in which Lily was allowed to live, ready to face life without the man she loves.

A Life of Her Own made its well-publicized premiere in theatres across the country in October 1950—to disappointing results. Most of the critics put the blame on its extremely verbose screenplay (the final script was an Isobel Lennart version). With sympathy directed towards Turner and Cukor, many felt that their initial collaboration deserved better than this well-mounted but very grim soap opera. Said *Cue*: "All the plush and polish can't turn this gushing goo into substantial drama."

In spite of—or perhaps, because of—the many script changes and character revisions involving the leading roles, the film's most plausible characters were those essayed by its supporting cast. Among the distaff side, especially, the parts of Mary Ashlon, the ill-fated model, and Mrs. Harleigh, the crippled wife, emerged the film's best-defined characters. Both roles were impressively delineated by, respectively, Ann Dvorak and Margaret Phillips.

Turner and Cukor, who enjoyed working together, have since expressed regrets that they did not have a better vehicle to work with. Its shortcomings notwithstanding, *A Life of Her Own*, like any Cukor work, exhibits much of the director's personal style and, consequently, the film has its share of admirers. Gavin Lambert in his book on Cukor, for instance, writes that director François Truffaut in his critic days saw in *A Life of Her Own* "the same 'beauty' of work as in Cukor's *Holiday* or *Little Women*." ★

As Lily James

With Barry Sullivan, Ann Dvorak and Louis Calhern

With Ray Milland

MR. IMPERIUM

A METRO·GOLDWYN·MAYER PICTURE
1951

CAST

LANA TURNER, *Fredda Barlo;* EZIO PINZA, *Mr. Imperium;* MARJORIE MAIN, *Mrs. Cabot;* BARRY SULLIVAN, *Paul Hunter;* SIR CEDRIC HARDWICKE, *Bernand;* DEBBIE REYNOLDS, *Gwen;* ANN CODEE, *Anna Pelan;* WILTON GRAFF, *Andrew Bolton;* GIACOMO SPADONI, *Giovanni;* JOSEPH VITALE, *Bearded Man;* DICK SIMMONS, *Air Corps Colonel;* CHICK CHANDLER, *George Hoskins;* ARTHUR WALSH, WILSON WOOD, BOBBY TROUP, ALLAN RAY, *Specialties in Band.* (Note: Singer TRUDY ERWIN supplied the singing voice for Miss Turner.)

CREDITS

Director, DON HARTMAN; Producer, EDWIN H. KNOPF; Screenplay, EDWIN H. KNOPF and DON HARTMAN; From the Play by EDWIN H. KNOPF; Photography (Technicolor), GEORGE J. FOLSEY; Color Consultants, HENRI JAFFA and JAMES GOOCH; Art Direction, CEDRIC GIBBONS and PAUL GROESSE; Set Decorations, EDWIN B. WILLIS with RICHARD A. PEFFERLE; Editors, GEORGE WHITE and WILLIAM GULICK; Sound, DOUGLAS SHEARER; Costumes, WALTER PLUNKETT; Makeup, WILLIAM TUTTLE; Hair Stylist, SYDNEY GUILAROFF; Miss Turner's Hair Styles, LARRY GERMAIN; Music, HAROLD ARLEN; Lyrics, DOROTHY FIELDS; Musical Direction, JOHNNY GREEN; Background Musical Score, BRONISLAU KAPER; Songs: "Andiamo," "Let Me Look at You," "My Love and My Mule"; Additional Song, "You Belong to My Heart," by RAY GILBERT and AUGUSTIN LARA. Running time, 87 minutes.

NOTES ABOUT THE FILM

A casual inspection of the cast and production names involved in the making of *Mr. Imperium* would immediately stack the cards in the film's favor. This was the picture that marked the screen debut of the Metropolitan Opera singer, Ezio Pinza, who had recently made such a hit co-starring with Mary Martin in the Broadway musical, *South Pacific.*

When Pinza arrived at MGM, the studio rolled out the red carpet for him, and amid much publicity, announced that his first leading lady would be their Golden Girl, Lana Turner. Since both stars literally oozed with their own respective brand of glamour, a screen merger gave all indications of being a box office natural and the start of big things in Hollywood for Pinza.

The picture chosen to serve as a showcase for Pinza began production on July 18, 1950. An original screenplay supplied the stars with a plot that had to do with a European prince who falls in love with an American nightclub singer while he is vacationing in Italy. He leaves her suddenly when it becomes time for him to assume the duties of the king. There is a sepa-

With Ezio Pinza

With Keenan Wynn in a scene that wound up on the cutting room floor

ration of twelve years, during which time the singer, Frederika Brown, has become the Hollywood star, Fredda Barlo. She is all set to marry her producer, Paul Hunter, when the king, traveling incognito, flies back into her life. They enjoy a Palm Springs weekend tryst, but eventually the king's conscience stirs him into returning to his country, but with the promise he'll be back again someday.

Mr. Imperium had been such a widely-heralded film that New York City's famed Radio City Music Hall scheduled it sight unseen, then cancelled the booking after the first preview when word got out that it was not

With Ezio Pinza in the "Andiamo" number

quite the felicitous event intended. Its release had been scheduled for the Spring of '51 but Metro shelved it until the end of the year to allow Pinza's second film at the studio, *Strictly Dishonorable*, the opportunity to go out first as his introduction to moviegoers. But although this Preston Sturges comedy was a mild improvement over *Mr. Imperium*, it was by no means strong enough to secure Pinza's future in films.

"Mr. Pinza had better stay away from Hollywood unless he takes his own writer out with him next time," warned the *New York World-Telegram*. And *Photoplay* commented: "Despite the grandeur that sweeps from the Mediterranean shores to Palm Springs gardens, the story

itself never jells. Lana Turner, who is seldom given material worthy of her, looks beautiful and does more than her share to tote this bale of nonsense. Pinza is just another middle-aged actor trying to prove himself, so far as this film is concerned. Certainly his magnificent voice is woefully neglected, the few songs given him far below his vocal ability."

Pinza had three songs, two of which ("Let Me Look at You" and "Andiamo") were originals by Harold Arlen and Dorothy Fields. His third and best, oddly enough, was a standard—"You Belong to My Heart" (which served as the picture's title when it was released in Great Britain). Another Arlen–Fields tune was "My Love and My Mule," with singer Trudy Erwin dubbing for Lana. In minor roles, Marjorie Main and Debbie Reynolds enlivened the proceedings considerably every time they appeared on the screen. However, footage containing Keenan Wynn as a motorcycle cop and veteran actress Mae Clarke as a secretary wound up on the cutting-room floor.

Seen today, *Mr. Imperium* comes off no better or worse than many of the other musical marshmallows MGM was producing at the time. In 1951, however, it had been such a ballyhooed event (the pre-release press coverage was enormous) that anything less than the celluloid equivalent of a *South Pacific* would have been a letdown.

Although the failure of *Mr. Imperium* signalled the beginning of the end of Pinza's cinema career, it had little or no effect on Lana's superstar status. In fact, it was on December 31, 1951, just two months after the release of the film, that MGM signed her to a new long-term contract.★

With Barry Sullivan

THE MERRY WIDOW

A METRO·GOLDWYN·MAYER PICTURE

1952

With Fernando Lamas

CAST

LANA TURNER, *Crystal Radek;* FERNANDO LAMAS, *Count Danilo;* UNA MERKEL, *Kitty Riley;* RICHARD HAYDN, *Baron Popoff;* THOMAS GOMEZ, *King of Marshovia;* JOHN ABBOTT, *Marshovian Ambassador;* MARCEL DALIO, *Police Sergeant;* KING DONOVAN, *Nitki;* ROBERT COOTE, *Marquis De Crillon;* SUJATA, *Gypsy Girl;* LISA FERRADAY, *Marcella;* SHEPARD MENKEN, *Kunjany;* LUDWIG STOSSEL, *Major Domo;* DAVE WILLOCK, *Attache;* WANDA McKAY, *First Girl;* ANNE KIMBELL, *Second Girl;* EDWARD EARLE, *Chestnut Vendor;* GWEN VERDON, *Specialty Dancer;* GREGG SHERWOOD, JOI LANSING, *Maxim Girls.*

With Robert Coote

CREDITS

Director, CURTIS BERNHARDT; Producer, JOE PASTERNAK; Screenplay, SONYA LEVIEN and WILLIAM LUDWIG; Based on the Operetta by FRANZ LEHAR and Authors VICTOR LEON and LEO STEIN; Photography (Technicolor), ROBERT SURTEES; Color Consultants, HENRI JAFFA and ALVORD EISEMAN; Art Direction, CEDRIC GIBBONS and PAUL GROESSE; Set Decorations, EDWIN B. WILLIS and ARTHUR KRAMS; Special Effects, A. ARNOLD GILLESPIE and WARREN NEWCOMBE; Costumes, HELEN ROSE and GILE STEELE; Makeup, WILLIAM TUTTLE; Hair Stylist, SYDNEY GUILAR-OFF; Music, FRANZ LEHAR; Lyrics, PAUL FRANCIS WEBSTER; Musical Direction, JAY BLACKTON; Musical Numbers Created and Staged by JACK COLE; Songs: "Vilia," "Night," "Girls, Girls, Girls," "I'm Going to Maxim's," "The Merry Widow Waltz," "Can-Can." Running time, 105 minutes.

With Una Merkel

NOTES ABOUT THE FILM

Of the thirty operettas composed by Franz Lehar, the military bandleader who became the outstanding light-opera composer of his day, the most imperishable is unquestionably *The Merry Widow.*

Lehar's celebrated musical enjoyed its first stage performance on December 30, 1905 in gay, prewar Vienna. America discovered it in 1907 when Donald Brian and Ethel Jackson starred in the New York stage production. On film, *The Merry Widow* became a 1912 two-reeler with Alma Rubens and Wallace Reid, and thirteen years later Erich von Stroheim directed a stunning full-length silent feature in which Mae Murray and John Gilbert gave striking performances. In 1934, another version with Jeanette MacDonald and Maurice Chevalier added sound and a mischievous mood of boudoir farce via the direction of Ernst Lubitsch.

When, on May 8, 1950, MGM announced its intentions to waltz the widow out once more, Joe Pas-

As Crystal Radek

ternak, the film's producer, stated that this version of Lehar's very adaptable property would be treated as a "love story with music" and that it would serve as a vehicle for Lana Turner and Ricardo Montalban.

When shooting began late in 1951, however, the coveted role of Danilo went to Fernando Lamas, a newly contracted Argentinian star. Although the score now took a back seat to the plot's sexual skirmishes, there was ample opportunity for Lamas to display his vocal talents. Almost all of the film's musical numbers fell his way and when *The Merry Widow* was released in September

1952, his dashing looks and romantic voice made quite an impression on both critics and moviegoers.

Sonya Levien and William Ludwig did the new screenplay and if it wandered considerably from the original Lehar–Stein–Leon book, the additions, subtractions and substitutions were very easy to take. The music was still Lehar's (with a dextrous set of modernized lyrics by Paul Francis Webster) under the direction of Jay Blackton, a Broadway recruit whose stage hits ranged from *Oklahoma!* to *Call Me Madam*. Another Broadway recruit was Jack Cole, one of the freshest and most inventive of choreographers, whose major contributions to the film included a brilliantly staged waltz finale and a rowdy can-can routine at Maxim's. Produced on a sumptuous scale in the best MGM–Joe Pasternak tradition and directed with taste and care by Curtis Bernhardt, this 1952 version of the operetta was the first to be photographed in Technicolor and its spectacular splashes of color played an important part in the picture's success.*

The all-important role of Lehar's heroine was carefully rewritten for its leading lady (including an Americanization of the character), with this fresh treatment discreetly relieving the widow of her musical requirements.† But the role did call for a display of poise, assurance and great beauty and Miss Turner easily filled its demands. She was dressed to the hilt in a handsome array of gowns, hats, negligees and hourglass corsets of those turn-of-the-century times (even her

With Una Merkel

shoes boasted jewelled heels), and if Mae Murray was merrier and Jeanette MacDonald more melodious, no Merry Widow—before or since, in *any* medium—has ever cut such a magnificent figure.

In this variation on the old theme, the heroine is Crystal Radek, the widow of an ex-Marshovian blacksmith who rose to industrial fame and fortune in the United States. Crystal is invited to Marshovia ostensibly to dedicate a statue to the memory of her late husband. Actually, the invitation is part of a scheme by the Marshovian king to have her fall in love with the dashing Lothario, Count Danilo, with the hopes of gaining access to her eighty million dollars in order to pay the national debt.

Danilo is loath to carry out his part in the plot,

----

*The '52 *Merry Widow* received two Oscar nominations in the Color division—for Best Art Direction/Set Decoration and for Best Costume Design.

†The widow does contribute one vocal selection when she shares a duet with Danilo at Maxim's. Her voice, however, was that of singer Trudy Erwin, again dubbing for Lana.

particularly when he mistakes Crystal's dour secretary, Kitty, for the wealthy widow, but patriotic pressure forces him to press an ardent suit. Discovering Danilo's mercenary motives, Crystal resolves to teach him a lesson. She leaves for Paris and, when pursued by Danilo, she poses as an impoverished chorus girl. It is at the famous Maxim's that the Count develops a genuine ardor for the "chorus girl" and then finds himself in the tragic predicament of having to renounce her for the rich woman he does not love. Soon his love becomes so strong that Danilo chooses arrest in preference to carrying out the king's scheme.

At the Embassy Ball, however, Crystal discloses her true identity and pays off Marshovia's national debt with a check for eight hundred million drankas. Danilo, not realizing that this is just one million dollars in American money, assumes the widow is now penniless. He rushes to Crystal, sweeps her in his arms and proposes to her, and together they dance to the romantic strains of *The Merry Widow Waltz*.

The third feature version of the famous operetta surprised everyone, including *The New York Times'* Bosley Crowther, by being a distinguished picture in its own right. "*The Merry Widow* never had it so good," wrote Crowther, who went on to call the production "the most colorful and exquisite it has ever had . . . the brilliance in Technicolor of the palaces, grand hotels and a replica of Maxim's in Paris that craftsmen at Metro have contrived is something to take your breath away, and the richness of the costumes and the staging of dance and choral groups will deal the knockout blow. No *Widow* in our recollection—and we've seen quite a few, including the memorable Ernst Lubitsch version —has been turned out as this one is."

Newsweek's critic agreed: "The assets of the new production, directed by Curtis Bernhardt, are legion. There are the great Lehar melodies, from the mesmeric waltz to "Vilia" and "I'm Going to Maxim's." There is Lana Turner, as a well-turned and glowing widow, and the Argentine importation Fernando Lamas, as a tall and ingratiating Count Danilo. There is a brisk new book, a deft new set of lyrics, and any amount of wonderfully baroque scenery in the mythical kingdom of Marshovia. . . Little else need be said . . . this is a first-class *Merry Widow* and a fine tribute to the last grand master of the Viennese waltz."

Admirable comic support was provided by Richard Haydn, Thomas Gomez, John Abbott, Robert Coote and especially by Una Merkel, whose youthful effervescence as the widow's companion belied the fact she had appeared as the queen in an earlier (1934) film version of the operetta.

For sheer chemistry, Señor Lamas was easily Miss Turner's most complimentary co-star since Gable and Taylor. For the more romantic patrons attending *The Merry Widow*, there was added interest in the fact that during the making of the film the two stars had been engaged in a much-publicized, off-screen romance.

Fortunately, the picture's box-office results were much happier than Lana's last two screen efforts. *The Merry Widow* won *Boxoffice* magazine's Blue Ribbon Award as the most widely-seen film during the month of September 1952. It still enjoys repeat showings throughout the world where its air of glamour and opulence make it a perennial favorite. Early in the 1970s, *Variety* reported that it had clicked heavily at the box office in a repeat showing in Lima, Peru.

More recently, Sweden's Ingmar Bergman has expressed hopes of directing a screen version of the operetta. ★

*With
Fernando
Lamas in
the "Merry
Widow
Waltz"
production
number*

177

THE BAD AND THE BEAUTIFUL

A METRO·GOLDWYN·MAYER PICTURE
1953

CAST

LANA TURNER, *Georgia Lorrison;* KIRK DOUGLAS, *Jonathan Shields;* WALTER PIDGEON, *Harry Pebbel;* DICK POWELL, *James Lee Bartlow;* BARRY SULLIVAN, *Fred Amiel;* GLORIA GRAHAME, *Rosemary Bartlow;* GILBERT ROLAND, *Victor "Gaucho" Ribera;* LEO G. CARROLL, *Henry Whitfield;* VANESSA BROWN, *Kay Amiel;* PAUL STEWART, *Syd Murphy;* SAMMY WHITE, *Gus;* ELAINE STEWART, *Lila;* IVAN TRIESAULT, *Von Ellstein;* KATHLEEN FREEMAN, *Miss March;* MARIETTA CANTY, *Ida;* JONATHAN COTT, *Assistant Director;* LUCILLE KNOCH, *Blonde;* STEVE FORREST, *Leading Man;* PERRY SHEEHAN, *Secretary;* ROBERT BURTON, *McDill;* FRANCIS X. BUSHMAN, *Eulogist;* SANDRA DESCHER, *Little Girl;* GEORGE LEWIS, *Actor in Screen Test;* BARBARA BILLINGSLEY, *Lucien;* WILLIAM "BILL" PHILLIPS, *Assistant Director;* DOROTHY PATRICK, *Arlene;* KAREN VERNE, *Rosa;* PEGGY KING, *Singer;* BEN ASTAR, *Joe;* BESS FLOWERS, *Joe's Friend at Party;* JEFF RICHARDS, *Young Man at Studio;* DEE TURNELL, *Linda Ronley;* ALYCE MAY, *Movie Extra.*

CREDITS

Director, VINCENTE MINNELLI; Producer, JOHN HOUSEMAN; Screenplay, CHARLES SCHNEE; Based on a Story by GEORGE BRADSHAW; Photography, ROBERT SURTEES; Art Direction, CEDRIC GIBBONS and EDWARD CARFAGNO; Set Decorations, EDWIN B. WILLIS and KEOGH GLEASON; Editor, CONRAD A. NERVIG; Sound, DOUGLAS SHEARER; Costumes, HELEN ROSE; Makeup, WILLIAM TUTTLE; Hair Stylist, SYDNEY GUILAROFF; Special Effects, A. ARNOLD GILLESPIE and WARREN NEWCOMBE; Music, DAVID RAKSIN; Assistant Director, JERRY THORPE; Running time, 117 minutes.

NOTES ABOUT THE FILM

In 1937, Lana Turner began her screen career as an extra in a film about Hollywood. Fifteen years later, as a star, she appeared in another in the Hollywood-on-Hollywood genre.

With Kirk Douglas

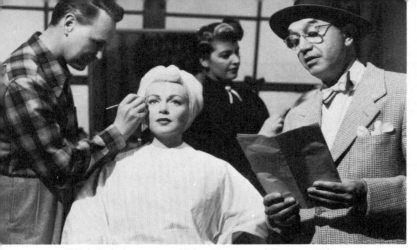

Like *A Star Is Born*, *The Bad and the Beautiful* is one of the best dissections of the film industry ever made. A January 1953 release, it was rushed into Los Angeles theatres one month earlier to qualify for 1952 Academy Award consideration and at the ceremonies in March '53 (the first such affair to be nationally televised), the picture won the evening's biggest total of awards with five Oscars: Best Supporting Actress (Gloria Grahame); Best Screenplay; Best Cinematography; Best Art Direction/Set Decoration; and Best Costume Design. (The film's sixth nominee, Kirk Douglas, lost in the Best Actor race to Gary Cooper for *High Noon*.)

With Del Armstrong, Helen Young and Sammy White

With Barbara Billingsley, Marietta Canty and Kirk Douglas

Georgia Lorrison in costume for her latest film

With Paul Stewart, Leo G. Carroll,
Walter Pidgeon and Gilbert Roland

With Kirk Douglas

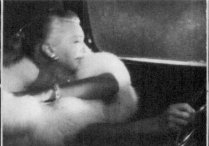

One of the most memorable moments in THE BAD AND THE BEAUTIFUL: *the*

MGM gave this movie about the movies an appropriately glossy and glamourous production, and from its opening shot to the final fadeout, *The Bad and the Beautiful* is a harvest of riches for movie fans who dote on behind-the-scenes atmosphere and all the other elements of the celluloid world. The sound stages, the dressing rooms, the Beverly Hills mansions; the "B" pictures in the making, the screen tests, the sneak previews; the Hollywood funeral, the Hollywood party, the Hollywood premiere—all were on display in what is probably the most exactingly detailed study of the dream factory ever presented on film.

All the standard Hollywood types were represented as well: the small-time agent; the money-conscious tycoon; the sexy starlet; the Latin lover. Although prefaced by the usual any-similarity-is-purely-coincidental line, Charles Schnee's screenplay was brimming with fascinating prototypes of many real-life Hollywood characters, a situation that prompted guessing games within the industry at the time of the film's release. Louella Parsons, in her widely syndicated column, openly stated that it was "difficult to believe some of the scenes were not suggested by events in the colorful David O. Selznick's life." Another prominent script character, the actress-daughter of a former Hollywood great,* is said to have been inspired by Diana Barrymore, and still another by producer Val Lewton.

For connoisseurs of "in" references, there were several of interest; e.g., Miss Turner's own personal makeup man (Del Armstrong) and hairdresser (Helen Young) appear as themselves performing the same duties for the actress-character she plays in the story. Her long-time stand-in, Alyce May, is a very visible extra as well, and in another scene, the staircase from Miss Turner's *Merry Widow* film is prominently used.

The Bad and the Beautiful's anti-hero is Jonathan Shields, the son of a movie magnate who died broke and was hated even into his grave. As the film opens, Fred Amiel, a noted director, James Lee Bartlow, a prize-winning author, and Georgia Lorrison, a big star, are gathered in the Hollywood sanctum of production tycoon Harry Pebbel. Jonathan, now bankrupt himself, is on the phone from Paris with financing for a colossal comeback feature provided he can enlist the services of director Amiel, writer Bartlow and actress Lorrison, all of whom he has ruthlessly double-crossed while pursuing his Hollywood career. As they ponder his plea, each reviews a crucial showdown with this driving but undeniably creative figure who is "more than a man —he's an experience."

The director tells the story of his great double-cross

first—Jonathan fostered his career, then took his "dream picture," the one he set his heart on, and gave it to a more celebrated director. The actress had been salvaged from a drunken obsession with her dead actor-father, transformed by Jonathan into a great star, but discarded when she fell in love with him. In the case of the author, Jonathan was also responsible for his success in Hollywood but equally instrumental in causing the death of his flighty young wife by fostering her romance with the studio Lothario.

To the three assembled in his office Harry Pebbel points out that despite the harm done by Jonathan Shields, without him they would never have attained their present stature. Unanimously, they turn down Jonathan's plea but as he relates his new idea to Pebbel over the transatlantic phone, they cannot help listening in. The film ends on this note, with all three apparently on the verge of succumbing to the old Shields magic.

The Bad and the Beautiful was directed by Vincente Minnelli and acted uncommonly well by a gilt-edged cast. The role of the glamourous Hollywood star quite naturally fit Miss Turner like a glove (or a tight sweater, as one critic quipped). It also provided her with that rare combination of a well-composed character, honest dialogue and a perceptive director. The result: it's one of her best played and most popular roles.

In *Film Quarterly* magazine, writer Albert Johnson called *The Bad and the Beautiful* Minnelli's "most brilliant piece of drama-direction." Here is his precise account of one of the film's truly memorable moments: "Robert Surtees, the cameraman for *The Bad and the Beautiful*, created one of the most exciting sequences of the decade for the picture: the car-hysteria episode. It is the section where Georgia Lorrison, the neurotic movie star (Lana Turner), yields to a fit of anguish while driving her automobile away from her lover's mansion. . . . Turner emerges from the mansion, dazed, in white ermine, and drives away. Her sobs soon build to hysteria, and lights of cars send flashes across the windows as she reaches a moment of unbearable frenzy, releases the steering wheel entirely, and screams in emotional agony. Her foot presses the brake. One hears only her screams, the honking of passing auto-horns, and suddenly, it is raining. The car bumps along uncontrollably for a second, then comes to a standstill. Turner falls over the wheel, still sobbing uncontrollably as the sequence fades. It is superb theater, one of the great moments of human despair shown in cinematic terms, and a prime example of the coordination of actress, director, and cameraman which can create a perfect visual moment of dramatic poetry upon the screen."

Vincente Minnelli recently commented on Miss Turner's work in this scene: "I found she had great imagination. She could do things I had no idea she could. She had great depth and color and rose to the

---

superbly-staged sequence in which Georgia attempts to drive home in a state of hysteria

part. That famous hysterical scene in the car was shot in one take. I had a special apparatus so the car revolved and the cameras moved in and out. I explained the whole routine to her, and she went in and did it in one take. She was a marvelous person as well as actress because if you were appreciative and responded to her doing a good job, she responded as well."

Equally at home in musicals or drama, Minnelli's handling of this scene and others in *The Bad and the Beautiful* is a smashing, raw testimonial to his versatility as a director, and it's regrettable—and somewhat astonishing—that he missed out on an Oscar nomination that year. Another glaring oversight involved composer David Raksin, a superior craftsman whose brilliant score for the film is one of his finest works.

In 1962, Vincente Minnelli directed another film in the Hollywood-on-Hollywood genre titled *Two Weeks in Another Town*. In it, he somewhat justifiably utilized footage from his own *The Bad and the Beautiful* as a specimen of exemplary filmmaking. ★

With Barry Sullivan and Dick Powell

LATIN LOVERS

A METRO·GOLDWYN·MAYER PICTURE
1953

CAST

LANA TURNER, *Nora Taylor*; RICARDO MONTALBAN, *Roberto Santos*; JOHN LUND, *Paul Chevron*; LOUIS CALHERN, *Grandfather Santos*; JEAN HAGEN, *Anne Kellwood*; EDUARD FRANZ, *Dr. Lionel Y. Newman*; BEULAH BONDI, *Woman Analyst*; JOAQUIN GARAY, *Zeca*; ARCHER MAC-DONALD, *Howard G. Hubbell*; DOROTHY NEUMANN, *Mrs. Newman*; ROBERT BURTON, *Mr. Cumberly*; RITA MORENO, *Christina*; TRISTRAM COFFIN, *Paul's Business Associate*.

CREDITS

Director, MERVYN LEROY; Producer, JOE PASTERNAK; Screenplay, ISOBEL LENNART; Photography (Technicolor), JOSEPH RUTTENBERG; Color Consultants, HENRI JAFFA and ALVORD EISEMAN; Editor, JOHN McSWEENEY, JR.; Sound, DOUGLAS SHEARER; Art Direction, CEDRIC GIBBONS and GABRIEL SCOGNAMILLO; Set Decorations, EDWIN B. WILLIS and JACQUE MAPES; Special Effects, A. ARNOLD GILLESPIE and WARREN NEWCOMBE; Music, NICHOLAS BRODSZKY; Lyrics, LEO ROBIN; Musical Direction, GEORGE STOLL; Dances Staged by FRANK VELOZ; Orchestrations, PETE RUGOLO; Assistant Director, ARVID GRIFFEN; Women's Costumes, HELEN ROSE; Men's Costumes, HERSCHEL McCOY; Makeup, WILLIAM TUTTLE; Hair Stylist, SYDNEY GUILAROFF; Songs: "Night and You," "I Had to Kiss You," "Come to My Arms," "A Little More of Your Amor," "Carlotta, You Gotta Be Mine." Running time, 104 minutes.

NOTES ABOUT THE FILM

This gorgeously Technicolored bit of fluff presented Lana as Nora Taylor, a Lady in the Dark–ish heroine who has everything in the world—including $37 million which she inherited from her father. Her one big problem: not even her psychoanalyst can tell her whether men love her for herself or her money. She isn't even sure of Paul Chevron, her stuffy fiance, who's worth $48 million in his own right. His reaction to her ardor is unenthusiastic, so when he goes off to Brazil with his polo team, she follows him in the hope that the change in climate will warm him up. Unfortunately for Nora, the land of romance does nothing for Paul, who is just as businesslike as ever.

But she does meet Roberto Santos, a young and handsome plantation owner, who sweeps her off her feet. At first, Nora is afraid that he'll refuse to marry her when he learns about her fortune, but she's even more upset when he expresses great delight in the discovery. What follows is a game of wits, resolved when, because she realizes Roberto truly loves her, Nora turns her entire fortune over to him so that after they are married, *he* can do all the worrying about the problems of having $37 million. To tie up further loose ends, Nora's sec-

With Ricardo Montalban

With Ricardo Montalban

retary, Anne, winds up with Paul Chevron for whom she's long had a secret passion.

Joe Pasternak produced *Latin Lovers* and Mervyn LeRoy directed Lana in it (for the fourth and to date

With John Lund

With Jean Hagen

last time). The picture can be likened to a multicolored parfait; but it's entertaining of its kind and not nearly as slight as it would have been in less capable hands. Archer Winsten in his *New York Post* review summed the whole thing up in this manner: "You shouldn't be too hard on a picture of this traditional slant. When it possesses such handsome people, so well dressed, and placed in such plushy surroundings, so beautifully Technicolored, you can lie back and let it surround you like a dream of sudden, enormous wealth. Why not? If you've paid for the pipe, no use complaining because you're having a pipe-dream you've had before."

In its advertising strategy for the picture, MGM tried to capitalize on the popularity of *The Bad and the Beautiful*. The ads for the film proclaimed: "The Bad and Beautiful girl is bad and beautiful again in a wonderful new musical." *Latin Lovers* was more a romantic comedy with music than one of MGM's traditional super-musicals of the period, but it did feature

five original Nicholas Brodsky–Leo Robin tunes, two of which were "sung" by Ricardo Montalban (actually they were extremely well dubbed for him by singer Carlos Ramirez). Other music included the rippling strains of several red-hot sambas, staged by Frank Veloz (of Veloz and Yolanda fame), which had even the critic for *The New York Times* tapping his toes and commenting: ". . . Miss Turner and Mr. Montalban dance to one of these numbers with professional aplomb, a talent that should not go unnoticed."

The film was still another great showcase for Turner the Clotheshorse. Helen Rose, who was Oscar-nominated for her work in both *The Merry Widow* and *The Bad and the Beautiful* (and who took home the prize for the latter film), came up with an unusual idea in designing the star's wardrobe. All of Lana's more than twenty costumes were created in black and white—or a combination of both—and pitted against the richly Technicolored backgrounds, it resulted in a striking and unusual effect. Joseph Ruttenberg, the cameraman assigned to the film, photographed Miss Turner to great advantage and in later years, he was the gentleman she most frequently requested to lens her non-Metro films.

Latin Lovers had two last-minute cast replacements in the male division. Ricardo Montalban stepped in for an equally virile Latin type, Fernando Lamas,* and John Lund took over for Michael Wilding, an MGM contractee who accepted a suspension rather than play the part of Paul Chevron which he considered a "secondary male lead." The cast also boasted Louis Calhern, Jean Hagen (good, even in a less-than-inspired role), Beulah Bondi, Rita Moreno, Eduard Franz and Dorothy Neumann, whose riotously funny cracks about psychoanalysis and its licensed practitioners added immeasurably to the fun.★

---

*The script of *Latin Lovers* had originally been tailored for Lana and Lamas as a follow-up to their *Merry Widow*. But when their real-life romance went kaput, MGM knew audiences would not be able to accept them romantically paired on-screen again. Thus, Montalban was substituted.

With Ricardo Montalban and Louis Calhern

FLAME AND THE FLESH

A METRO·GOLDWYN·MAYER PICTURE

1954

CAST

LANA TURNER, *Madeline*; PIER ANGELI, *Lisa*; CARLOS THOMPSON, *Nino*; BONAR COLLEANO, *Ciccio*; CHARLES GOLDNER, *Mondari*; PETER ILLING, *Peppe*; ROSALIE CRUTCHLEY, *Francesca*; MARNE MAITLAND, *Filiberto*; ERIC POHLMANN, *Marina Proprietor*; CATHARINA FERRAZ, *Dressmaker*; ALEXIS DE GALLIER, *Playboy*.

CREDITS

Director, RICHARD BROOKS; Producer, JOE PASTERNAK; Screenplay, HELEN DEUTSCH; Based on a Novel by AUGUSTE BAILLY; Photography (Technicolor), CHRISTOPHER CHALLIS; Editors, ALBERT AKST and RAY POULTON; Sound, A. W. WATKINS; Art Direction, ALFRED JUNGE; Technicolor Color Consultant, JOAN BRIDGE; Music, NICHOLAS BRODSZKY; Lyrics, JACK LAWRENCE; Musical Direction, GEORGE STOLL; Songs: "No One But You," "Peddler Man," "Languida," "By Candlelight." Running time, 104 minutes.

NOTES ABOUT THE FILM

A "new" Lana Turner and some beautiful location work in Italy were the major points of interest in this hard-breathing romantic drama about a pleasure-loving adventuress who breezes into town just long enough to ruin a few lives and, in the process, discovers the one true love of her life. The picture was set in Naples, and to play the Neapolitan lady tramp Lana had to become a brunette.

As the picture's most exploitable asset, MGM slanted almost all of its promotional and advertising efforts on behalf of the film towards Lana's "new look." Months before *Flame and the Flesh* was released, magazines and wire services were issued pictures of her in her new hair

During the film's title credits, a little girl apes Lana's sexy walk

color and when the movie premiered in May 1954, the ads blared: "Lana Turner—even more exciting now as a brunette!"

Flame and the Flesh was loosely based on an Auguste Bailly novel. It had already been the inspiration for a 1937 French film titled *Naples au Baiser de Feu* starring Viviane Romance, Tino Rossi and Mireille Balin. The picture opens with Lana, as Madeline Douvane, being tossed out of her apartment by a disapproving landlady. Eventually, she gets picked up on the street by a

With Carlos Thompson

With Charles Goldner

Flame and the Flesh was MGM's unabashed attempt at imitating those earthy Italian-made sex dramas that helped to popularize European stars like Gina Lollobrigida and which usually centered on the shenanigans of a shady lady. It's one of Richard Brooks' earliest directorial efforts and although he made a valid attempt to achieve a suggestion of neo-realism in the picture, for most critics the end result contained more flesh (Lana's) than flame.

In the *New York Herald Tribune*, Otis L. Guernsey, Jr. wrote: "Lana Turner has done the chic thing—she has made a movie in Italy and she plays a loose woman in it . . . Director Brooks concentrates on making Miss Turner look sexy in all kinds of settings from cabarets to a stuffy bedroom. This is not hard to do, and he does it very well. But he cannot make much out of the inner meanings of the story . . . From its adult beginning the film moves to the only logical ending allowed in

kind-hearted musician who feeds her and gives her a room. In no time at all, however, the lady sets her cap for her benefactor's roommate, Nino, a handsome singer with a reputation as a heart-breaker.

Although he resists her obvious advances, Nino ultimately succumbs to Madeline's sultry charms and off they go together on the eve of his marriage, to the consternation of both his fiancée, Lisa, and the lovelorn musician who up to now had notions of marrying Madeline and making an honest woman of her.

Once the novelty of life with her handsome but impecunious lover has worn off, and the struggle for existence becomes more marked each time he obtains a job only to lose it because he is jealous of the attention paid his lady by patrons or proprietors of these establishments, it's not long before Madeline picks out a more prosperous "protector."

Nino makes a final attempt to win her back but Madeline, even though she really loves him, knows he would be happier with Lisa. She sends him back to Naples and the fadeout sees Madeline, awakened to real love for the first time, traipsing off into the fog, ready for whatever life has to offer her next.

American movies. In short, the fire of Italian neo-realism which permeates the situation doesn't mix at all with the watered-down morals code of the producers association. Thus, story-wise, the proceedings are weak. Taken on the isolated sequence basis, however, fans of the Turner School of Histrionics may be satisfied."

Newsweek limited the film to "unreconstructed and patient Turnerphiles," adding: "Helen Deutsch's script is chiefly an opportunity for Miss Turner to ogle the boys. There are many fine views of Vesuvius, but the star herself does most of the smoking."

Flame and the Flesh was Lana's first European venture and was made on location in and around Naples (to scenically magnificent effect) with interiors filmed at MGM's Elstree Studios in London. Joe Pasternak, best known for his musicals, produced the movie and managed to inject four excellent new Nicholas Brodszky—Jack Lawrence songs into the plot.★

With Pier Angeli

BETRAYED

A METRO·GOLDWYN·MAYER PICTURE

1954

As Carla Van Oven

CAST

CLARK GABLE, *Col. Pieter Deventer;* LANA TURNER, *Carla Van Oven;* VICTOR MATURE, *"The Scarf";* LOUIS CALHERN, *Gen. Ten Eyck;* O. E. HASSE, *Col. Helmuth Dietrich;* WILFRID HYDE WHITE, *Gen. Charles Larraby;* IAN CARMICHAEL, *Capt. Jackie Lawson;* NIALL MacGINNIS, *"Blackie";* NORA SWINBURNE, *"The Scarf's" Mother;* ROLAND CULVER, *Gen. Warsleigh;* LESLIE WESTON, *"Pop";* CHRISTOPHER RHODES, *Chris;* LILLY KANN, *Jan's Grandmother;* BRIAN SMITH, *Jan;* ANTON DIFFRING, *Capt. Von Stanger.* (Note: Singer DIANA COUPLAND supplied the singing voice for Miss Turner.)

CREDITS

Director/Producer, GOTTFRIED REINHARDT; Screenplay, RONALD MILLAR and GEORGE FROESCHEL; Photography (EastmanColor), F. A. YOUNG; Editors, JOHN DUNNING and RAYMOND POULTON; Sound, A. W. WATKINS; Art Direction, ALFRED JUNGE; Miss Turner's Costumes by BALMAIN-PARIS; Makeup, JOHN O'GORMAN; Song: "Johnny, Come Home." Music by WALTER GOEHR and Lyrics by RONALD MILLAR; Running time, 111 minutes.

NOTES ABOUT THE FILM

It's a bit unfortunate that three of the four Clark Gable–Lana Turner co-starring vehicles have had World War II backgrounds. Certainly two such Beautiful People warranted more glamourous trappings. Their fourth and final film together, *Betrayed*, had them back in combat suits and steel helmets for a cloak-and-dagger melodrama, the script of which provided too few love scenes to suit the fans of this charismatic duo. But

With Clark Gable

With Victor Mature

although the clinches didn't come as often as in the past and the fireworks weren't as loud, the romantic moments did occasionally contain certain rewards, including a recitation of that classic line, ". . . you're beautiful when you're angry" (Gable to Turner, of course).

Gottfried Reinhardt (son of the famous Max Reinhardt), who had been the associate producer on *Homecoming*, persuaded Gable and Turner, both of whom had been filming in Europe, to remain abroad for this film which he produced as well as directed. The location site was Holland, and F. A. Young's exquisite EastmanColor cameras lovingly captured all the atmospheric beauty and old-world charm of the Netherlands, giving the film a genuine James Fitzpatrick travelog look. Competing with the scenery for front-and-center attention was the film's third co-star, Victor Mature, out of togas and sandals for a change and, during this period of his career, almost overdressed in peasant garb for the highly colorful role of "The Scarf," a dashing resistance leader with an acute case of Momism.

Betrayed (which began production under the title *The True and the Brave*) opens as Colonel Pieter Deventer is captured by the Nazis. A resistance group led by "The Scarf" liberates him, and he escapes to England where he enlists playgirl Carla Van Oven as a spy. She is a Dutch widow who had been friendly with the enemy, and by way of redeeming herself, she agrees to become an agent for the British. Deventer trains her for the task and the two fall in love, but their romance is disrupted by a dangerous leak in security with the finger pointing to Carla as the traitor who had sold out to the Germans. Carla herself suspects "The Scarf," even though he has also expressed love for her.

Ultimately, "The Scarf," numbed by the fact that his own people have condemned his beloved mother as a collaborator, is revealed as the traitor. As he tries to escape, he is shot by Deventer, who is then reunited with Carla.

In Philip T. Hartung's review for *The Commonweal*, he wrote: "In real life I'd be a little suspicious of the characters in *Betrayed*, an American film made in Holland and England. During long parts of it one is never quite sure for whom Clark Gable, Lana Turner and Victor Mature are spying and chasing. But director Gottfried Reinhardt does manage to work up some good suspense at times, and even though your loyalties are splattered all over the place, you get keyed up to quite a pitch. Perhaps a little better motivation in the characterization and a little more honesty in the mystery part of the script would have resulted in a better picture. But of course a Gable–Turner movie is not entirely without interest and the EastmanColor photography is very beautiful too."

For Bob Brock of the *Dallas Times-Herald*, the film had another significance: "If nothing else, *Betrayed* marks a couple of milestones—one major and one minor. In the major sense, *Betrayed* is Clark Gable's last picture for MGM, writing finis to an association that spanned two decades of moviemaking. In a minor sense—maybe major to some—*Betrayed* will probably mark Miss Turner's last time as a brunette. Rumblings from Culver City where the cameras are now turning on her next film are that Miss Turner is her old blonde self again."

As critic Brock noted, *Betrayed* was indeed Gable's last picture as a Metro contractee. The new studio regime under Dore Schary prompted a virtual dissolution of their huge stable of high-priced contract talent, which included actors, producers, directors and technicians. Gable was among the first to leave and he never again worked at Metro, even on a free-lance basis.

As for Miss Turner's hair, it had been her own decision to retain the brunette shade of *Flame and the Flesh* for this film. Fortunately, she soon realized that her fans preferred her as a blonde, and although years later she did go dark for a few scenes of *Madame X*, after *Betrayed* she was never again totally brunette for a film.★

THE PRODIGAL

A METRO·GOLDWYN·MAYER PICTURE

1955

CAST

LANA TURNER, *Samarra;* EDMUND PURDOM, *Micah;* LOUIS CALHERN, *Nahreeb;* AUDREY DALTON, *Ruth;* JAMES MITCHELL, *Asham;* NEVILLE BRAND, *Rhakim;* WALTER HAMPDEN, *Eli;* TAINA ELG, *Elissa;* FRANCIS L. SULLIVAN, *Bosra;* JOSEPH WISEMAN, *Carmish;* SANDRA DESCHER, *Yasmin;* JOHN DEHNER, *Joram;* CECIL KELLAWAY, *Governor;* PHILIP TONGE, *Barber-Surgeon;* DAVID LEONARD, *Blind Man;* HENRY DANIELL, *Ramadi;* PAUL CAVANAGH, *Tobiah;* DAYTON LUMMIS, *Caleb;* TRACEY ROBERTS, *Tahra;* JARMA LEWIS, *Uba;* JAY NOVELLO, *Merchant;* DOROTHY ADAMS, *Carpenter's Wife;* PETER DeBEAR, *Carpenter's Son;* PHYLLIS GRAFFEO, *Miriam;* PATRICIA IANNONE, *Deborah;* EUGENE MAZZOLA, *David;* GEORGE SAWAYA, *Kavak;* RICHARD DEVON, *Risafe;* ANN CAMERON, *Lahla;* GLORIA DEA, *Faradine;* JOHN ROSSER, *Lirhan;* CHARLES WAGENHEIM, *Zubeir;* REX LEASE, *Purveyor;* DOROTHY NEUMANN, *Mother;* GEORGE LEWIS, *Guard;* ALMIRA SESSIONS, *Old Lady;* GEORGE ROBOTHAM, *Chosen Martyr;* JO GILBERT, *Mother;* ARGENTINA BRUNETTI, *Woman.*

CREDITS

Director, RICHARD THORPE; Producer, CHARLES SCHNEE; Screenplay, MAURICE ZIMM; Adaptation from the Bible Story by JOE BREEN, JR. and SAMUEL JAMES LARSEN; Photography (CinemaScope and EastmanColor), JOSEPH RUTTENBERG; Editor, HAROLD F. KRESS; Sound, WESLEY C. MILLER; Art Direction, CEDRIC GIBBONS and RANDALL DUELL; Set Decorations, EDWIN B. WILLIS and HENRY GRACE; Costumes, HERSCHEL McCOY; Makeup, WILLIAM TUTTLE; Hair Stylist, SYDNEY GUILAROFF; Special Effects, A. ARNOLD GILLESPIE and WARREN NEWCOMBE; Music, BRONISLAU KAPER; Assistant Director, ARVID GRIFFEN; Running time, 115 minutes.

NOTES ABOUT THE FILM

After two consecutive pictures as a brunette, *The Prodigal* returned Lana to the famous blonde hair shade most recognizable—and most preferable—to her public. Here, she was cast as Samarra, the lightly-clad temptress who incited history's first juvenile delinquent to leave home. It was her first appearance in CinemaScope and George Bourke of *The Miami Herald* called the role "just about the most form-fitting she's had since she first sashayed before a movie camera in a memorable sweater."

The Prodigal was based on the Biblical story of the prodigal son as told by St. Luke in Chapter XV of his gospels. There, in fewer than 300 words is the bare suggestion of a youth who "wasted his substance in riotous living," later to return repentant to farm and father. MGM, with much elaboration, turned this handful of words into a huge and costly ($5,000,000) spectacle, and made it their most ambitious project of 1955. When the original fifty-six page outline by Samuel James Larsen, a twenty-eight year-old victim of cerebral palsy, reached Dore Schary, then head of production, Schary expressed hopes of making *The Prodigal* one of the "really significant Biblical spectacles of all time." Joe Breen, Jr. then collaborated with Larsen on the final treatment and Maurice Zimm fashioned it into a screenplay.*

With Edmund Purdom

In amplifying the twenty-two verses from Luke into a scenario two hours long, the writers portrayed the prodigal as Micah, the model son of a Hebrew patriarch named Eli. As the film begins he has honored his father by becoming engaged to Ruth, a gentle girl of his own faith. While visiting Damascus, however, the youth enters the tent of Samarra, the high priestess of Astarte, goddess of the flesh, and he is dazzled by her beauty. To his father's bitter dismay, he demands his share of the family fortune, leaves his fiancee on the eve of their marriage, and goes off to the city in pursuit of the pagan woman, whose duties include presiding over human sacrificial rites.

Amidst the fleshpots of Damascus, Micah's uncontrollable infatuation for the priestess plunges him into a variety of mishaps. He is victimized by Nahreeb, the

---

*Although its writers claimed that their version was a fresh treatment, the 1955 *Prodigal* bears a striking resemblance in form and in incidental characters to a 1926 silent film based on the same Biblical parable. Titled *The Wanderer*, it starred William Collier, Jr. and Greta Nissen (as the pagan temptress), under the direction of Raoul Walsh.

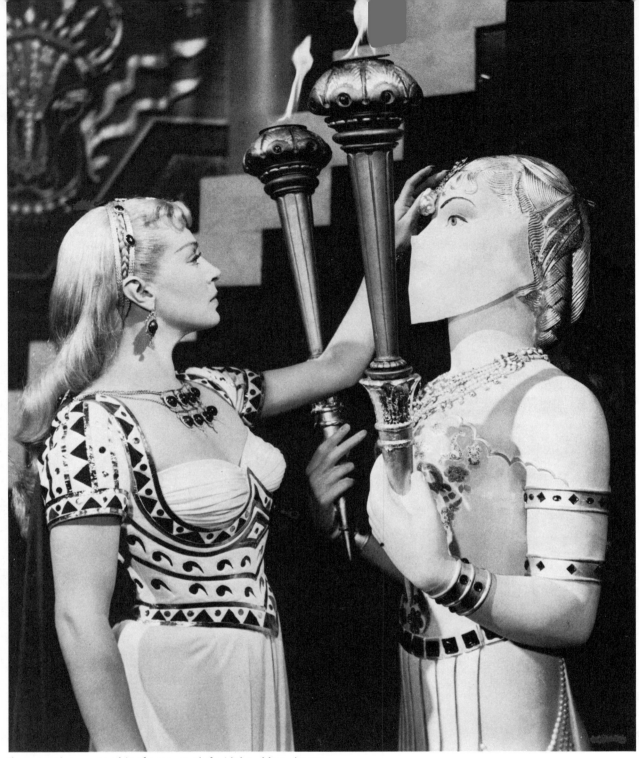

Samarra places a pearl in the crown of the idol-goddess Astarte

sinister high priest of Baal, who conspires to destroy him for his irreverent interest in Samarra; by Bosra, an unscrupulous moneylender; and even by Samarra herself, who withholds her love until he produces a certain valuable pearl as a gift for her goddess.

After squandering all his money on the woman, Micah winds up penniless and is sold into slavery to pay his debts. In prison, he is offered his freedom if he will publicly renounce his faith but he refuses and is thrown to the vultures. Finally, Micah escapes and with the famine-ridden people of Damascus, he leads a successful revolt against the dynasty of Baal and its idol-worshippers. The film here has an actionful climax as an

enraged mob stones Samarra, who then topples into the sacrificial fires that had previously claimed so many of her victims.

Repentant, the prodigal son then makes his way homeward and the final scene shows Eli, his father, welcoming him and extending his forgiveness by preparing a feast of the fatted calf.

The Prodigal was one of the biggest spectacles filmed in its entirety in Hollywood. Appropriately enough, when the movie was released in May 1955, critics found its flavor much more Hollywood than Biblical. Jesse Zunser of *Cue*, for example, felt the religious element of the well-loved parable had been all but smothered by what he described as "$5,000,000 worth of gigantic sets, garish costumes, eye-popping spectacle, vulgarity, sin, seduction and a generous display of flesh."

Charles Schnee, who scripted *The Bad and the Beautiful,* made his bow here as a producer and, in appraising the film, *Variety* felt that MGM had "filled the picture so full of scene and spectacle that Richard Thorpe's direction is hard put to give it any semblance of movement or to get life and warmth into the characters and incidents." As the saying goes, the bigger they are, the harder they fall. *The Prodigal* was roundly panned by the critics.

Today, this big Biblical potboiler, which *Newsweek* once likened to a "combination of the old Ziegfeld Follies and a traveling carnival," is something of a high-camp television perennial and, in recent years, even Miss Turner has had some amusing comments to make about it. ("It should have played Disneyland," she told one interviewer.)

For some, there are rewards, however. As the high priestess, Miss Turner wears as few strategically distributed beads as the 1955 Production Code would permit, and on frequent occasions the camera follows her as she saunters majestically among her subjects or up and down lavish staircases in a manner very suggestive of a Ziegfeld Girl on parade.

Said W. Ward Marsh in the *Cleveland Plain Dealer*: "Lana Turner, glorifying the flesh, also exhibits plenty of her own for glorification. I have never seen her walk better in my life." And Sidney Skolsky, in his syndicated

*With Louis
Calhern and
Edmund Purdom*

*With
George Robotham*

column, wrote: "That long walk Lana takes through the Temple of Love in *The Prodigal* is the best reason for seeing the picture. Pure poetry in motion. . . ."

Herschel McCoy, whose wardrobe credits included *Joan of Arc*, *Quo Vadis* and *Julius Caesar*, was the costumer on the picture. Authentically copied from excavations of the period (70 B.C.)—with a number of his own Hollywood elaborations—McCoy's costumes for Lana were among the most eye-popping ever worn by a major star at the time and although they look comparatively modest in these X-rated days, they were very provocative by 1955 standards. One number in particular, accurately described by a reviewer as "an astonishment of beads and jeweled G-strings," created such a ruckus when featured in the ad campaign that several straight-laced theatre owners ordered special retouching on their billboard art in an effort to make the costume seem less sensational.

As part of the film's publicity campaign, Eric Carpenter, the still photographer assigned to the picture, shot some of the most gorgeous pin-up art ever devised for motion picture exploitation purposes. His publicity shots have since become popular collectors' items among Lana Turner fans; and while MGM's big, glamourized version of the Prodigal Son is hardly a Sunday school lesson, for "cheesecake" connoisseurs, it indelibly remains the best showcase ever provided for the famous Turner figure. ★

With Edmund Purdom

In the spectacular finish to THE PRODIGAL, *high priestess Samarra plunges to her death in a pool of fire*

One of the breathtaking pin-up photos of Lana as Samarra, Goddess of Love

CAST

JOHN WAYNE, *Karl Ehrlich;* LANA TURNER, *Elsa Keller;* DAVID FARRAR, *Commander Napier;* LYLE BETTGER, *Kirchner;* TAB HUNTER, *Cadet Wesser;* JAMES ARNESS, *Schlieter;* RICHARD DAVALOS, *Cadet Walter Stemme;* JOHN QUALEN, *Chief Schmitt;* PAUL FIX, *Max Heinz;* LOWELL GILMORE, *Capt. Evans;* LUIS VAN ROOTEN, *Matz;* ALAN HALE, JR., *Wentz;* WILTON GRAFF, *Hepke;* PETER WHITNEY, *Bachman;* CLAUDE AKINS, *Winkler;* JOHN DOUCETTE, *Bo'sun;* ALAN LEE, *Brounck;* GLORIA DEA, *Spanish Girl.* (Note: Singer BONNIE LOU WILLIAMS supplied the singing voice for Miss Turner.)

CREDITS

Producer and Director, JOHN FARROW; Screenplay, JAMES WARNER BELLAH and JOHN TWIST; From the Novel by ANDREW GEER; Photography (CinemaScope and WarnerColor), WILLIAM CLOTHIER; Editor, WILLIAM ZIEGLER; Sound, FRANCIS J. SCHEID; Art Direction, FRANZ BACHELIN; Set Decoration, WILLIAM WALLACE; Wardrobe, MOSS MABRY; Makeup, GORDON BAU; Music, ROY WEBB; Orchestrations, MAURICE DEPACKH and LEONID RAAB; Assistant Directors, EMMETT EMERSON and RUSSELL LLEWELLYN; Running time, 117 minutes.

NOTES ABOUT THE FILM

Under the Louis B. Mayer regime, it was a rare occasion indeed when the studio that boasted "more stars than there are in the heavens" permitted the loan-out of one of their stellar contractees to a rival studio.

Lana Turner's first such arrangement occurred in the summer of 1954 when she had been part of the Metro fold for sixteen years, working there exclusively. Dore Schary had by then replaced Mayer as head of production on the Culver City lot and the loan-out, ironically, returned Lana to Warner Brothers, the studio where she first attracted attention as the Sweater Girl. By another small coincidence, Mervyn LeRoy, the man responsible for her initial break in films, was working there at the very same time directing *Mister Roberts* on an adjoining sound stage.

The film that lured the actress back to her former studio was *The Sea Chase,* a John Wayne vehicle with a World War II background. Her role: a mink-coated lady with an unseemly past—cool on the outside but inwardly smoldering—who finds regeneration in love. Warners offered MGM more than $300,000 for Lana's services and the very attractive deal included a location trip to Hawaii where almost all of the picture's exterior scenes were filmed.

The screenplay derived from a popular Andrew Geer novel with a strong, insistently masculine tone. However, once negotiations between MGM and Warners had been settled and Lana firmly signed for the picture, the story underwent heavy rewriting in an effort to strengthen the feminine role. The movie's added emphasis on the romantic element may not have pleased the admirers of Geer's action-packed best-seller but it did add immeasurably to the picture's ticket-selling potential. In fact, Wayne and Turner proved to be such a popular box-office team that at the end of the year *The Sea Chase* made a surprising appearance on *Variety*'s list of the ten top-grossing pictures of 1955, in the company of such heavily promoted blockbusters as *Oklahoma!, Mister Roberts* and *Battle Cry.*

The film's plot, as the title indicates, utilized one of the staunchest standbys of the motion picture medium —the chase. Wayne played Karl Ehrlich, an anti-Nazi, German sea captain. He despises the new regime but as a loyal citizen of the Fatherland he feels he must save his ship from destruction. At the outbreak of World War II, he slips the steamer—a rusty old 5,000-ton freighter named the *Ergenstrasse*—out of Sydney harbor just before news reaches Australia that the Nazi armies have moved into Poland. But a British man-of-war, the H.M.S. *Rockhampton*, takes off in hot pursuit. From that point on it takes all of Ehrlich's skill to keep his ship from falling into the hands of the British. Adding to his problems are both the *Ergenstrasse*'s shortage of fuel and supplies and the presence of Elsa Keller, a German spy and international adventuress, whom he'd been forced to take along by official orders. Once Ehrlich's mistress, Elsa is now engaged to Jeffrey Napier of His Majesty's Navy, who just happens to be in command of the pursuing *Rockhampton.*

Midway into the film as the *Ergenstrasse* is being refuelled at an island outpost, Kirchner, its ruthless first mate, callously murders a group of shipwrecked fishermen, thereby reflecting dishonor on Ehrlich and his crew. Ehrlich is outraged at Kirchner's action but his

With John Wayne

As Elsa Keller

With Lyle Bettger

determination to remain loyal to his country is in no way weakened. Eventually, the ship arrives at Valparaiso where its captain receives a hero's welcome from the German colony. But Napier, still in pursuit, learns of the massacred fishermen and resolves more than ever to capture the ship.

When the *Ergenstrasse* once more sets sail for home, Elsa, now in love with Ehrlich, is still aboard. Kirchner, meanwhile, has been forced to write a full account of the island killings in the ship's log. The *Ergenstrasse* finally meets her nemesis when the *Rockhampton* intercepts her. Struck by British shells, Ehrlich insists on remaining aboard his sinking freighter. Elsa decides her own fate and remains with him. But on the one remaining lifeboat that gets away with a few survivors, she has managed to stow the logbook which reveals in Kirchner's own handwriting Ehrlich's innocence in the island atrocities.

Although it seemed virtually impossible for the star-crossed lovers of *The Sea Chase* to escape their watery fate, Warners tacked onto the film's ending some optimistic words from Captain Napier (David Farrar, who had been narrating throughout). Added apparently for romantics who deplore unhappy endings, the film concludes with Napier commenting: "We searched for survivors but all that we found was a riddle of the sea . . . Had the sea taken them or had they reached the nearby shore where the fiords could hide a secret? . . . Who can say? . . . There are only two people who can answer that,

With Trudie Wyler

With John Wayne

wherever they are . . . but knowing Karl Ehrlich as I did, I have my own opinion . . ."

In addition to its unorthodox ending, *The Sea Chase* offered a storm at sea, a shark attack, a suicide and a near mutiny. John Farrow, a practiced hand with this sort of material, directed and as an adventure film, *The Sea Chase* is good entertainment. For some critics, the presence of its stars introduced a note of unreality in an otherwise fairly valid portrait of one man's allegiance to his country. One reviewer called it "the oddest casting of the year. John Wayne, that all-American hunk of man, is a German sea captain and Lana Turner, that all-American hunk of woman, is a German secret agent! Of course," she continued, "once you accept this, you settle back, your tongue anchored firmly in your cheek, to enjoy a suspenseful drama which doesn't neglect a fire-meets-fire romance between John and Lana. Neither one bothers with a German accent. Both stars are content to be themselves and that's just dandy with moviegoers."

In the *Saturday Review*, Lee Rogow noted that Miss Turner boarded the *Ergenstrasse* "with a cruise wardrobe that will have all the lady spies in town asking their governments for more charge accounts." Her one bag for the long and arduous trip included all the necessary *femme fatale* accouterments: mink; diamonds; and a form-fitting white gown. And to make the picture complete, designer Moss Mabry also included a few sweaters —which seemed to be obligatory garb for Lana at Warners.★

A TWENTIETH CENTURY·FOX PRODUCTION
1955

CAST

LANA TURNER, *Edwina Esketh;* RICHARD BURTON, *Dr. Safti;* FRED MacMURRAY, *Tom Ransome;* JOAN CAULFIELD, *Fern Simon;* MICHAEL RENNIE, *Lord Esketh;* EUGENIE LEONTOVICH, *Maharani;* GLADYS HURLBUT, *Mrs. Simon;* MADGE KENNEDY, *Mrs. Smiley;* PAUL H. FREES, *Sundar;* CARLO RIZZO, *Mr. Adoani;* BEATRICE KRAFT, *Oriental Dancer;* KING CALDER, *Mr. Smiley;* ARGENTINA BRUNETTI, *Mrs. Adoani;* JOHN BANNER, *Ranchid;* IVIS GOULDING, *Louise;* RAM SINGH, *Major Domo;* LOU KRUGMAN, *Courier;* RAMA BAI, *Lachmaania;* TRUDE WYLER, *Guest;* NAJI GABBAY, *Wagonlit Porter;* JUGAT BHATIA, *Head Hunter;* PHYLLIS JOHANNES, *Nurse Gupta;* GEORGE BRAND, *Mr. Simon;* ELIZABETH PRUDHOMME, *Nurse Patel;* RAM CHANDRA, *Satter.*

CREDITS

Director, JEAN NEGULESCO; Producer, FRANK ROSS; Screenplay MERLE MILLER; Based on the Novel *The Rains Came* by LOUIS BROMFIELD; Photography (CinemaScope and DeLuxe Color), MILTON KRASNER; Editor, DOROTHY SPENCER; Sound, ALFRED BRUZLIN and HARRY M. LEONARD; Art Direction, LYLE R. WHEELER and ADDISON HEHR; Set Decorations, WALTER M. SCOTT and PAUL S. FOX; Costumes, TRAVILLA; Miss Turner's Gowns, HELEN ROSE; Makeup, BEN NYE; Hair Stylist, HELEN TURPIN; Assistant Director, ELI DUNN; Special Effects, RAY KELLOGG; Music, HUGO FRIEDHOFER; Conducted by LIONEL NEWMAN; Orchestrator, MAURICE DePACKH; Choreography, STEPHEN PAPICH; Running time, 104 minutes.

NOTES ABOUT THE FILM

The Rains Came was a popular Louis Bromfield novel about the effect that a devastating earthquake has on the emotions of an assorted group of saints and sinners. In 1939, when 20th Century-Fox and director Clarence Brown were casting their screen version, an eighteen-year-old Lana Turner had been a strong contender for the role of one of Bromfield's "saints," Fern Simon, the young, brimming-with-idealism daughter of a missionary. When a loan-out arrangement fell through between Fox and Metro, Lana's home studio, Brown used a new Fox contractee, Brenda Joyce, in the role adding her to a cast that already included Tyrone Power, Myrna Loy and George Brent.

Sixteen years later, the same studio spent money like water on a lavish, CinemaScope and DeLuxe color remake of the film, titled *The Rains of Ranchipur.* Its producer was Frank Ross, whose production of *The Robe* pioneered the CinemaScope era. Coincidentally, the second film adaptation had Miss Turner in the casting

With Richard Burton

With Fred MacMurray

With Michael Rennie

With Fred MacMurray, Joan Caulfield and Michael Rennie

race once more, but this time for the major role of Bromfield's most prominent "sinner," Lady Edwina Esketh, the rich, spoiled woman whose regeneration is effected by true love. In an interview he gave at the time, director Jean Negulesco stated that there were only three women in Hollywood in 1955 capable of playing Lady Esketh—Lana Turner, Ava Gardner and Rita Hayworth. When the role eventually went to Miss Turner, *The Rains of Ranchipur* became her second loan-out assignment of the year and her first appearance in a Fox film.

Miss Turner was cast opposite Richard Burton, then several years away from *Cleopatra*, Elizabeth Taylor and superstardom, as well as Fred MacMurray and Michael Rennie, all actors she had not performed with at Metro. The story was set in India and although that country was reluctant to admit junketeering occidental film-makers, producer Ross did receive the consent and cooperation of the Pakistan Government. The actors didn't go there but a location company did, for one month of background shooting prior to the studio-filmed scenes which began in August 1955. For Miss Turner, the Bromfield heroine was changed from a Britisher to an American married to a titled Englishman. The woman, Lady Edwina Esketh, is beautiful, wealthy, and blatantly man-hunting, the sort that finds it expedient to take her husband along on her wanderings. When the married couple arrive in Ranchipur as guests of the Maharani, they meet Dr. Safti, a young Hindu who is the ruler's protege and in whom the Maharani has recognized the greatness that will be all-important to her country. Edwina, however, decides then and there that she must add this young man to her "collection."

The Maharani does, of course, try to prevent the doctor from falling in love with Edwina, whose reputation as an amoral woman has preceded her to India. But as he becomes harder to get, Edwina becomes more and more determined to have him and, out of her yearning, there is born to her the first stirrings of genuine emotion. Soon, Dr. Safti admits his love for her and tells the woman he is prepared to go away with her.

But the seasonal rain begins. An earthquake destroys the bridge, the dam disintegrates and the onrushing waters threaten disaster to all. Dr. Safti leaves Edwina's side to attend the injured and dying and in doing so realizes that his place is in India with his own people. Resignedly, the woman accepts his decision, rejoins her husband and leaves the country, somewhat ennobled by the experience.

Interwoven with all this was a secondary love story concerning a hard-drinking, disillusioned American engineer named Tom Ransome, who wins back his self-respect as well as the love of Fern Simon, an uninhibited local girl drawn to him in her desperation to make something of her life. The latter role, a mixture of *Claudia* and Debbie Reynolds, was played by Joan Caulfield (Mrs. Frank Ross).

Brought in on a $4,000,000 budget, *The Rains of Ranchipur* was Fox's Christmas 1955 attraction and like its '39 predecessor, drew mixed reviews. While many critics complained of a "superficial treatment," the New York *Daily News* was awarding the film its highest rating (four stars) and *Redbook* magazine was selecting it as their "Picture of the Month." Today, it is generally snubbed by film buffs who venerate the earlier screen version, but as Steven H. Scheuer critiqued: ". . . the pace is smooth, the spectacle lavish and the stars attractive."

The critic for *The Commonweal* said *Ranchipur* "has

With Richard Burton

been produced on such an elaborate and definitive scale that I doubt if it will ever be made again." Ray Kellogg was the special effects director on this early "disaster" film and his work on the picture won him an Oscar nomination.

Miss Turner was by now something of a specialist at battling the elements. She had weathered an equally devastating earthquake just eight years earlier in *Green Dolphin Street*, and just prior to filming *Ranchipur*, she had some stormy moments on the high seas in *The Sea Chase*. Unlike the ill-fated heroine of Bromfield's novel and Myrna Loy of the initial film version, Lana's Lady Esketh is allowed to survive at the finish of *Ranchipur* looking, it should be added, beautifully intact. Fox's Milton Krasner photographed the star here for the first and only time, and his soft DeLuxe color lensing was extremely flattering. Some of Miss Turner's staunchest admirers think she has never been better photographed during the '50s, even by the craftsmen at MGM.

Lady Esketh, whose character is established in the film's first five minutes when her husband calls her "greedy," "selfish," "decadent," and "corrupt" all in one breath, is probably the most determined, straightforward *femme fatale* the star has ever essayed on the screen ("I just *look* at what I want," she tells the Hindu doctor), and Merle Miller's screenplay is, more than anything else, a documentation of her viciousness in the early segments and her regeneration in the end. The film's final scene—a juicy, climactic confrontation between Lady Esketh and the Maharani—gave Lana the oppor-

With Richard Burton, Michael Rennie and Eugenie Leontovich

tunity to spout that attention-getting line: "I don't give a damn!" Although the line didn't have nearly the same shocking impact on moviegoers that it did when Rhett Butler used it to tell off Scarlett O'Hara sixteen years earlier, it was still something of an eyebrow-raiser for audiences in 1955. Eugenie Leontovich, an actress with a strong bravura style, very effectively played the Maharani and greatly suggested Maria Ouspenskaya, the Maharani of the '39 version.★

DIANE

A METRO·GOLDWYN·MAYER PICTURE
1956

CAST

LANA TURNER, *Diane;* PEDRO ARMENDARIZ, *King Francis I;* ROGER MOORE, *Prince Henri;* MARISA PAVAN, *Catherine de Medici;* SIR CEDRIC HARDWICKE, *Ruggieri;* TORIN THATCHER, *Count de Breze;* TAINA ELG, *Alys;* JOHN LUPTON, *Regnault;* HENRY DANIELL, *Gondi;* RONALD GREEN, *The Dauphin;* SEAN McCLORY, *Count Montgomery;* GEOFFREY TOONE, *Duke of Savoy;* MICHAEL ANSARA, *Count Ridolfi;* PAUL CAVANAGH, *Lord Bonnivet;* MELVILLE COOPER, *1st Court Physician;* IAN WOLFE, *Lord Tremouille;* BASIL RUYSDAEL, *Chamberlain;* CHRISTOPHER DARK, *Gian-Carlo;* MARC CAVELL, *Piero;* GENE REYNOLDS, *Montecuculli;* JOHN O'MALLEY, *Marechal de Chabannes;* PETER GRAY, *Sardini;* MICKY MAGA, *Charles;* RONALD ANTON, *Francis;* PERCY HELTON, *Court Jester;* JAMES DRURY, *Lieutenant;* BOB DIX, *Young Officer;* STUART WHITMAN, *Henri's Squire;* ALICIA IBANEZ, ANN BRENDON, FAY MORLEY, BARBARA DARROW, ANN STAUNTON, BUNNY COOPER *(Ladies-in-Waiting).*

CREDITS

Director, DAVID MILLER; Producer, EDWIN H. KNOPF; Screenplay, CHRISTOPHER ISHERWOOD; Based on the Story by JOHN ERSKINE; Photography (CinemaScope and EastmanColor), ROBERT PLANCK; Editor, JOHN McSWEENEY, JR.; Sound, DR. WESLEY C. MILLER; Art Direction, CEDRIC GIBBONS and HANS PETERS; Set Decorations, EDWIN B. WILLIS and HENRY GRACE; Costumes, WALTER PLUNKETT; Makeup, WILLIAM TUTTLE; Hair Stylist, SYDNEY GUILAROFF; Music, MIKLOS ROZSA; Assistant Director, RIDGEWAY CALLOW; Special Effects, A. ARNOLD GILLESPIE and WARREN NEWCOMBE; Running time, 110 minutes.

NOTES ABOUT THE FILM

Diane de Poitiers was the French courtesan who became the mistress of King Henri II of France and virtually supplanted his wife, Catherine de Medici, as the power behind the throne. Writers have alternately described her as "the most cultivated woman of the French Renaissance" and as "a sixteenth-century silken tramp."

In the MGM film loosely based on her life, we first see Diane as she appears at the court of Francis I to plead for the life of her husband, Count de Breze, who has been falsely accused of plotting against the King. She succeeds in having him spared but at the same time alienates the affection of her husband who suspects she

A publicity photo showing Lana surrounded by the gowns and the original costume sketches used for DIANE

With Roger Moore and Marisa Pavan

With Torin Thatcher

With Marisa Pavan

obtained his release by infidelity. When the King sends for her, the Count feels his suspicions are confirmed. However, the real reason Diane has been summoned is to teach the King's son, Prince Henri, the graces of court life in preparation for his marriage to Catherine de Medici. Impressed by her beauty, charm and political sageness, as well as her ability to cope with his son, the King keeps her at court. In the course of the tutorship, Diane and Henri fall in love and even after his marriage to Catherine, Diane stays on at the palace as the mistress of the young Prince.

When the King is killed in battle, Henri ascends the throne and Catherine soon comes to hate the woman who is her husband's real love and the power behind him as well. But Henri's rule is short-lived. Due to de Medici treachery, he is murdered in a jousting tournament. Catherine, in mourning, orders the elimination of

the Italian plotters and sees in Henri's death the opportunity to destroy her rival. She plans the woman's execution but relents, and after a brief scene of reconciliation between the two women, the film ends with Catherine instead banishing Diane to her country home.

This battle of wits between wife and mistress was exquisitely produced, recreating the glitter of throne rooms and the splendor of court costumes with an air of authenticity. Although not a precise account of the Countess's life and loves, the film was of distinguished literary heritage, having been based upon a story by John Erskine, with its screenplay by Christopher Isherwood. (A foreword conveniently acquitted Mr. Isherwood of historical inaccuracies; apart from some de Medici whitewashing, his most noteworthy liberty was the fact that Henri II, who was only fourteen when he was married to Catherine, actually was twenty years younger than his mistress, Diane, and she was sixty when he met his untimely death.)

Diane was directed by David Miller and although he injected plenty of action into the film (a stag hunt, an exciting encounter with a wild boar, and a thrilling climactic jousting sequence), Arthur Weiler of *The New York Times* found the end result "more stately than exciting, more pageant than play." In direct contrast, the *Mirror*'s Frank Quinn called *Diane* "a brilliant Renaissance film" while the critic for *The Commonweal* offered this assessment: "Well-primed with political intrigue, and surprisingly frank in portraying the king-mistress relationship, *Diane* is no more inaccurate than most historical films; and it is far more entertaining." In other evaluations, there was special mention for the supporting performance of Marisa Pavan, who in *Diane* had possibly the best role of her film career as Henri's menacing yet pitiable wife, Catherine de Medici; and for Miklos Rozsa's musical score, which is one of his most eloquently beautiful.

Underneath the pomp and pageantry, *Diane* is basically a variation on the familiar vagabond-of-love pattern established by former Turner romantic heroines. The sixteenth-century milieu provided a change of scenery, however, and despite the fact that Diane is the third corner of the triangle, Isherwood's screenplay portrays her as a somewhat sympathetic figure. As usual, MGM spared nothing in the way of haute couture to showcase their star and her soft blondness contrasted brilliantly with the dramatic black costumes she wore through most of the film (since Diane is always in mourning for someone).

Diane was a property that MGM had originally purchased in the '30s for Greta Garbo. When the story finally reached the screen two decades later, costume dramas were fast losing favor at the box office. MGM continued to produce them nonetheless (*Quentin Durward, The King's Thief* and *Moonfleet* were some of the others released with *Diane* in the mid-'50s) but moviegoers were turning to more relevant themes. In the case of *Diane*, MGM used a modernized, extremely sexy ad campaign to bolster its appeal ("Lana Turner dares the devil in *Diane*" was the film's slogan), but it was still rough going at the box office.

Released in January 1956, *Diane* proved to be a significant film in Miss Turner's career. One month later,

while budget-conscious MGM was in the midst of disbanding its expensive star system, Miss Turner terminated her eighteen-year association with the studio. While not specifically mentioning *Diane*, in an interview she gave at the time she complained of the "costume stinkers" MGM had been saddling her with. Interestingly enough, *Diane* was not only her final film as an MGM contractee,* but it has also proven to be her last appearance to date in a costume picture.

Although frankly sentimental about the studio that had been her home since 1938, her departure from Metro was a judicious move. Her next film—and her first as a free-lance actress—could hardly be termed a "costume stinker." It would, in fact, mark another turning point in her career and ultimately bring her an Oscar nomination. ★

The Rains of Ranchipur, which was filmed at Fox after *Diane* but released before it, was the last film Lana made under her MGM contract. *Diane*, however, was the last picture she actually filmed at her home studio.

With Roger Moore

PEYTON PLACE

A JERRY WALD PRODUCTION FOR TWENTIETH CENTURY·FOX RELEASE
1957

CAST

LANA TURNER, *Constance MacKenzie;* HOPE LANGE, *Selena Cross;* LEE PHILIPS, *Michael Rossi;* LLOYD NOLAN, *Dr. Swain;* DIANE VARSI, *Allison;* ARTHUR KENNEDY, *Lucas Cross;* RUSS TAMBLYN, *Norman Page;* TERRY MOORE, *Betty Anderson;* BARRY COE, *Rodney Harrington;* DAVID NELSON, *Ted Carter;* BETTY FIELD, *Nellie Cross;* MILDRED DUNNOCK, *Mrs. Thornton;* LEON AMES, *Harrington;* LORNE GREENE, *Prosecutor;* ROBERT H. HARRIS, *Seth Bushwell;* TAMI CONNER, *Margie;* STAATS COTSWORTH, *Charles Partridge;* PEG HILLIAS, *Marion Partridge;* ERIN O'BRIEN-MOORE, *Mrs. Page;* SCOTTY MORROW, *Joey Cross;* BILL LUNDMARK, *Paul Cross;* ALAN REED, JR., *Matt;* KIP KING, *Pee Wee;* STEFFI SIDNEY, *Kathy;* TOM GREENWAY, *Judge;* MICHAEL LALLY, *Bailiff.*

CREDITS

Director, MARK ROBSON; Producer, JERRY WALD; Screenplay, JOHN MICHAEL HAYES; From the Novel by GRACE METALIOUS; Photography (CinemaScope and DeLuxe Color), WILLIAM MELLOR; Editor, DAVID BRETHERTON; Sound, E. CLAYTON WARD and FRANK MORAN; Art Direction, LYLE R. WHEELER and JACK MARTIN SMITH; Set Decoration, WALTER M. SCOTT and BERTRAM GRANGER; Executive Wardrobe Designer, CHARLES LeMAIRE; Costumes, ADELE PALMER; Makeup, BEN NYE; Hair Styles, HELEN TURPIN; Assistant Director, HAL HERMAN; Music, FRANZ WAXMAN; Orchestrations, EDWARD B. POWELL; Special Effects, L. B. ABBOTT; Running time, 157 minutes.

NOTES ABOUT THE FILM

On April 15, 1957, Louella Parsons' "exclusive" of the day informed movie fans that Hollywood's erstwhile Sweater Girl was about to undertake her first role as the mother of a teen-ager.

Turner fans did not take the news lightly, of course. First and foremost, it seemed to indicate the end of Lana's gilt-edged glamour days and that henceforth she would be destined exclusively for maternal roles. None of the movies' celebrated World War II Love Goddesses had yet succumbed to playing the mother of a teen-ager and, at thirty-six, Lana was still younger than all of the others. But it took little persuasion on the part of producer Jerry Wald to convince her to sign for the part. The picture was one of the year's most important—the screen version of the sensational best-seller *Peyton Place* —and the role of Constance MacKenzie was easily the best Lana had been offered in years. When *Peyton Place* was eventually released—during the Christmas, 1957 movie season—her performance as Constance was so well received by press and public alike that the character did

in fact create a new and popular Turner image: the elegant, emotionally wounded mother figure struggling for happiness within a troubled milieu. Furthermore, the role became the forerunner of several screen heroines she would portray in the future.

Louella Parsons Writes:

Luscious Lana Signs to Play Mother Role!

BY LOUELLA O. PARSONS

HOLLYWOOD, Apr. 15—By the time this is in print, Lana Turner will have put her name on a contract to play Connie in "Peyton Place" for Jerry Wald. In fact, it may be signed now.

I know that Buddy Adler, Jerry and director Mark Robson have had several meetings with Lana, who is intrigued with the idea of playing the mother of a girl of 18. Remember, it was Jerry who brought Joan Crawford back in "Mildred Pierce," which won her an Academy Award as the mother of a daughter played by Ann Blyth.

This would be the first time that Lana has stepped out of glamor roles, but this is going to be such a big picture she'd be foolish not to accept it pronto.

LANA TURNER
Switches from glamor.

Louella Parsons' "exclusive" of the day for April 15, 1957

Jerry Wald was the same producer who a dozen years earlier had lured Joan Crawford into playing *Mildred Pierce*, a mother role that won Miss Crawford an Oscar and rejuvenated her career as well. If *Peyton Place* was not the great star vehicle that *Mildred* was, it nonetheless provided Lana Turner with a character of some substance for a change and under Mark Robson's direction she gave it enough to garner an Oscar nomination. Although she lost in the final Oscar race (to Joanne Woodward for *The Three Faces of Eve*), the recognition from her peers, coming as it did on the heels of her departure from Metro, had particular significance on both a personal and professional level.

As a novel, *Peyton Place* had been a first effort on the part of Grace Metalious, a New Hampshire housewife, and while it may not have been the finest example of distinguished writing its phenomenal popular success is still a minor legend in the book industry. According to a statistic taken at the time, one out of every thirty-seven Americans bought a copy of *Peyton Place*. Because of the censorship problems regarding the more sensational aspects of Mrs. Metalious' novel, the book quite obviously couldn't be filmed as written. Instead, in the hands of producer Wald and screenwriter John Michael Hayes, her story was turned into an extremely tasteful portrait of an American town, with an intelligent, sensitive concern for its characters. Its director, Mark Robson, did a superior job of evoking the feeling of small town life in the film and there are a host of first-rate performances. At award time, *Peyton Place* drew nine Oscar nominations. Included besides that of Miss Turner for Best Actress, were nominations for Best Picture, director Robson, screenwriter Hayes and pho-

tographer William Mellor. And in what was then a record for supporting performances within the same film, four players from *Peyton Place* (Hope Lange, Diane Varsi, Russ Tamblyn and Arthur Kennedy) were nominated in that category. (Not until 1974's *The Godfather Part II* did another film draw as many supporting player nominations.)

Among the outstanding attributes of *Peyton Place* was its great pictorial beauty. The exterior scenes of the film were photographed in Camden, Maine and magnificently captured the special charm of a small New England town. The story takes place in the late '30s and begins as the new school principal, Michael Rossi, arrives in town to assume his duties. In quick succession, many of the town's local inhabitants are introduced.

Constance MacKenzie is an attractive widow who owns a dress shop, runs it efficiently and persists in keeping her teen-aged daughter, Allison, insulated from the world.

Allison's best friend is Selena Cross, who lives in a shack on the wrong side of town with her worn-out

With Diane Varsi

With Edwin Jerome, Lloyd Nolan and Lee Philips

With Diane Varsi

With Hope Lange

mother, Nellie (who is Constance's housekeeper), and her brutal stepfather, Lucas.

There is also Norman Page, a sensitive, insecure, mother-dominated adolescent; Rodney Harrington, the arrogant son of the town's biggest tycoon; Betty Anderson, the school flirt; Ted Carter, the boy friend of Selena Cross; and Doc Swain, a well-liked medic. These are the most prominent characters among a large assortment of townspeople whose lives form a pattern of love, hate and destruction.

The first of the narrative's dramatic occasions is set one evening after a graduation dance when Ted proposes to Selena and she promises to wait for him to become a successful lawyer. That night when she returns to her ramshackle home, Selena finds her stepfather, Lucas, alone, drunk, and abusive. He attacks her, as a result of which she becomes pregnant. Doc Swain immediately confronts Lucas with his crime, obtains a written confession from him and orders the man to leave Peyton Place for good. Later, the doctor is forced to perform an abortion on Selena which he lists officially as an appendectomy.

The plot then shifts to the emotional conflict between school principal Rossi and Constance. He has been making a romantic bid for her but she bitterly rejects his love in her continued retreat from any emotional commitment. Constance's guilty secret, the fact that has chilled her own life and threatens to freeze that of her only child, is that she has never married.

When Constance is told by the town gossip that Allison has been swimming in the nude with Norman Page, she confronts her daughter with the story. An angry scene follows, and the truth about Allison's illegitimacy is revealed. By this time the girl has grown so hostile towards her mother that she decides to leave home to live in New York.

A chaotic series of events follows: Nellie Cross commits suicide; Rodney Harrington joins the army when war breaks out and is among the first to be killed; Constance finally admits her love for Michael Rossi as he is about to leave town; Norman Page is brought out of the shell in which his narrow-minded mother has encased him. Lastly, Lucas Cross returns to town and when he attempts to attack Selena again, she kills him and hides the body in fear.

This latter event progresses into a court trial in which the case against Selena becomes so strong that Doc Swain is forced to expose Lucas's real nature by producing the confession note as evidence. Selena is then acquitted and the trial brings about a reconciliation between Constance and Allison, who has returned to town to stand by her friend.

Peyton Place was strong stuff in its time but due to the masterful screenplay of John Michael Hayes, the film offered wholly unobjectionable entertainment while retaining all of the strong dramatic qualities of the novel. So skillful was Hayes' launderization job that the usually strict Catholic Legion of Decency rated the film in its "A" (acceptable for all) category. In addition, the National Board of Review cited the film as "an example of how a fine motion picture can be made out of a cheap and dirty book." In the New York *Daily News*, Wanda Hale wrote: "Putting *Peyton Place* on the screen was a gigantic undertaking. And from it, 20th Century-Fox has made a picture that is better than the book. It is less shocking, although it is as candid as a French drama, as unreserved as Italian neo-realism. Nobody, not even the author, can complain of the few changes made and Grace Metalious couldn't ask for a better cast to bring her characters to life."

As Constance MacKenzie

Equally enthusiastic was Bosley Crowther who thought Lana's role was played "remarkably well." And Stanley Kauffman of the *Saturday Review* wrote: "Lana Turner, given a chance with a role of some depth, proves that she can be as persuasive as some of the Method-dedicated girls flocking into the movies these days."

Predictably, *Peyton Place* was a rousing financial success. It was in fact 1957's largest-grossing film. Its popularity started a trend for a whole succession of movies devoted to small American towns and the shady secrets of their inhabitants. But *Peyton Place* remains the best of this genre. The success of the film fostered a 1961 sequel titled *Return to Peyton Place* (in which Eleanor Parker essayed the role of Constance), a TV series which ran several seasons during the '60s (with Dorothy Malone), and even a daytime soap opera (with television actress Bettye Ackerman in the role). ★

215

THE LADY TAKES A FLYER

A UNIVERSAL·INTERNATIONAL PICTURE
1958

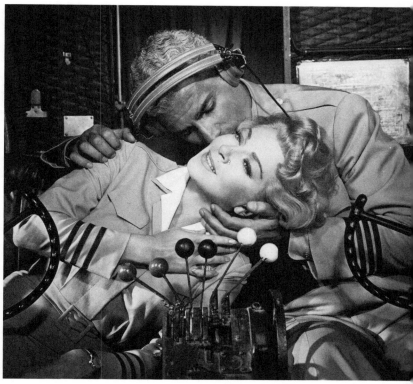

With Jeff Chandler

As Maggie Colby

CAST

LANA TURNER, *Maggie Colby;* JEFF CHANDLER, *Mike Dandridge;* RICHARD DENNING, *Al Reynolds;* ANDRA MARTIN, *Nikki Taylor;* CHUCK CONNORS, *Phil Donahue;* RETA SHAW, *Nurse Kennedy;* ALAN HALE, JR., *Frank Henshaw;* JERRY PARIS, *Willie Ridgley;* DEE J. THOMPSON, *Collie Minor;* NESTOR PAIVA, *Childreth;* JAMES DOHERTY, *Tower Officer.*

CREDITS

Director, JACK ARNOLD; Producer, WILLIAM ALLAND; Screenplay, DANNY ARNOLD; Story, EDMUND H. NORTH; Photography (CinemaScope and EastmanColor), IRVING GLASSBERG; Editor, SHERMAN TODD; Sound, LESLIE I. CAREY and CORSON JOWETT; Costumes, BILL THOMAS; Makeup, BUD WESTMORE; Art Direction, ALEXANDER GOLITZEN and RICHARD H. RIEDEL; Set Decoration, RUSSELL A. GAUSMAN and OLIVER EMERT; Music, HERMAN STEIN; Music Supervision, JOSEPH GERSHENSON; Assistant Director, DAVID SILVER; Technical Advisor, JACK FORD; Running time, 93 minutes.

With Jeff Chandler

NOTES ABOUT THE FILM

Free from her Metro contract, the first film deal Miss Turner accepted was at Universal* where she was given the right co-star but a less-than-ideal vehicle.

The leading man selected for her was the tall and virile Jeff Chandler, an actor whose characteristic ruggedness was a perfect foil for her pronounced femininity. There was interesting chemistry in this star combination and Universal should have utilized the pair to the fullest, possibly in a sparring-of-the-sexes drama in the tradition of the early Gable–Turner vehicles.

Instead, the script selected for them was a lightweight domestic comedy called *The Lady Takes a Flyer*. It had its share of engaging moments (a *New York Times* critic in a retrospective review found the film "surprisingly ingratiating"), but Turner and Chandler deserved much better. The screenplay was inspired by a real-life couple named Mary and Jack Ford, who were then known in flight circles as "the flying Fords." The Fords were the founders of the world's busiest airplane ferrying service and, in true Hollywood tradition, they bore not the slightest physical resemblances to their more illustrious film counterparts.

The story opens with ex-Air Force Colonel Mike Dandridge flying a crippled surplus aircraft to a delivery point in California where he finds his best friend, Al Reynolds, operating a flying school. Through Al, Mike meets Maggie Colby, a flying instructress, and Mike and Maggie "discover" each other when a ferrying trip to Japan throws them together. They marry, and when Al resigns to return to the Air Force, Mike takes over the company. Meanwhile, Maggie becomes pregnant.

Bored by his desk duties, Mike finds someone else to handle them and returns to the air as a pilot. After Maggie's child is born, she becomes a stay-at-home, much to the dismay of Mike, who finds responsibility and fatherhood an unbearable strain. In due time, he seeks companionship with Nikki Taylor, one of his lady pilots. This prompts Maggie, in a temper, to take a

---

*Although *The Lady Takes a Flyer* was filmed a few months prior to *Peyton Place*, the latter film was released to theatres first when 20th Century-Fox rushed out their picturization of the Grace Metalious best-seller as their Christmas '57 attraction.

ferrying assignment to England, leaving Mike to tend the baby. But Mike, determined to reach England before Maggie does, packs up the baby and takes her along. He succeeds in getting there first, and saves Maggie's life when, with the airstrip closed in by fog, he instructs her by radio to parachute from her disabled plane. Because of the danger that develops during her escapade, Mike comes to his senses, realizes just how much he loves his wife, and prepares to embrace domesticity.

A publicity photo showing Lana and Jeff Chandler with their real-life counterparts, Mary and Jack Ford

With Richard Denning

With two such attractive people as Turner and Chandler on hand, the scriptwriters were wise enough to inject this connubial conflict with some crackling good romantic moments. The film's most effective love scene: Chandler romancing Lana while perched on the rim of her bathtub.

Wanda Hale in the New York *Daily News* called *The Lady Takes a Flyer* a "pleasing, honest comedy" and said that Lana "moves and expresses herself just right as the woman torn between being a practical mother and a sweetheart to her husband."

The Lady Takes a Flyer had two working titles while in production: *Lion in the Sky* and *Wild and Wonderful*.★

ANOTHER TIME, ANOTHER PLACE

A LANTURN PRODUCTION FOR PARAMOUNT RELEASE
1958

CAST

LANA TURNER, *Sara Scott;* BARRY SULLIVAN, *Carter Reynolds;* GLYNIS JOHNS, *Kay Trevor;* SEAN CONNERY, *Mark Trevor;* TERRENCE LONGDON, *Alan Thompson;* SIDNEY JAMES, *Jake Klein;* MARTIN STEPHENS, *Brian Trevor;* DORIS HARE, *Mrs. Bunker;* JULIAN SOMERS, *Hotel Manager;* JOHN LeMESURIER, *Dr. Aldridge;* CAMERON HALL, *Alfy;* JANE WELSH, *Jonesy;* ROBIN BAILEY, *Capt. Barnes;* BILL FRASER, *R. E. Sergeant.*

CREDITS

Director, LEWIS ALLEN; Producer, JOSEPH KAUFMAN; Assistant Producer for Lanturn Productions, DEL ARMSTRONG; Screenplay, STANLEY MANN; Based on a Novel by LENORE COFFEE; Photography (VistaVision), JACK HILDYARD; Editor, GEOFFREY FOOT; Sound, GERRY TURNER and J. B. SMITH; Production Designer, TOM MORAHAN; Wardrobe, LAURA NIGHTINGALE; Makeup, STUART FREEBORN; Hairdressing, ANN BOX; Assistant Director, RENE DuPONT; Associate Producer, SMEDLEY ASTON; Music, DOUGLAS GAMLEY; Conducted by MUIR MATHIESON; Title Song by JAY LIVINGSTON and RAY EVANS; Running time, 98 minutes.

NOTES ABOUT THE FILM

This picture was filmed in England under the banner of Miss Turner's own production outfit, the appropriately named Lanturn Productions, in association with a British firm.

The screenplay was by Stanley Mann from a Lenore Coffee novel titled *Weep No More* in Britain, and published under the film title in America. It centered around the struggle of two women for possession of the memory of a dead man whom both loved, and producer Turner had great hopes that the story would make an effective "woman's picture."

Its heroine, Sara Scott, is a chic, mink-coated American newspaper woman stationed in England during the closing days of World War II. Although engaged to her publisher, Carter Reynolds, she is obsessively in love with

With Sean Connery

With Martin Stephens

With Barry Sullivan

Mark Trevor, a BBC commentator, whom she learns in time has a wife and child living on the coast of Cornwall.

After Mark's death in an airplane crash, Sara has a nervous breakdown and remains so obsessed with the memory of her dead lover that she decides to make a pilgrimage to the Cornish town where he lived. Falling ill there, she meets by chance Mark's widow, Kay, and accepts the hospitality of the woman, who knows nothing of Sara's association with her late husband. Spellbound by memory, Sara stays on at the house and soon becomes fast friends with Kay, who had suspected that her husband had been unfaithful to her while he was in London during the war but had no evidence to justify it.

Ridden with guilt, Sara ultimately reveals that she had been Mark's mistress but, by the film's end, she has managed to convince Kay that Mark's heart was always with his wife, his son and his home. Kay accepts this, and it brings her a tranquility she has not known since Mark's death. And Sara, realizing she cannot live in the past, goes back to New York with her understanding fiance, Carter Reynolds.

Paramount rushed *Another Time, Another Place* into release four months ahead of schedule to cash in on the notoriety surrounding Lana's real-life tragedy of 1958, which had been dominating the front pages for over a month. But the public was clearly more interested in the drama taking place off screen. The film's box-office returns were less than enthusiastic and its cool critical reception did not help matters either.

If nothing else, *Another Time, Another Place* did call some attention to the young Sean Connery who played the part of the ill-fated Mark Trevor. Connery, who had just scored a success in a BBC television production of *Requiem for a Heavyweight*, was one of three British actors screentested for the role and although he had appeared in a few films prior to this one, he was given "introducing" billing here.

Another Time, Another Place was shot in the tiny fishing village of Polperro, Cornwall, with interiors done at the Elstree Studios in London. Britain's crack cameraman, Jack Hildyard, whose work won him an Oscar for *The Bridge on the River Kwai*, was at his usual high-caliber best with some interesting subjects to train his lens on: the rugged and picturesque locations of Cornwall and, of course, the producer-star herself. ★

With Glynis Johns

With Sean Connery

IMITATION OF LIFE

A UNIVERSAL·INTERNATIONAL PICTURE

1959

CAST

LANA TURNER, *Lora Meredith*; JOHN GAVIN, *Steve Archer*; SANDRA DEE, *Susie (age 16)*; DAN O'HERLIHY, *David Edwards*; SUSAN KOHNER, *Sarah Jane (age 18)*; ROBERT ALDA, *Allen Loomis*; JUANITA MOORE, *Annie Johnson*; MAHALIA JACKSON, *Herself*; KARIN DICKER, *Sarah Jane (age 8)*; TERRY BURNHAM, *Susie (age 6)*; JOHN VIVYAN, *Young Man*; LEE GOODMAN, *Photographer*; ANN ROBINSON, *Show Girl*; TROY DONAHUE, *Frankie*; SANDRA GOULD, *Receptionist*; DAVID TOMACK, *Burly Man*; JOEL FLUELLEN, *Minister*; JACK WESTON, *Stage Manager*; BILLY HOUSE, *Fat Man*; MAIDA SEVERN, *Teacher*; THAN WYENN, *Romano*; PEG SHIRLEY, *Fay*; CICELY EVANS, *Louise*; BESS FLOWERS, *Geraldine Moore*; PAUL BRADLEY, *Preston Mitchell*; NAPOLEON WHITING, *Kenneth*; MYRNA FAHEY, *Actress*; EDDIE PARKER, *Policeman*.

CREDITS

Director, DOUGLAS SIRK; Producer, ROSS HUNTER; Screenplay, ELEANORE GRIFFIN and ALLAN SCOTT; Based on the Novel by FANNIE HURST; Photography (Eastman-Color), RUSSELL METTY; Art Direction, ALEXANDER GOLITZEN and RICHARD RIEDEL; Set Decoration, RUSSELL A. GAUSMAN and JULIA HERON; Editor, MILTON CARRUTH; Sound, LESLIE I. CAREY and JOE LAPIS; Costumes, JEAN LOUIS and BILL THOMAS; Makeup, BUD WESTMORE; Assistant Directors, FRANK SHAW and WILSON SHYER;

With Juanita Moore

223

Lora Meredith searches for her daughter on the beach at Coney Island

Music, FRANK SKINNER; Music Supervision, JOSEPH GERSHENSON; Title Song by SAMMY FAIN, Lyrics by PAUL FRANCIS WEBSTER, Sung by EARL GRANT; Song: "Empty Arms," by ARNOLD HUGHES, Lyrics by FREDERICK HERBERT; Running time, 125 minutes.

NOTES ABOUT THE FILM

Fannie Hurst's prolific pen has been responsible for over a dozen novels, more than 400 short stories, and other works including a play. Although it is estimated she has been read by a half billion people, an even greater number have seen the movies made from her stories, which include *Back Street* (made three times), *Imitation of Life* (twice), *Humoresque* (twice), *Symphony of Six Million*, *Lummox*, *Appassionata*, and *Four Daughters* (which was based on a Hurst novel titled *Sister Act*).

In *Imitation of Life*, Miss Hurst turned out what is referred to in show business phraseology as a four-handkerchief tear-jerker. Her novel was first used as the

basis for a Universal film in 1934, one year after the book was published. Claudette Colbert, Warren William, Rochelle Hudson, Louise Beavers and Fredi Washington starred in the movie, which was premiered to great success at New York's Roxy theatre. A quarter of a century later, a new generation of moviegoers stormed the same Roxy for a second adaptation of the Hurst novel—a revised, modernized, and glamourized version that Bosley Crowther of the *New York Times* labelled "the most shameless tear-jerker in years."

Despite lukewarm reviews (quite a few critics felt the film was appropriately titled), *Imitation of Life* scored so heavily at the box office that it singlehandedly put the ailing Universal Pictures back into business. It was one of the company's largest-grossing pictures of all time and it continued to make money on subsequent reissues. One who benefited greatly from its success was its star, Lana Turner (playing the role originally essayed by Claudette Colbert). Just one year before, Miss Turner's private life had been engulfed in tragedy, and *Imitation of Life* marked an important career comeback for her. In lieu of a large salary, her contract called for 50% of the picture's profits and the result was one of the largest fees ever received by a film actress at the time.

In *Imitation of Life*, Miss Turner looked like a million as well. Universal and producer Ross Hunter gave her the full star treatment for the film and she was bedecked in a dazzling wardrobe and more than a million dollars worth of jewelry.

Directed by Douglas Sirk, this 1959 remake of Miss Hurst's overwhelmingly sentimental hymn to mother love epitomizes the Hunter–Sirk '50s brand of melodrama, slick with shining production values that included lush sets, dazzling costumes, and a dramatic use of color. But beneath the glossy surface and the elaborate soap opera overtones, it also contained an interesting exploration of race relations given considerable depth and style through Sirk's polished direction. To reporter James Bacon, Miss Turner herself paid the film its highest accolade. "This," she said, "is the way Louis B. Mayer used to make movies."

Penned for the screen by Eleanore Griffin and Allan Scott and photographed impeccably by Russell Metty,

the major script revisions included the change of the central character from the "pancake queen" business woman of the original to the more characteristic (for Miss Turner) occupation of a resplendent Broadway actress. Her black business partner was transformed into the actress's housekeeper-companion (to bring her character out of the outmoded "colored mammy" stereotype of the original).

Even the credits for *Imitation of Life* have an expensive look. As the Universal logo fades, a handful of diamonds slowly fall from the top of the screen in the manner of raindrops. By the time the credits have finished, the entire screen is ready to overflow with them. From this blinding introduction, the film suddenly shifts to the beach at Coney Island where its four chief protagonists meet. Lora Meredith, an attractive widow with theatrical aspirations, has lost her daughter, Susie, in the crowds. She finally locates her in the company of Annie Johnson, a kind but impoverished black woman, and her light-skinned daughter, Sarah Jane, who had been playing with Susie. Before long Annie goes to work

With Dan O'Herlihy

With John Gavin

With Robert Alda and Than Wyenn

With Sandra Dee

UNIVERSAL-INTERNATIONAL presents

LANA TURNER
JOHN GAVIN

Imitation of Life

in *Eastman* **COLOR**

FANNIE HURST'S IMITATION OF LIFE

co-starring

SANDRA DEE · DAN O'HERLIHY · SUSAN KOHNER
ROBERT ALDA · JUANITA MOORE
MAHALIA JACKSON singing "Trouble of the World"

Hear
EARL GRANT
sing "Imitation of Life"

Directed by DOUGLAS SIRK · Produced by ROSS HUNTER · Screenplay by ELEANORE GRIFFIN and ALLAN SCOTT

"Although by no means a religious film, *Imitation of Life* has the slick and problem-laden properties that pass so often as a religious-minded soap opera. Those who remember Fannie Hurst's novel or the first film version won't mind the changes made in this updated script. The picture is now all glamour and tears—and the troubles that beset two mothers . . . Ross Hunter has given his picture a handsome production, and Douglas Sirk has guided his good-looking cast in performances that fit the many trying situations. Needless to say, *Imitation of Life* is a tear-jerker; and when Mahalia Jackson sings "Trouble of the World" in the finale episode, a veritable flood sweeps through the theater. Come prepared."

Imitation of Life was the first of three highly lucrative Lana Turner–Ross Hunter collaborations. It was also a marvelous showcase for the talents of Juanita Moore and Susan Kohner, both of whom won Academy Award nominations in the category of Best Supporting Actress. Miss Moore was one of more than forty who had been considered for the role of Annie Johnson. Others included Pearl Bailey and Marian Anderson.★

With Dan O'Herlihy

With John Gavin

as a housekeeper for Lora and a deep bond of affection develops between them and their children.

Encouraged by Allen Loomis, an agent, Lora gets a good role in a play by David Edwards. In the years that follow, she becomes the darling of Broadway and appears in one Edwards smash after another. But success means work and work means neglecting Susie, now sixteen, who must endure the loneliness of a youngster whose mother is too busy being a star. A good-looking photographer, Steve Archer, is the determined, admiring love of Lora's life but he too must wait and starve for her affection.

Meanwhile, Annie has her problems as well. Surrounded by luxury, her daughter, Sarah Jane, is resentful of the segregation and restrictions on her future imposed by her race. She even disclaims her mother to camouflage her ancestry and eventually she runs away to become a showgirl. Broken-hearted, Annie grows ill.

With fame no longer a novelty, Lora turns to Steve, then discovers that Susie is also in love with him. The shock reveals to her the emptiness of her existence, and she realizes at last just how much her success as a star has cost in terms of personal happiness. Eventually, Annie succumbs to her long illness. At the elaborate funeral she requested with her dying breath, the strength she imparted to others becomes evident. Sarah Jane, repentant, returns and begs for forgiveness and the tragedy brings the others closer together.

Time described *Imitation of Life* as "still a potent onion", and the critic for *The Commonweal* opined:

PORTRAIT IN BLACK

A UNIVERSAL·INTERNATIONAL PICTURE
1960

With Sandra Dee and Anthony Quinn

With Anthony Quinn

With Anna May Wong

CAST

LANA TURNER, *Sheila Cabot;* ANTHONY QUINN, *Dr. David Rivera;* SANDRA DEE, *Catherine Cabot;* JOHN SAXON, *Blake Richards;* RICHARD BASEHART, *Howard Mason;* LLOYD NOLAN, *Matthew Cabot;* RAY WALSTON, *Cob O'Brien;* VIRGINIA GREY, *Miss Lee;* ANNA MAY WONG, *Tani;* DENNIS KOHLER, *Peter Cabot;* PAUL BIRCH, *Detective;* JOHN WENGRAF, *Dr. Kessler.*

CREDITS

Director, MICHAEL GORDON; Producer, ROSS HUNTER; Screenplay (based on their play), IVAN GOFF and BEN ROBERTS; Photography (EastmanColor), RUSSELL METTY; Art Direction, RICHARD H. RIEDEL; Set Decoration, JULIA HERON; Editor, MILTON CARRUTH; Sound, WALDON O. WATSON and HENRY WILKINSON; Gowns for Lana Turner, JEAN LOUIS; Jewels, DAVID WEBB; Makeup, BUD WESTMORE; Hair Stylist, LARRY GERMAIN; Assistant Director, PHIL BOWLES; Music, FRANK SKINNER; Music Supervision, JOSEPH GERSHENSON; Musical Theme, BUDDY PEPPER and INEZ JAMES; Running time, 112 minutes.

NOTES ABOUT THE FILM

Portrait in Black was derived from a stage opus with an ill-starred theatrical history. Leland Hayward produced the original stage production which premiered late in 1945 in New Haven, Connecticut, with Geraldine Fitzgerald in the lead. It opened on Broadway in May 1947 wth Claire Luce, Donald Cook and Sidney Blackmer in the leads, and had a run of sixty-one performances. Shortly thereafter, producers Jack Skirball and Bruce Manning, who owned the film rights, announced that Joan Crawford would appear in their screen version with Carol Reed directing for Universal release. When their project fell through, Universal purchased the film rights from them. However, *Portrait in Black* didn't reach the screen until thirteen years later when it was reactivated as a vehicle for Lana by Ross Hunter who had been shopping around for a good commercial follow-up to their highly successful *Imitation of Life.*

Hunter rounded up a fine array of talent to whip the property into shape, including director Michael Gordon, who had just scored a resounding success with Hunter's *Pillow Talk;* art director Richard Riedel, who won an Academy Award nomination for his sets on the same film; cinematographer Russell Metty, who photographed *Imitation of Life;* and designer Jean Louis, another Hunter regular.

Sandra Dee, who played Lana's daughter in *Imitation,* was in the cast (this time she was Lana's stepdaughter); also aboard was veteran actress Virginia Grey, whom Hunter has often referred to as his "good luck charm." A familiar Hunter staple, the casting of members of Hollywood's Old Guard, was realized with the selection of the famed Oriental beauty, Anna May Wong, whom the producer lured out of an eleven-year retirement to portray an enigmatic housekeeper.

The scenario, which was rewritten for the screen by Ivan Goff and Ben Roberts, who penned the stage original, utilized the ever-popular triangle murder as its theme. The setting of the film was San Francisco and the home of Matthew Cabot, a tyrannical shipping tycoon, bedridden by an incurable disease, who meets his death

in what appears to be a "perfect" murder planned by his wife, Sheila, and her lover, Dr. David Rivera. The homicidal couple appear safe until an anonymous letter arrives, revealing their crime is well known to someone else. Among those who may or may not have wielded the threatening pen are Catherine Cabot, the tycoon's daughter; Howard Mason, the family lawyer; Cob, the chauffeur; and Tani, the Chinese housekeeper.

When suspicions keep centering on Mason, Dr. Rivera decides that he, too, must be killed, and with Sheila's assistance, he murders him with the guilt thrown on Blake Richards, Catherine's boyfriend. But the anonymous letters *still* keep coming.

In the film's climax, Dr. Rivera manages to wrest the truth from Sheila, who admits that she herself penned the notes. Her reason had been fear that Rivera would leave her, and the hope that a belief on his part that someone knew that they had committed murder would bind him firmly to her. Because Catherine has overheard the revelation, Rivera goes after her but she escapes unharmed while the crazed doctor falls to his death from a window ledge. At the fadeout, Sheila is left to face the

With Lloyd Nolan

grim consequences for the crimes their passion nurtured and Blake Richards is absolved of the murder of Howard Mason.

Like its Broadway predecessor, the screen version of *Portrait in Black* drew largely negative notices. *Daily Variety* described the film as "a contrived murder melodrama with psychological character interplay that is more psycho than logical", while *Cue* found it "highly polished but generally incredible."

Portrait in Black is the only hard-breathing exercise in adultery and homicide to boast the name of Ross Hunter, a producer generally associated with romantic film fare. Its theme notwithstanding, the picture unmistakeably bears the Hunter brand and, consequently, can go down on record as being the most glistening, glittering, and glamourous murder mystery ever produced. As *Cue* further noted: "the high class killings are done amid the lushest settings and most expensive costumes— and photographed in the most gorgeous pastelled EastmanColor."

and upwards at the box office. Without Miss Turner and Hunter, it could have been a different story."

In Great Britain, *Portrait in Black* had once served as a stage vehicle for Diana Wynyard. This is how Susan Mann of the British periodical *Women's Mirror* summed up the heroine of the film version: "This week, I'm celebrating the return of a very dear friend. There she is in *Portrait in Black*, as rich, ravishing and wildly improbable as ever. The moment she slipped her mink coat carelessly round her shoulders and rushed out to meet a secret lover leaving her bedridden husband behind, I breathed a sigh of luxurious relief. To me, she's the *grande dame* of tormented heroines. She used to turn up in film after film. Joan Crawford played her to perfection; so did Bette Davis. Neither Joan or Bette have been filming lately. So Lana Turner has taken over as top representative of my favorite species of celluloid queen bee. But, after Lana, who else is left in films to stride across the screen, diamonds flashing, passions exposed, behaving as if she believed every word of a plot as incredible as anything in Hans Andersen? It takes a special kind of star to do it. And it grieves me that they don't make stars like that these days." ★

With Richard Basehart

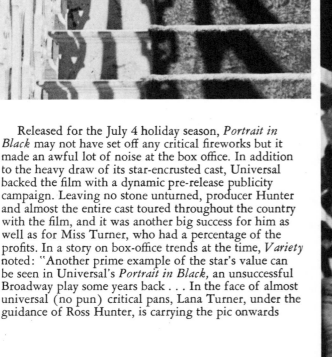

Released for the July 4 holiday season, *Portrait in Black* may not have set off any critical fireworks but it made an awful lot of noise at the box office. In addition to the heavy draw of its star-encrusted cast, Universal backed the film with a dynamic pre-release publicity campaign. Leaving no stone unturned, producer Hunter and almost the entire cast toured throughout the country with the film, and it was another big success for him as well as for Miss Turner, who had a percentage of the profits. In a story on box-office trends at the time, *Variety* noted: "Another prime example of the star's value can be seen in Universal's *Portrait in Black,* an unsuccessful Broadway play some years back . . . In the face of almost universal (no pun) critical pans, Lana Turner, under the guidance of Ross Hunter, is carrying the pic onwards

BY LOVE POSSESSED

MIRISCH PICTURES, INC. IN ASSOCIATION WITH SEVEN ARTS PRODUCTIONS, INC.
FOR UNITED ARTISTS RELEASE
1961

With Efrem Zimbalist, Jr.

CAST

LANA TURNER, *Marjorie Penrose;* EFREM ZIMBALIST, JR., *Arthur Winner;* JASON ROBARDS, JR., *Julius Penrose;* GEORGE HAMILTON, *Warren Winner;* SUSAN KOHNER, *Helen Detweiler;* BARBARA BEL GEDDES, *Clarissa Winner;* THOMAS MITCHELL, *Noah Tuttle;* EVERETT SLOANE, *Reggie;* YVONNE CRAIG, *Veronica Kovacs;* JEAN WILLES, *Junie McCarthy;* FRANK MAXWELL, *Jerry Brophy;* GILBERT GREEN, *Mr. Woolf;* CARROLL O'CONNOR, *Bernie Breck.*

CREDITS

Director, JOHN STURGES; Producer, WALTER MIRISCH; Screenplay, JOHN DENNIS; Based on the Novel by JAMES GOULD COZZENS; Photography (Color by DeLuxe), RUSSELL METTY; Art Direction, MALCOLM BROWN; Set Decoration, EDWARD G. BOYLE; Editor, FERRIS WEBSTER; Sound, FRANKLIN HANSEN; Wardrobe, BILL THOMAS; Makeup, DEL ARMSTRONG and LAYNE BRITTON; Assistant Director, SAM NELSON; Music, ELMER BERNSTEIN; Running Time, 115 minutes.

NOTES ABOUT THE FILM

Although *By Love Possessed*'s screenplay is attributed to John Dennis, the name is actually a pseudonym. Originally the scenario was written by Charles Schnee, the Academy Award-winning writer who won his Oscar for Lana's *The Bad and the Beautiful.* During production, however, three other writers—Isobel Lennart, Bill Roberts and Ketti Frings—were called in and when Schnee saw the finished product he threatened to sue unless his name was removed from the screen credits.

In attempting to translate the novel into a motion picture, Schnee clearly had his work cut out for him. *By Love Possessed* was published in 1957, headed the best-seller lists for months, and ultimately became the recipient of the coveted William Dean Howells Award as "the most distinguished work of American fiction published during the last five years." Its author, James Gould Cozzens, spent eight years turning it into an exhaustive, sensitive, frequently obscure study of what love does to people, and vice versa. Despite its acclaim, it is estimated that few of its readers ever made it to the end of the 575th page. The book covered twenty-five years in a soul-searching way which, through the use of flashbacks and introspection, Cozzens related over a period of three days' time. The film version, on the other hand, dealt solely with the "now" story; i.e., what happened in those three days.

The time is the present and the place is New England. The people belong to the elite of the town, and are among its most upstanding citizens. But underneath, their lives are a seething mass of discontent and shattered emotions. Arthur Winner, for instance, is a solid resident with a good law practice. He has married the girl everyone said he would, joined the right clubs and taken his rightful place in community activities. In his profession, he is devoted to the letter of the law, seldom, if ever, making allowances for circumstances. Carefully reserved in his relationships with all, including his wife and son, he has arrived at his present position in life believing himself content and well-adjusted, convinced of the rightness of his course. Then, the events of a few short days put his composure and convictions to severe trial.

He begins to suspect that a respected senior partner in his firm, Noah Tuttle, is guilty of embezzling trust funds to pay a debt of honor. At the same time, the chill that he feels in his marriage leads him into an adulterous interlude with Marjorie, the dipsomaniac wife of his other law partner, Julius Penrose. Impotent as the result of an automobile accident, Julius is too proud to ask for his wife's affection on the grounds it might be construed as pity. Yet he refuses to give her a divorce and tells Marjorie to "go find what you want somewhere else. Just don't tell me about it."

The climax comes when Arthur's son, Warren, gets involved in a rape charge, the shock of which leads to the suicide of Helen Detweiler, the girl Warren had been expected to marry. In the end, the emotional upheaval of Helen's death causes both Arthur and his wife, Clarissa, and Julius and Marjorie Penrose to rediscover each other.

The screen version of the Cozzens novel, which a *Time* critic described as "the worst good novel of the last decade," was in respectable hands. Its director was John Sturges, whose notable films included *Bad Day at Black Rock, The Magnificent Seven* and *The Old Man and the Sea*, and its cast was large and distinguished. Producer Walter Mirisch gave the film a handsome production, and although common report placed the setting of the book in Doylestown, Pennsylvania, the film shifted the locale to New England to allow some

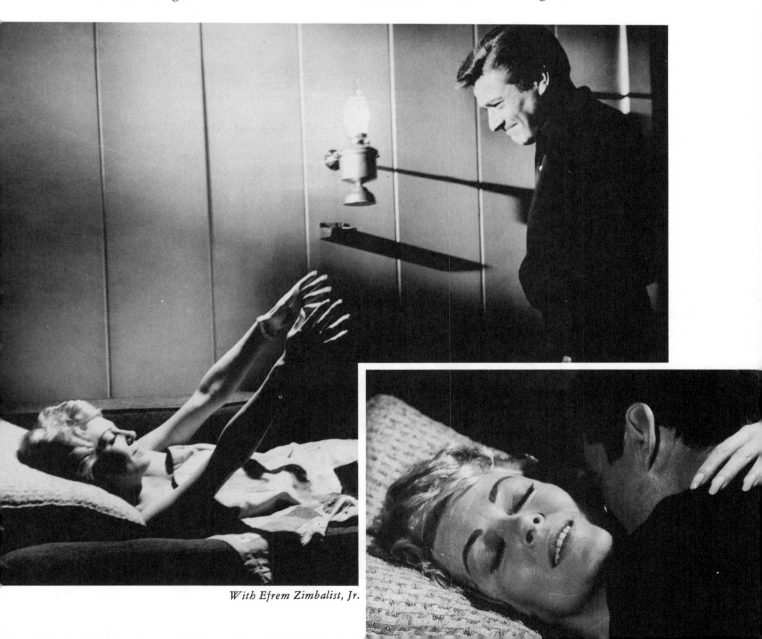

With Efrem Zimbalist, Jr.

With Efrem Zimbalist, Jr.

excellent landscapes in DeLuxe color. Backgrounds for the town used in *By Love Possessed* were photographed in Groton and Fitchburg, Massachusetts, and the bulk of the film was directed by Sturges in the surprisingly short period of thirty-two days.

The result, as premiered in the Spring of 1961, was a mixture of uneven Cozzens and slick soap opera. Moreover, with its multi-character plotting, its "sensational" elements (rape, suicide, embezzlement), the New England setting, and the presence of Lana Turner, *By Love Possessed* was an open invitation to comparisons with the earlier *Peyton Place* or to one of the many

imitations fostered by that very successful film. Unlike *Peyton Place*, however, *By Love Possessed* is a rather talky affair, closer to a television drama than to something cinematic.

While admiring the film's handsome production values and the fact that "almost everyone concerned with *By Love Possessed* appears to have been honorably determined to do his best," Brendan Gill in his *New Yorker* review felt its producers were dealing with "a work that contained few traces of filmable material."

Just as in the novel, the character most thoroughly explored in the film is Cozzens' middle-aged hero, Arthur Winner (played with a touch of gray in his hair by Efrem Zimbalist, Jr.). Although she has far less screen time, Miss Turner is top-billed in the picture and has a few good moments as hard-drinking, love-hungry Marjorie Penrose. Bob Freund, a Fort Lauderdale, Florida reviewer called it "a role she does well—the dame with a surface elegance glossing a wanton brassiness." ★

With George Hamilton

234

With Jason Robards, Jr.

BACHELOR IN PARADISE

A METRO·GOLDWYN·MAYER RELEASE OF A TED RICHMOND PRODUCTION

1961

With Paula Prentiss and Bob Hope

With Bob Hope

CAST

BOB HOPE, *Adam J. Niles;* LANA TURNER, *Rosemary Howard;* JANIS PAIGE, *Dolores Jynson;* JIM HUTTON, *Larry Delavane;* PAULA PRENTISS, *Linda Delavane;* DON PORTER, *Thomas W. Jynson;* VIRGINIA GREY, *Camille Quinlaw;* AGNES MOOREHEAD, *Judge Peterson;* FLORENCE SUNDSTROM, *Mrs. Pickering;* CLINTON SUNDBERG, *Rodney Jones;* JOHN McGIVER, *Austin Palfrey;* ALAN HEWITT, *Backett;* RETA SHAW, *Mrs. Brown;* VINCE SCULLY, *Announcer;* JERRY DOGGETT, *Himself;* LEE GOODMAN, *Leland Quinlaw;* ROBERTA SHORE, *Ginny;* MARY TREEN, *Mrs. Freedman;* JOY MONROE, *Voluptuous Girl;* WILLIAM "BILLY" McLEAN, *Cab Driver.*

CREDITS

Director, JACK ARNOLD; Producer, TED RICHMOND; Screenplay, VALENTINE DAVIES and HAL KANTER; Based on the Novel by VERA CASPARY; Photography (Cinema-Scope and MetroColor), JOSEPH RUTTENBERG; Art Direction, GEORGE W. DAVIS and HANS PETERS; Set Decoration, HENRY GRACE and KEOGH GLEASON; Editor, RICHARD W. FARRELL; Sound, FRANKLIN MILTON; Wardrobe, HELEN ROSE; Makeup, DEL ARMSTRONG; Assistant Director, ERICH VON STROHEIM, JR.; Music, HENRY MANCINI; Title Song Lyrics, MACK DAVID; Running time, 108 minutes.

NOTES ABOUT THE FILM

In the Spring of '61, Miss Turner returned to her former studio, MGM, to pick up her pension and to finish off an old contractual commitment by joining Bob Hope in a comedy he was doing there called *Bachelor in Paradise*. Over the years, Hope had always wanted to add Lana to his long and impressive list of glamourous leading ladies but because of their respective studio ties, their screen-teaming was never realized. They were hardly strangers, however, having worked together many times on radio and television and in later years Miss Turner accompanied the comedian on his annual Christmas tour to entertain the servicemen overseas.

Vera Caspary, the author of *Laura*, wrote the story for *Bachelor in Paradise*, which examined the mores of contemporary suburbia with considerable accuracy and satiric relish. Hope played an income-tax afflicted writer named Adam J. Niles, who is sent by his publisher to Paradise Village, a modern housing development, to write a book on "How the Americans Live," the proceeds of which he hopes will clear his debt. He moves into a house formerly occupied by Rosemary Howard, the only bachelor girl in the development—and that's when the trouble starts.

In the course of his research for the book, he enlists the aid of many of the local housewives, which does not endear him to the local husbands who, each and every one of them, suspect their wives of having affairs with Adam. Three of the men finally accuse their spouses of infidelity, naming Adam as co-respondent. But bliss is restored to the domestic disharmony in a final courtroom scene when Adam confesses his love for Rosemary and prepares to leave bachelorhood behind him.

In addition to the traditional Hope punch lines, many of the laughs in *Bachelor in Paradise* were visual ones deriving from such familiar phenomena of the American way of life as supermarkets, baby-sitters, garbage disposal machines and the hazards of freeways. The funniest moment: when an entire ranch house slowly fills with soap bubbles from an automatic washer into which helpless bachelor Hope has poured too much detergent.

Writer Bob Considine, in his review of the film, called *Bachelor in Paradise* "Bob Hope's funniest comedy ever" and while he may have overrated it quite a bit this very funny poke at suburban living is certainly one of the best of the comedian's latter-day vehicles. In the New York *Daily Mirror*, H. V. Coren critiqued: "It is Bob Hope's special talent that he needs no story to be funny. Master of the ridiculous, he can send an audience howling with a lifted eyebrow, a one-step strut. In *Bachelor in Paradise*, he *has* a funny situation to work with, and the comic results are happily predictable. In addition, he's got Lana Turner, who does a complete about-face from her recent heavy dramatics and plays 'straight man' to Hope's antics."

Not too straight, however. In one nightclub scene, when she's had too much tequila, Lana clears the dance floor with a lively—and extremely agile—hula. She looks lovely throughout the film, incidentally, and was fortunate enough to have two of her favorite associates from her contract years at MGM on the picture as well, photographer Joe Ruttenberg and costume designer Helen Rose.

Henry Mancini's title song, with lyrics by Mack David, won him an Academy Award nomination.★

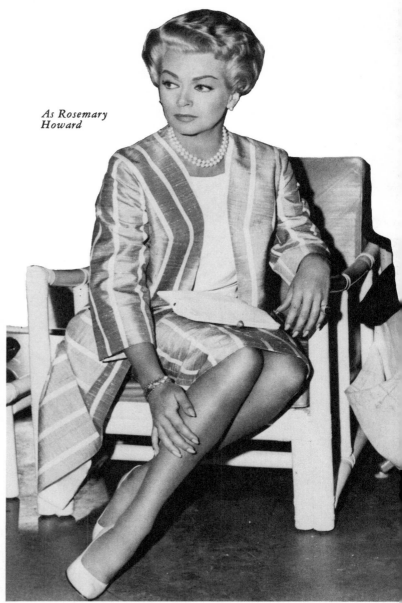

As Rosemary Howard

With Bob Hope

CAST

DEAN MARTIN, *Steve Flood;* LANA TURNER, *Melanie Flood;* EDDIE ALBERT, *Clint Morgan;* NITA TALBOT, *Saturday Knight;* WALTER MATTHAU, *Tony Gagoots;* MARGO, *Roza;* PAUL FORD, *Judge Boatwright;* LEWIS CHARLES, *Clutch;* JOHN McGIVER, *Judge Fogel;* DAN TOBIN, *Sanford;* ALEXANDER ROSE, *Goody;* JACK ALBERTSON, *Hodges;* HILLARY YATES, *Hoxie;* EDDIE QUILLAN, *Dingo;* JAY ADLER, *Driver;* BENNY GILL, *Violinist;* WILBUR MACK, *Octogenarian;* JUNE WILKINSON, *Bride;* KAREN VON UNGE, *Young Starlet;* HOUSE PETERS, JR., *Cop in Elevator.*

CREDITS

Director, DANIEL MANN; Producer, JACK ROSE; Screenplay, JACK ROSE; Based on the Novel *Four Horseplayers Are Missing* by ALEXANDER ROSE; Photography (Technicolor and Panavision), JOSEPH RUTTENBERG; Art Director, ARTHUR LONERGAN; Editor, HOWARD SMITH; Sound, HUGO GRENZBACH; Wardrobe, EDITH HEAD; Makeup, DEL ARMSTRONG; Assistant Director, ARTIE JACOBSON; Music, GEORGE DUNING; Running time, 93 minutes.

NOTES ABOUT THE FILM

With her sleek glamour and his characteristic casualness, Lana and Dean Martin were something of an "odd couple" when they teamed for this wacky racetrack yarn. Equally off-beat was the selection of Daniel Mann as director, since Mann's previous credits consisted exclusively of heavy dramatic films like *I'll Cry Tomorrow, The Rose Tattoo* and *Butterfield Eight.* The bestselling book, *Four Horseplayers Are Missing,* by Alexander Rose, was the source for the screenplay by Jack Rose (no relation), who also produced. Author Rose also contributed a small but zany cameo to the on-screen horseplay.

Lana played Melanie Flood, a slightly dizzy socialite turned authoress, who is concerned over her husband Steve's preoccupation with horses and the money losses that go with them. With the help of Steve's law partner, Clint Morgan, Melanie hits on a scheme to enable him to give vent to his addiction without losing money: she secretly becomes his "bookie." Her ideal plan goes wrong, however, since Steve has a winning streak and Melanie has to honor his bets even if it means pawning her jewelry and denuding their home of its furniture. The situation is worsened when Steve urges his friends to contact his lucky bookie.

Meanwhile, the syndicate boss, Tony Gagoots, is enraged about losing bets and decides to track down the unknown bookie. Gagoots's girl, nightclub singer Saturday Knight, just happens to be the Floods' next door neighbor and also the purchaser of many of their pos-

With Dean Martin

With Dean Martin

With Dean Martin

sessions. All involved end up at the Floods' apartment, where Melanie is packing to leave town before Steve finds out the truth. When matters are all straightened out, Melanie is forgiven, and Gagoots, in trouble with the law, is persuaded by Steve to marry the nightclub singer who knows all about his bookmaking syndicate so she can't testify against him. Finally, Steve charges Gagoots enough for the legal advice to get Melanie out of hock and reclaim their furniture.

This Runyonesque comedy-of-complications garnered a mixed reaction from critics, some of whom felt its best intentions never left the starting gate. Others, like *Time*, liked it very much: "The syndicate has the last laugh in this yak derby, but the customers get most of the others . . . *Action* is not the merriest oatsmobile that ever came down the track, but Dean and Lana make a surprisingly smooth entry; Paul Ford is hilarious as a birdbrained, spaniel-eyed, llama-lipped pony player; and Walter

Matthau has his moments as the big hair-ball who runs the syndicate—among them the deathless moment when, with a casual flick of his manicured fingers, he announces superbly: 'Give dis genulman eighteen tousan' dolluhs frum petty cash.' The whole cast obviously enjoyed making the picture, and most spectators will find that the pleasure is mutuel.''

Betty Bronson, who created the role of Peter Pan in the Paramount movie of 1925, had been signed to play a small but good bit as a Pasadena society matron in a party scene at the Flood apartment, but due to production delays her scenes were never shot and the role was eventually scrapped.

For those who dote on Turner trivia, *Who's Got the Action?* displayed Lana in her fourth screen bathtub scene—and a highly elaborate one it was. Her previous dunkings occurred in *Ziegfeld Girl, The Merry Widow* and *The Lady Takes A Flyer.* ★

With Dean Martin and Jack Albertson

With Eddie Albert

LOVE HAS MANY FACES

A JERRY BRESLER PRODUCTION FOR COLUMBIA PICTURES RELEASE
1965

With Cliff Robertson

With Hugh O'Brian

CAST

LANA TURNER, *Kit Jordan;* CLIFF ROBERTSON, *Pete Jordan;* HUGH O'BRIAN, *Hank Walker;* RUTH ROMAN, *Margot Eliot;* STEFANIE POWERS, *Carol Lambert;* VIRGINIA GREY, *Irene Talbot;* RON HUSMANN, *Chuck Austin;* ENRIQUE LUCERO, *Lt. Riccardo Andrade;* CARLOS MONTALBAN, *Don Julian;* JAIME BRAVO, *Manuel Perez;* FANNIE SCHILLER, *Maria;* RENE DUPREYON, *Ramos.*

CREDITS

Director, ALEXANDER SINGER; Producer, JERRY BRESLER; Screenplay, MARGUERITE ROBERTS; Photography (EastmanColor by Pathé), JOSEPH RUTTENBERG; Art Director, ALFRED SWEENEY; Editor, ALMA MACRORIE; Sound, CHARLES J. RICE and JESUS GONZALES GANCY; Set Decoration, NOLDI SCHRECK, Mexico City; Miss Turner's Wardrobe, EDITH HEAD; Jewels by KIOR, INC. of Beverly Hills, California; Makeup, DEL ARMSTRONG and DEL

In the melodramatic climax of LOVE HAS MANY FACES, *Kit is gored by a wild bull*

As Kit Jordan, one of the wealthiest women in the world

ACAVEDO; Makeup Supervised by BEN LANE; Hair Stylist, NAOMI A. CAVIN; Assistant Director, RICHARD MODER; Music, DAVID RAKSIN; Title Song Lyrics by MACK DAVID; Sung by NANCY WILSON; Running time, 105 minutes.

NOTES ABOUT THE FILM

Filmed in the ultra-luxury Mexican resort of Acapulco, *Love Has Many Faces* cast Lana as Kit Jordan, a jaded American millionairess who has been everywhere, done everything, and makes her own rules. Wronged in her teens by an overpossessive mother and frustrated now by her inability to have children, her past is filled with aimless affairs with the local young American gigolos known as "beach boys." As the film opens, we learn she is presently the wife of Pete Jordan, a former beach boy who married her for her money and who now is guilt-ridden because of it.

A subplot involves another beach boy, Hank Walker, a former pal of Pete's and still a gigolo living on the gifts he woos from lonely women. His current target is Margot Eliot, a middle-aged *turista*, but his ultimate goal is Kit herself, and as her marriage to Pete founders, Hank is waiting on the sidelines ready to move in on her beauty and money.

When a third beach boy—and a former lover of Kit's—is found dead on the beach, an apparent suicide, Kit pays for his funeral. This mystery serves to introduce to Acapulco's jet-set Carol Lambert, a young girl from Detroit, who is the dead boy's fiancee. Although Pete advises her to go back home, her hatred of Kit, whom she considers responsible for her boyfriend's death, keeps her on. With each meeting, Carol falls more in love with Pete, who, tormented by the thought his wife had carried on her affair with the dead boy after their marriage, is himself attracted to the girl.

The climax of the film takes place on a ranch where young bulls are being trained for the ring. Here, Kit, who has watched the relationship between Pete and the younger girl deepen, jumps her horse suicidally into the ring where she falls and is gored by a bull. Her ex-beach boy husband, however, risks his life to save hers and she is rushed to a hospital in time.

This near-tragic turn of events rescues the marriage of Kit and Pete, who has suddenly realized how much he loves his wife, while the third corner of the triangle, Carol Lambert, goes back to Detroit, a little older and wiser.

Love Has Many Faces was directed by Alexander Singer, who four years earlier had made a somewhat auspicious debut with *A Cold Wind in August*, a film that also dealt with a woman in love with a younger man. Singer's subsequent films like *Psyche 59* did not live up to his initial promise, nor did *Love Has Many Faces* which is more interesting as an exercise in the clothes-horse school of the "woman's picture" than for its dramatic merits. Released in February 1965, this Jerry Bresler production was one of the last of an endangered, if not quite extinct, genre which Hollywood, catering to the feminine trade, used to turn out in such profusion in the '30s and '40s and even into the '50s.

To properly underline the character of Kit Jordan, *Love Has Many Faces'* super-rich flaunter of conventions ("who has almost as many problems as wardrobe changes" said Howard Thompson of *The New York Times*), Edith Head, the Academy Award-winning designer, created one of the most razzle-dazzle costume displays of her long career. Since it ultimately proved to be the picture's most exploitable asset, Columbia elevated Miss Head's wardrobe to "star" billing—right along with the performers—in the film's advertisements ("Lana Turner's Million Dollar Wardrobe by Edith Head," read the posters).

Not surprisingly, more than one reviewer felt that although Lana was flanked by two stalwart leading men (Cliff Robertson and Hugh O'Brian), her real co-star in *Love Has Many Faces* was her "Million Dollar Wardrobe." It even became the theme of a short subject previewing Miss Head's costumes with comments by the designer herself. Titled, appropriately enough, *Million Dollar Wardrobe*, this five-minute color featurette played most first-run theatres one week prior to the scheduled showings of *Love Has Many Faces* and was devised as a means of luring patrons back the following week to see the full-length feature.

By 1965, however, audiences did not show much enthusiasm for the what-will-she-wear-next approach to drama. And the critics were even more apathetic. One reviewer described *Love Has Many Faces* as "a lushly wrapped, dime-novel escapade," while Judith Crist, snapping at its soapy melodramatics, called it "the kind of movie that over the decades has given the term 'a woman's picture' all the opprobrium it bears."

If few could take the glitter and the gloss seriously, *Love Has Many Faces* was nonetheless perfect fodder for Turner fans for it more than generously displayed the star doing the things they loved best: (a) changing costumes with great frequency; (b) suffering nobly throughout.

Since its sale to television, *Love Has Many Faces* has found another, equally responsive audience. One TV critic recommended the film be restricted to mid-afternoon telecasts since it is "the perfect antidote for bored housewives who thrive on the sight of beautiful clothes and emotional turmoil in opulent surroundings." ★

With Stefanie Powers

Lana's fabulous wardrobe in LOVE HAS MANY
FACES *was the subject of a Columbia featurette
entitled* MILLION DOLLAR WARDROBE. *In it she
modelled her Edith Head fashions while Miss
Head supplied the narration*

MADAME X

A ROSS HUNTER·ELTEE·UNIVERSAL PICTURE
1966

CAST

LANA TURNER, *Holly Parker;* JOHN FORSYTHE, *Clay Anderson;* RICARDO MONTALBAN, *Phil Benton;* BURGESS MEREDITH, *Dan Sullivan;* CONSTANCE BENNETT, *Estelle Anderson;* KEIR DULLEA, *Clay Anderson, Jr.;* JOHN VAN DREELEN, *Christian Torben;* VIRGINIA GREY, *Mimsy;* WARREN STEVENS, *Michael Spalding;* CARL BENTON REID, *Judge;* TEDDY QUINN, *Clay, Jr. as a boy;* FRANK MAXWELL, *Dr. Evans;* KAREN VERNE, *Nurse Riborg;* JOE DeSANTIS, *Carter;* FRANK MARTH, *Combs;* BING RUSSELL, *Sgt. Riley;* TENO POLLICK, *Manuel Lopez;* JEFF BURTON, *Bromley;* JILL JACKSON, *Police Matron;* NEIL HAMILTON, *Party Guest.**

CREDITS

Director, DAVID LOWELL RICH; Producer, ROSS HUNTER; Screenplay, JEAN HOLLOWAY; Based on the Play by ALEXANDRE BISSON; Photography (Technicolor), RUSSELL METTY; Art Directors, ALEXANDER GOLITZEN and GEORGE WEBB; Editor, MILTON CARRUTH; Sound, WALDON O. WATSON and CLARENCE SELF; Set Decorations, JOHN McCARTHY and HOWARD BRISTOL; Miss Turner's and Miss Bennett's Gowns, JEAN LOUIS; Makeup, BUD WESTMORE; Hair Stylist, LARRY GERMAIN; Assistant Director, DOUG GREEN; Music, FRANK SKINNER; Musical Supervision, JOSEPH GERSHENSON; Running time, 100 minutes.

NOTES ABOUT THE FILM

In more ways than one, *Madame X* is a lady who's "been around." Written originally for the French stage in 1909 by Alexandre Bisson, this celebrated old warhorse about a fallen woman was first discovered by Hollywood in 1916 when Pathé brought it to the screen with Dorothy Donnelly in the title role. Since then, the lady has hit the skids with regularity: in 1920, Samuel Goldwyn produced an adaptation starring Pauline Frederick; in 1929, MGM released the initial sound version which Lionel Barrymore directed and which made its star, Ruth Chatterton, the first major new dramatic actress of the talking screen; and in 1937, MGM filmed it again with Gladys George.

Approximately twenty-five years later, Lana Turner was looking for a vehicle with which to reactivate her independent production company. Someone suggested a remake of *Madame X* and a screening of the Gladys George version was arranged for the actress at MGM. After viewing the film, Miss Turner, with much enthusiasm, brought the property to the attention of Ross Hunter. Hunter, the last of the producers to specialize in "women's pictures," had been having a difficult

With John Forsythe

With Constance Bennett and John Forsythe

With Ricardo Montalban

*Although most of Neil Hamilton's footage was deleted from the final print of *Madame X*, he can still be briefly spotted in the wedding reception sequence early in the film.

time himself locating material for the screen. At the start of the Sixties, stories for feminine stars were becoming increasingly scarce and the only recourse seemed to be the reworking and updating of old properties. Although reaching back to a 1909 tear-jerker was really digging deep, Hunter had little trouble selling the idea of refilming *Madame X* to the executives at Universal. His track record as far as remakes were concerned had been lined with box-office gold, and two of his films—*Imitation of Life* and *Magnificent Obsession*—were credited with keeping the studio open when it was in a very critical condition. Now Hunter's sharp commercial instinct told him that *Madame X*'s potent blend of

With Teddy Quinn

With Constance Bennett

With Burgess Meredith

glamour and tears would make an ideal vehicle for Miss Turner and prove to be another box-office winner for Universal.

Early in 1962, Turner and Hunter purchased the story rights to *Madame X* from MGM and entered into a co-production deal in which the picture would be jointly filmed under the banner of Hunter's film outfit and Miss Turner's own newly rechristened Eltee Productions. With production scheduled for October of that same

year, Hunter assigned the screenplay to Jean Holloway, a writer he knew from his days as a radio actor in the early '40s. However, production snags—principally centering on the concept of the script—held the picture up. The film did not go before the cameras until three years later —in April 1965—and although *Madame X* was clearly designed for a far less cynical age, Miss Holloway's treatment of the Bisson play, with but the barest updating, remained precisely what it always has been—a shameless blend of hokum and honest sentiment.

The heroine is Holly Anderson, the young wife of a rich diplomat. Neglected by her husband, she is driven in boredom into the arms of Phil Benton, a playboy. When he is killed in an accident during one of their trysts, she appeals to her matriarchal mother-in-law for help. But the older woman, who has always resented her introduction into the family, convinces her the indiscretion will cost her husband his career and wreck their young son's life. To save her loved ones from scandal, the wife flees to Europe, leaving them to think she is dead.

Over the years, she slowly drifts into a life of absinthe and prostitution, sinking lower and lower until, in a Mexican hotel, she meets Dan Sullivan, a smooth-talking con-man, and agrees to join him in a blackmail scheme. When she discovers too late that the intended victim is her husband, she shoots the blackmailer and goes on trial for murder, known only as Madame X. Unaware of her true identity, the young lawyer assigned to defend her is her own son, now grown to manhood. He takes to her instantly and almost wins the case, but before the verdict the woman dies of heart failure, never revealing to the defense that she was his mother.

In the Ross Hunter tradition, this 1966 remake was mounted with splendor and overloaded with the usual come-ons for women, such as Jean Louis creating Madame's wardrobe—right down to the handkerchiefs for her to cry into. David Lowell Rich, a newcomer to films with a lot of television experience, directed in a speedy thirty-five days and moved the film's twenty-five-year time span along at a cracking pace.* The new role of the aristocratic mother-in-law was played with great style by Constance Bennett, one of the most glamourous and high-priced stars of the 1930s who returned to the screen after a twelve-year absence at Ross Hunter's behest. Sadly, the film was Miss Bennett's last; she died shortly before it was released.

Madame X was released in March 1966 at a time when the movies were fast shrugging off all the shackles of censorship. Since its plotful of woes had been rather

---

*After purchasing the property in 1962, Ross Hunter approached Douglas Sirk about directing *Madame X*. But Sirk, who had successfully guided so many of Hunter's previous soapers on to box-office glory, declined because of ill health. Three years later, when the picture was finally ready for production, Sirk was still favored for the job but by then he was in definitive retirement from films.

outmoded at the time of *Madame*'s last (1937) reworking, in the permissive atmosphere of 1966 its sentiments seemed really antique. Cynics with pretensions to sophistication had a field day mocking the picture's tear-jerking mechanisms. ("If you haven't seen a movie since 1930, you may think it's great," sneered one critic.)

Others, like Chicago reviewer Ann Marsters, were not quite as hardhearted: "Corny, perhaps, and mawkish, too, but it plays with a kind of dramatic splendor. I haven't cried so much in years." Several critics felt it took courage to resuscitate a hymn to mother-love and self-sacrifice at a time when moviegoers were lining up for sex and violence and films that focused on the seamier side of human relationships. James Powers in *The Hollywood Reporter* wrote: "Only Ross Hunter would dream, would dare to do a remake of *Madame X*, and it has turned out to be an electrifyingly right

Holly shoots the blackmailer who threatens to reveal her identity to her family

With Warren Stevens and Keir Dullea. John Forsythe and Constance Bennett are seated in the back row, left.

decision . . . a superb cast of players take this rather shabby old piece and give it immediacy, vigor and credibility. It plays, and it plays beautifully." And the critic for the *London Evening Standard* added: "We should be grateful that Hollywood still has the face to make an unabashed weepie with the sluices open."

But *Madame X* was not the big financial blockbuster that the Turner–Hunter collaborations of just a half-dozen years earlier had been. Much of its intended female audience had gravitated to television soap opera for emotional release. Nor did *Madame X* launch a rebirth of ultra-glamorous tear-jerkers on the screen. As writer René Jordan recently described the period: "Even the carefully resurrected dreamworld of the Lana Turner–Ross Hunter rhinestone melodramas became passé in the 'serious' late Sixties. Fakery had permeated the real life of the public beyond the saturation point. Blatantly glamourous movies were being rejected with a wave of the hand . . ."

If the vehicle itself, so dear to the hearts of an earlier

generation, was hardly up to the moment at the time of this 1966 incarnation it nonetheless afforded Lana Turner one of her most demanding acting assignments. Although she faced some severe critics in perennial detractors like Pauline Kael, Lana's performance in the title role won more than its share of plaudits. Dorothy Manners, Abe Greenberg of the *Hollywood Citizen News*, and the critic for the *Independent Film Journal*, for instance, were just a few of the writers who felt she would have been Oscar-nominated had it not been for the picture's indifferent critical reception.

The first half of *Madame X* puts its audience in familiar Turner territory. Dressed to the teeth, she marries one man, dallies illicitly with another, and endures considerable agony along the way—all against the meticulous Technicolored trappings synonymous with Ross Hunter productions.

But the picture's second half is another matter entirely. Although hokey and manipulative of its audience in the extreme, this section of the film contains

*The two faces
of Madame X*

what many consider some of Miss Turner's finest screen moments. Here, responding to David Lowell Rich's sensitive direction and supported by an excellent cast, she carries off a number of very difficult scenes, making her tear-drenched heroine a remarkably credible character. Her final moments—on the skids in Mexico, the famous courtroom scene, and the truly harrowing death-bed confrontation with her long-lost son—are genuinely moving and, in the words of Charles Champlin of the *Los Angeles Times*, "the unsparing, guileless honesty of her performance is very touching."

But Lana's most significant recognition came from abroad. There, she was the recipient of both the David Di Donatello Award (as "Best Foreign Actress" at the annual Taormina Film Festival) and La Perla Verde (the Green Pearl trophy, presented to her by the Theatre Owners of Italy).

When *Madame X* was released in Great Britain, critic David Quinlan offered this interesting analysis of the picture: "Producer Ross Hunter may not be a miner who strikes original veins, but he's an efficient, careful man who, give him due credit, ambles tidily along with his little pick and strikes a tear-duct every time. Here he picks up the definitive weepie plot and, with the help of a strong, discerning director, David Lowell Rich, holds it firmly and wisely to the spirit of the silent era, building up to an out-with-your-handkerchiefs climax which is all the more effective for being handled in a strictly old-fashioned manner. The film has an uneasy first twenty minutes when it seems to be struggling against its own natural trappings. But once it finds its own metier, not a trick is missed—the juvenile saying his prayers, the wicked stepmother framed in a window during a storm, Madame X collapsing in snow and catching pneumonia—and one can almost see the silent credits. Yet still, a lot depends on the star and one can never remember a more affecting performance from Lana Turner, especially in the latter half of the film, when she is so much more impressive than one could ever imagine that one is almost entirely captive to a portrayal in which she is utterly deglamourised, and says so much with brown eyes that seem old and fathomless."

Since she is usually impeccably coiffed and costumed in her films, Lana's willingness to make herself unattractive for many scenes in *Madame X* came as quite a shock to some observers. Writing of her deglamourized appearance in the film, Clifford Terry in *The Chicago Tribune* said: ". . . when she takes the stand in the final

courtroom scene, her face resembling a dust bowl victory garden, it's the most devastating denouement since Barbara Fritchie poked her head out the window."

When *Madame X* was released in the Spring of 1966, Lana toured extensively throughout the country on behalf of the film. In many of the interviews she gave at the time, she told the press she had never worked harder on a characterization.* To one reporter, she related: "I'm not a method actress, but the only way I can reach that kind of emotion is to call on situations and experiences in my own life. It's not easy to do because you lock them away. But it's the only way to get to that same level of intensity."

Lana Turner has since stated that the role of Madame X is one of her own personal favorites. Among her fans as well, Miss Turner's interpretation of Alexandre Bisson's martyred mama has taken its place—along with Sheila Regan (*Ziegfeld Girl*), Cora Smith (*The Postman Always Rings Twice*) and Georgia Lorrison (*The Bad and the Beautiful*)—as one of the star's best-liked movie heroines. ★

---

*Depite some well-publicized on-set discord between Lana and Ross Hunter, when *Madame X* completed shooting, the actress took out a full-page ad in a Hollywood trade paper thanking Hunter and all seventy-five members of the cast and crew for helping her get through the difficult role.

With Keir Dullea

THE BIG CUBE

A WARNER BROS. · SEVEN ARTS RELEASE
OF A FRANCISCO DIEZ BARROSO PRODUCTION

1969

CAST

LANA TURNER, *Adriana Roman;* GEORGE CHAKIRIS, *Johnny Allen;* RICHARD EGAN, *Frederick Lansdale;* DANIEL O'HERLIHY, *Charles;* KARIN MOSSBERG, *Lisa Winthrop;* PAMELA RODGERS, *Bibi;* CARLOS EAST, *Lalo;* AUGUSTO BENEDICO, *Dr. Lorenz;* VICTOR JUNCO, *Delacroix;* NORMA HERRERA, *Stella;* PEDRO GALVAN, *University Dean;* THE FINKS, *Themselves;* REGINA TORNE, *Queen Bee.*

CREDITS

Director, TITO DAVISON; Producer, LINDSLEY PARSONS; Screenplay, WILLIAM DOUGLAS LANSFORD; Story, TITO DAVISON and EDMUNDO BAEZ; Photography (Eastman-Color), GABRIEL FIGUEROA; Art Director, MANUEL FONTANALS; Editor, CARLOS SAVAGE, JR.; Sound, JAMES L. FIELDS; Recorders, MANUEL TOPETE and G. SAMPERIO; Gowns, TRAVILLA; Makeup, ANA GUERRERO and ROSA GUERRERO; Hair Stylist, ESPERANZA GOMEZ; Music, VAL JOHNS; Song, "Lean on Me" by VAL JOHNS with Lyrics by HOWARD FINKELSTEIN; Special Effects, CHARLATAN PRODUCTIONS, INC.; Assistant Director, WINFIELD SANCHEZ; Running time, 98 minutes.

NOTES ABOUT THE FILM

The Big Cube is a mixture of a standard Turner plot formula (the stepmother vs. stepdaughter theme) and "now" touches (drug parties, psychedelic sequences, rock music and flashes of nudity) designed to convert what is basically an old-fashioned soap opera into a movie for the tastes of the current commercial scene. The title refers to sugar cubes spiked with LSD.

Here Miss Turner is a stage actress named Adriana Roman, who as the film opens, is retiring from her profession to marry millionaire Charles Winthrop. Once they wed, she incurs the resentment of Winthrop's daughter, Lisa, just back from boarding school and involved with a group of hippies.

When her husband drowns in a yachting accident, Adriana is left in control of the family fortune, much to the chagrin of her stepdaughter since Winthrop's will stipulates that Lisa must have Adriana's approval to wed before she receives her share. Lisa is in love with Johnny Allen, a schemer working his way through medical school by peddling LSD to his friends. When Adriana refuses to permit their marriage, they initiate a plan to drive her mad by mixing LSD with her sedative pills. In a short time, she succumbs to amnesia and Johnny and Lisa wed.

On her wedding night, when Lisa discovers Johnny is only after her money, she confesses everything to

With Daniel O'Herlihy

With Karin Mossberg and George Chakiris

253

As Adriana Roman

Frederick Lansdale, a stage director who is in love with Adriana. Lansdale's form of therapy is to write a play recreating the actual experiences that put Adriana into her amnesia. By inducing her to play in it, and reliving the chain of events, he brings her back to her normal state.

In the end, the play becomes a great hit; Adriana marries the loyal director who stood by her, and is reunited with her stepdaughter as well; and Johnny Allen becomes a victim of his own vices. When last seen, he is writhing on the floor of a basement slum after taking an overdose of LSD.

The Big Cube, which Maurice Forley in his *Motion Picture Daily* review described as "Peyton Place with generous doses of LSD," was filmed in Mexico and co-produced by ANCO Productions, a Mexico firm, and Motion Pictures International, an American outfit. The American contingent, besides Miss Turner, included actors George Chakiris, Richard Egan and Daniel O'Herlihy. Other prominent names involved in the making of the film were Gabriel Figueroa, Mexico's fore-most cinematographer and Travilla, the former 20th Century-Fox costume designer.

Commercially, *The Big Cube* did very well south of the border. However, it was far less fortunate Stateside where it bears the dubious distinction of being one of the most poorly distributed Turner films of all. Shortly after filming finished, it was acquired for U.S. distribution by Warner Bros.–Seven Arts. When released in May 1969, it had major playdates in Boston, Cleveland and Chicago. But midway into its release schedule it was lost in the shuffle with other foreign-made pickups of the period when the Kinney Corporation took over Warners. Among the "lost" films in this package are Peter O'Toole's *Great Catherine*, Tony Curtis's *On My Way to the Crusades*, and Rita Hayworth's *Sons of Satan*. Some of these films were shelved, others were dropped and never released in America. A few, like *The Big Cube*, were unceremoniously booked into neighborhood theatres and drive-ins across the country on the lower halves of double bills in support of more favored product made under the Kinney regime.

In 1972, a dubbed-in-Spanish version of *The Big Cube*, titled *El Terron de Azucar*, showed up in the States. Released by Cimex Distributing Agency, it played over 500 Spanish-language houses throughout the country. Meanwhile, English-speaking Turner fans, who have never seen the film, are scanning their television listings daily watching for its inevitable small-screen destination. ★

PERSECUTION

A TYBURN FILM PRODUCTION
RELEASED IN THE U.S.A. BY THE FANFARE CORPORATION
1974

With Mark Weavers

With Trevor Howard

With Olga Georges-Picot

CAST

LANA TURNER, *Carrie Masters;* TREVOR HOWARD, *Paul Bellamy;* RALPH BATES, *David Masters;* OLGA GEORGES-PICOT, *Monique Kalfon;* SUZAN FARMER, *Janie Masters;* PATRICK ALLEN, *Robert Masters;* MARK WEAVERS, *Young David;* CATHERINE BRANDON, *Mrs. Deacon;* SHELAGH FRASER, *Mrs. Banks;* RONALD HOWARD, *Doctor Ross;* JENNIFER GUY, *Waitress;* JOHN RYAN, *Gardener.*

CREDITS

Director, DON CHAFFEY; Producer, KEVIN FRANCIS; Associate Producer, HUGH ATTWOOLL; Original Story and Screenplay, ROBERT B. HUTTON and ROSEMARY WOOTTEN; Additional Scenes and Dialogue, FREDERICK WARNER; Photography (EastmanColor), KENNETH TALBOT; Art Direction, JACK SHAMPAN with PETER WILLIAMS; Sound, JACK BROMMAGE; Editor, MIKE CAMPBELL; Miss Turner's Costumes, ANTHONY MENDLESON (Executed by BERMANS of London); Miss Turner's Makeup, ROY ASHTON; Miss Turner's Hair Stylist, JOAN CARPENTER; Music, PAUL FERRIS; Assistant Director, ANTHONY WAYE; Makeup, JIMMY EVANS; Hairdressing, GORDON BOND; Production Manager, ROBIN DOUET; Assistant to the Producer, LORRAINE FENNELL; Running time, 92 minutes (U. S. running time, 88 minutes).

NOTES ABOUT THE FILM

After her well-publicized excursions into the worlds of television and the legitimate theatre, Lana Turner returned to moviemaking in a British-made psychological suspense drama titled *Persecution.* It was filmed late in 1973 at Pinewood Studios in England as the first production of a new independent outfit called Tyburn Films. The company was founded by Kevin Francis, the twenty-eight-year-old son of veteran horror film director and cult favorite, Freddie Francis.

At a pre-production press conference, Miss Turner told the British press that the film was "something very foreign to anything I've attempted before. It's an

entirely different characterization and I'm sure I'll get a lot of hate mail."

In *Persecution*, Miss Turner plays Carrie Masters, a rich American émigré and the possessive mother to end all possessive mothers. Crippled (apparently by a husband who has since left her), she has grown to resent her young son, David, whom she blames solely for her crippled state. Her cruelest form of vengeance involves her obsession with a series of Persian cats all named Sheba, whom she introduces into the most terrifying situations to frighten the boy.

At the age of ten, David rebels by drowning Carrie's present cat in its own milk. Carrie, however, totally crushes any rebellion left in her son by conducting a bizarre funeral for the cat and by giving David the cat's coffin as a Christmas present.

At twenty-four, David has married and his wife, Janie, has also become a victim of Carrie's persecution. Carrie, of course, never wanted the marriage to take place and does everything possible to break it up. Finally, when their baby is accidentally suffocated in its crib by the latest Sheba, the mental state of both David and Janie begins to deteriorate. Carrie, sensing this is the time to drive home the wedge between her son and his wife, engages a beautiful prostitute as a "nurse" to Janie, who has not yet recovered from the death of the baby.

Just as Carrie had intended, David falls for the charms of the girl and they are discovered making love by Janie. Rushing blindly out of the room, she stumbles over Sheba and falls down the stairs to her death. After the death of the baby and now his wife, David's mind finally gives way. He kills the prostitute and goes out into the garden to dig up the cats' graves. There, he discovers the bones of Carrie's husband, Robert Masters.

Now at the mercy of her deranged son, Carrie is forced to admit that she murdered Masters years ago and that it was her lover, Paul Bellamy (David's real father), who was responsible for crippling her. In David's crazed mind his mother and Sheba, her cat, reverse roles and in the film's ironic finale, Carrie is drowned by her son in the cat's milk.

Persecution is, of course, Miss Turner's first fling at Grand Guignol, the genre popularized by the success of the Bette Davis–Joan Crawford starrer, *Whatever Happened to Baby Jane?*, and ultimately tackled by virtually every veteran actress of the screen. Unlike her cinema sisters, Miss Turner is not required to don a fright wig or wield an ax for the role of the felinely wicked Carrie Masters. Even amidst the bizarre happenings of *Persecution* she is handsomely costumed (by Britain's award-winning designer Anthony Mendleson) and set against her customary rich world milieu. The exquisite interior and exterior sets used as the Masters home in the film are actually part of the real-life domain of Harry Saltzman, producer of the James Bond films. The estate was previously used in the Bond saga, *Thunderball*, as well as in *The Hireling*, the Sarah Miles–Robert Shaw starrer.

Although *Persecution* was poshly produced, beautifully photographed and in the hands of an efficient director (Don Chaffey), the results, unfortunately, left much to be desired. When the picture opened in Great Britain in November 1974, Margaret Hinxman of the London *Daily Mail* wrote: "Silly as it seems, here is the spectacular Lana Turner playing a crippled, cat-loving mother dominating the life of her unfortunate son (Ralph Bates, who deserves a better fate). Given a more astute script I imagine that able director Don Chaffey would have done justice to his star. As it is the film is surprisingly stodgy, barely a gasp of surprise in it."

As Carrie Masters

Variety's review was negative as well, its critic describing the film as an "old-fashioned meller riddled with ho-hum and sometimes laughably trite scripting. Also, it's very tame in the shock-horror department."

Despite the downbeat reviews, Miss Turner herself drew good personal notices.* Added *Variety*: "Routine playing, for the most part, is an inevitable consequence of the limp story. But under the circumstances, Turner's performance as the perverted dame of the English manor has reasonable poise. Both she and story become especially effective in the waning sequences."

In the *Monthly Film Bulletin*, Geoff Brown said of the star: ". . . one can only admire the lady's fortitude. Even though she is playing a crippled, crazy lady who ages twenty-five years and dies imitating a cat, she strives to exhibit the same mad dignity of *Portrait in Black* and *Madame X* . . . Lana Turner apart, there is little of interest."

Like *The Big Cube, Persecution* has had scant theatrical showings in America. Late in '74, the Fanfare Corporation (who had the U.S. distribution rights)

released the film in a few situations under the title *Sheba*. Six months later, with a revised ad campaign stressing the "horror" elements of the plot, it was put out again as *The Terror of Sheba*.

In April '75, Lana surprised her fans—and, no doubt, the picture's distributors—by publicly labelling the film "a bomb." While praising the work of director Chaffey, she placed the movie's unsatisfying results on the poor editing job done on its completion. ★

---

*On October 28, 1975, at the Sitges (Spain) Festival of Horror Films, Lana won the Silver Carnation award for best actress for her performance in *Persecution*.

With Ralph Bates

LANA

TV

AND
OTHER
APPEARANCES

SHORT SUBJECTS & OTHER APPEARANCES

In addition to her feature films, Lana Turner also appeared in the following short subjects:

PICTORIAL REVUE NO. 6 (Vitaphone, 1938). This issue of the Revue series was divided into three segments. The first sequence showed scenes of the Kellogg ranch in the west where the finest breed of Arabian horses are raised. Besides an exhibition by several of the highly trained horses, some visitors from Hollywood are seen including Dick Foran, Marie Wilson, Ronald Reagan, Kenny Baker and a very young, dark-haired Lana. The second sequence, narrated by Clem McCarthy, focuses on an ice hockey game at Madison Square Garden in New York. The final sequence, photographed in color, follows the manufacture of ladies' shoes from the designing stage to the completed product. The first and third segments were narrated by Alan Kent. Running time, 10 minutes.

RHUMBA RHYTHM (MGM, 1939). Directed by Sammy Lee, produced by Louis Lewyn, and featuring Sally Payne, Mary Treen and a "Galaxy of Stars." Filmed in Sepia, this one-reeler centered around two girls who go to Hollywood to see the local sights, meet a number of movie personalities and conquer in a rhumba contest staged in one of the screen capital's night spots. The payoff comes when the girls are presented with an exorbitant bill from their dancing partners, who, unknown to them, are professional instructors. Off-the-record shots of some of the film personalities present include (in order of their appearance) a turbanned Lana (at a ringside table with Chester Morris), Frank Albertson, June Lang, James Dunn, Arleen Whelan, Alex D'Arcy, George Murphy (who is also the judge of the dancing contest), Arthur Lake, Marsha Hunt, John Carroll and Lionel Stander. Filmed at Hollywood's La Conga nightclub, the short featured Eduardo Chavez and his band and the Theodores, a popular dance team. Running time, 10 minutes.

SHOW BUSINESS AT WAR (20th Century-Fox, 1943; Volume IX, Issue #10 of "The March of Time"). Produced by the Editors of *Time* and directed by Louis de Rochemont, this star-studded segment of the popular series pictured various Hollywood personalities doing their part for the war effort. Lana was shown selling defense stamps at the Los Angeles Victory House. Listed alphabetically, the other celebrities appearing in the short were Eddie (Rochester) Anderson, Louis Armstrong and His Band, Phil Baker, the Ballets Russes de Monte Carlo, Ethel Barrymore, Robert Benchley, Jack Benny, Edgar Bergen (with Charlie McCarthy), Irving Berlin, Joe E. Brown, James Cagney, Lt. Col. Emanuel Cohen, Bing Crosby, Michael Curtiz, Linda Darnell, Bette Davis, Olivia de Havilland, Marlene Dietrich, Walt Disney, Irene Dunne, Deanna Durbin, W. C. Fields, Errol Flynn, Lt. Comdr. John Ford, Kay Francis, Clark Gable, John Garfield, Bert Glennon, Rita Hayworth, Alfred Hitchcock, Lou Holtz, Bob Hope, Al Jolson, Brenda Joyce, Kay Kyser and His Band, Hedy

Lamarr, Dorothy Lamour, Carole Landis, Gertrude Lawrence, Lt. Col. Anatole Litvak, Mary Livingston, Carole Lombard, Myrna Loy, Alfred Lunt, Fred Mac-Murray, Victor Mature, Mitzi Mayfair, the Mills

With Ronald Reagan in PICTORIAL REVUE NO. 6

With Chester Morris in RHUMBA RHYTHM

In SHOW BUSINESS AT WAR

Brothers, George Murphy, Eugene Ormandy and the Philadelphia Symphony Orchestra, Lily Pons, Tyrone Power, Lt. Col. Robert Presnell, the Ritz Brothers, Ginger Rogers, Mickey Rooney, Ann Rutherford, Anne Shirley, Ginny Simms, Frank Sinatra, Lt. Gregg Toland, Maj. Anthony Veiler, Hal B. Wallis, Jack L. Warner, Orson Welles, Don Wilson, Loretta Young, and Col. Darryl F. Zanuck. Running time, 18 minutes.

MILLION DOLLAR WARDROBE (Columbia, 1965). The spectacular wardrobe created by Academy Award-winning designer Edith Head for Lana to wear in *Love Has Many Faces* was the subject of this Eastman-Color featurette for both theatrical and TV release. With Miss Head supplying the narration, Lana put on a one-woman fashion show as she paraded the individual costumes before the cameras in new footage filmed expressly for the short. Co-star Stefanie Powers modeled her less elaborate wardrobe as well, and male leads Cliff Robertson and Hugh O'Brian were seen briefly in new studio footage on the Acapulco location sets and in scenes from the film. Running time, 5 minutes.

Clips from Lana Turner movies have appeared in numerous Metro films; e.g., *Down in San Diego* (1941), *The Stratton Story* (1949) and *Watch the Birdie* (1951).

Other clips have resurfaced from time to time in short subjects like MGM's popular *Passing Parade* series as well as in the many "compilation" films produced by the studio throughout the years. The first of these films was *Some of the Best*, a featurette commemorating Metro's twenty-fifth anniversary. Released in the fall of '49, it offered highlights from studio product both old and new. The final moments of *Some of the Best* presented a roll call of all the Metro players and the film ended with a huge close-up of Lana's face (the clip used was from *Cass Timberlane*).

Another compilation film was *The MGM Story* (1951). A featurette with two reels in black and white and four reels in color, it previewed highlights from twenty-five upcoming Metro films including the Turner–Pinza *Mr. Imperium*. Dore Schary (introduced by Lionel Barrymore) supplied the narration.

Finally, in *That's Entertainment*, the nostalgic 1974 feature saluting the numerous musicals made by MGM, there were two brief clips of Lana and Clark Gable from *Honky Tonk*. This time commemorating the studio's fiftieth anniversary, *That's Entertainment* was produced by Jack Haley, Jr. and released through United Artists. It was so successful at the box-office that in 1976 a sequel, titled *That's Entertainment, Part 2*, was issued. In it, there is some footage from *The Merry Widow* and *Ziegfeld Girl*.

In addition to these films, old footage on Lana appeared in such non-MGM features as *The Love Goddesses* (1965), a documentary homaging the screen's greatest sex symbols. Here, Lana's sweater girl scenes from *They Won't Forget*—including her memorable walk across the screen—were prominently featured.

And in *Hollywood Babylon*, a 1972 documentary based on Kenneth Anger's book about the film colony's wild and woolly past, there is some old newsreel footage of the star.

In the nearly forty years since she first became a household name, Lana has been "name-dropped" in the dialogue of a score of movies, the titles of which are too numerous to list. Some of the films include: *Cairo* ('42); *Lucky Jordan* ('43); *Anchors Aweigh* ('45); *Without Reservations* ('46); *The Senator Was Indiscreet* ('48); *Luxury Liner* ('48); *Music Man* ('48); *Father Was a Fullback* ('49); *The Milkman* ('50); *I Love Melvin* ('53); *Dream Wife* ('53); *Top Banana* ('54); *Crime in the Streets* ('56); *The Goddess* ('58); *Dondi* ('61); *Mary, Mary* ('63); *Myra Breckenridge* ('70); *Women in Revolt* ('72); *Mixed Company* ('74); *Alice Doesn't Live Here Anymore* ('74); and *Crazy Mama* ('75).

As an MGM contract star, she was consistently alluded to in their features. In *Meet the People* ('44), there's a boat named "The Lana Turner"; in *Small Town Girl* ('53), she decorates a billboard during a production number; in *I Love Melvin* ('53), she gets a full screen close-up as a *Look* cover girl; and she's even been mentioned in the limited dialogue of the studio's Tom and Jerry cartoons as well as the Pete Smith specialties.

More recently the scripts of such made-for-TV movies as *The Girl on the Late, Late Show* (1974) and *The Entertainer* (1976) have made references to her.

An ad for one of the many compilation features which utilized clips from Turner movies

261

Miss Turner has over the years been mentioned for many other film projects. As in the case of all major stars, for every one film that got before the cameras, there were dozens that for one reason or another never materialized. It's well known, for instance, that Lana was one of the many young starlets who tested for the role of Scarlett O'Hara in *Gone With the Wind*; that she was very close to playing Amber in *Forever Amber*.

Here is a year-by-year account of just some of the projects that trade papers, Hollywood columnists or studio press releases suggested she would appear in. Films that were never made; roles that because of conflicting commitments on her part were ultimately played by other actresses; roles that she herself reneged on doing.

1938: HAVING WONDERFUL TIME. Lana was to have been one of Ginger Rogers' girl friends in this romantic comedy set at a summer resort but a loanout deal with RKO fell through.

I TAKE THIS WOMAN. A sudden appendectomy forced Miss Turner from the cast even before her scenes were filmed. Laraine Day replaced her in this trouble-plagued Spencer Tracy–Hedy Lamarr vehicle.

SNUG HARBOR. Ray Bolger, Florence Rice, Dennis O'Keefe, Nat Pendleton, Reginald Gardiner, George Givot and E. E. Clive were also in the cast of this project that was cancelled only a week prior to its filming. Edwin L. Marin was to have directed.

IDIOT'S DELIGHT. Lana was to have been one of Harry Van's (Clark Gable) dancing girls in this 1939 release but the State Department of Education stepped in and declared her ineligible for work until her schooling was completed!

1939: THUNDER AFLOAT. Unable to get Barbara Stanwyck for the feminine lead of this Wallace Beery starrer, MGM made tests of the much younger Lana, Laraine Day and Virginia Grey (who won the role).

THE RAINS CAME. Lana was a hot bet for the ingenue role of Fern Simon (which served to introduce Brenda Joyce to the screen). Sixteen years later, Miss Turner played in a remake of the film (titled *The Rains of Ranchipur*) playing the role of its predatory heroine, Lady Edwina Esketh.

A DAY AT THE RACES. In this Marx Brothers comedy, Florence Rice eventually played the feminine lead that Lana was rumored for.

LIVING IN A BIG WAY. Originally purchased for Jean Harlow, this project was to have been directed by S. Sylvan Simon. Although the film was never made, the title was later used for a Gene Kelly starrer in 1947.

THE HUNCHBACK OF NOTRE DAME. Trade papers indicate that Lana was one of director William Dieterle's top choices for the role of Esmeralda (which Maureen O'Hara eventually played on screen).

1940: 20 LITTLE WORKING GIRLS. Based on a story by Bradford Roper, this never-filmed project at MGM was to have co-starred John Carroll.

TROPICAL HURRICANE. An unrealized Hunt Stromberg production which for a time was part of Metro's campaign to hoist Lana to stardom. Robert Taylor was to have co-starred from a script by John Lee Mahin.

BETHEL MERRIDAY. A proposed Turner starrer from a Sinclair Lewis novel.

WITCH IN THE WILDERNESS. About a

lady and a lumberjack, this Gable–Turner story would have been their first co-starring picture.

PRESENTING LILY MARS. A Booth Tarkington story about a playwright who transforms a little shopgirl into one of Broadway's most glamourous actresses. In 1940, MGM said it would serve as Lana's first major starring vehicle. One year later, although retitled *Lulu*, it was still on her film schedule until finally the studio decided to rework the script to fit the musical talents of Judy Garland.

1941: THE HARVEY GIRLS. MGM purchased this original story by Eleanore Griffin and William Rankin and the *New York Times* announced, in November 1941, that it would come to the screen with Lana, Hedy Lamarr, Ruth Hussey, Patricia Dane and Marsha Hunt. But nothing came of the project and in 1943 the studio put the property up for sale. In the end, however, MGM retained it, musicalized it for Judy Garland (just as they had done with *Presenting Lily Mars*)—and they had a big hit on their hands.

THEY LIVE BY NIGHT. This Jane Hall story was going to be Joe Pasternak's first production for MGM in his shift from Universal. The story was about a girl night club photographer and Walter Pidgeon was going to play the club's operator. Another vehicle placed on Lana's schedule that year (and never filmed) was *Flying Blonde*, in which she would have played a lady test pilot.

1942: BEST FOOT FORWARD. The role of the movie star in the screen version of the Broadway hit had been penciled in for Lana until she bowed out due to pregnancy. Lucille Ball stepped in for her.

MARY SMITH, U.S.A. A story by Mildred Cram about a small town girl who kills a politician for disloyalty to the U.S. The picture was to have co-starred Walter Pidgeon, with Arthur Hornblow, Jr. producing and Mervyn LeRoy directing. In 1942, it was also printed that MGM would loan Lana to Columbia for their upcoming Robert Fellows production of *The Petty Girl* (the picture was postponed and did not reach the screen until 1950 with Nat Perrin producing and Joan Caulfield in the title role); that MGM had offered Warners $100,000 for the script of Irwin Shaw's *The Hard Way* for Clark Gable, Joan Crawford and Lana (Warners turned down the deal and made the film themselves with Dennis Morgan, Ida Lupino and Joan Leslie); and that *Cry Havoc*, MGM's tribute to women in uniform would feature "every big girl name on the lot including Joan Crawford, Lana Turner, Ann Sothern, Donna Reed, Marsha Hunt and Susan Peters" (when the film was made only Sothern and Hunt were part of the all-feminine cast).

1943: JENNY WAS A LADY. Based upon the career of Nellie Bly, an early newspaper woman, MGM's writers could not obtain a suitable story from her adventures and the idea was abandoned.

MUSIC FOR MILLIONS. In the fall of '43, MGM issued press releases stating that Lana's first film after the birth of her baby would be *Music for Millions*. But she returned to the screen instead in *Marriage Is a*

Private Affair and *Music* starred Margaret O'Brien and June Allyson (in, presumably, a considerably reworked version of the role intended for Lana). Another script submitted to Lana right after Cheryl's birth was *Frankie From Frisco*, a dramatic musical about a gal raised on the Barbary Coast who falls in love with a socialite from Nob Hill. Arthur Hornblow, Jr. was to have produced but Miss Turner reportedly turned down the script.

1944: MIDNIGHT IN BOMBAY. With India as the setting, this Louis Bromfield story was being prepared for Lana and Van Johnson.

EARLY TO WED. When the film finally went before the cameras, only two of the four originally announced stars remained in the cast—Lucille Ball and Keenan Wynn. The parts that were to have been played by Lana and Gene Kelly were done by Esther Williams and Van Johnson and the title became *Easy to Wed*.

1945: JOSEPHINE. A Booth Tarkington story about a small town girl who gets her clutches on a returned soldier until he wakes up to her tricks and gives her the gate. Before the film was called off, Van Johnson had been announced as co-star and the cast was to have included Marsha Hunt, Agnes Moorehead, Cecil Kellaway and Angela Lansbury.

1946: LUCKY BALDWIN. A yarn about a gambler and his lady intended as the first postwar Gable–Turner film. However, neither star was happy with the script—or its many revisions—and the whole thing was cancelled.

COQUETTE. Mary Pickford sold this property to MGM, Albert Hackett and Frances Goodrich did the script, and Albert Lord was slated to produce. Throughout 1946, MGM publicity insisted that Lana's next picture would be a remake of this Pickford oldie, but the film was never made.

1949: MADAME BOVARY. On September 9, 1947, MGM announced that a screenplay of the Gustav Flaubert novel was being prepared for Miss Turner. Late in '48, it was believed that the project would serve as her return vehicle (she had been off the screen for a year after marrying millionaire Henry J. "Bob" Topping). By the time the film was ready to roll, pregnancy forced her from the cast and she was replaced in the lead by Jennifer Jones. Other announced "comeback" vehicles that year: *The Reformer and the Redhead* (later filmed with June Allyson); *The Running of the Tide*, based on an

A trade paper ad for a Turner film that was never made

263

Esther Forbes novel with Elizabeth Taylor and Margaret O'Brien co-starring, Charles Vidor directing and Edwin Knopf producing; and *Born Yesterday* (eventually Judy Holliday's Academy Award-winning role).

THREE GUYS NAMED MIKE. Lana was originally set to play the airline hostess heroine that Jane Wyman portrayed when the picture finally came to the screen in '51. Arlene Dahl had been mentioned as a co-star.

NOTHING DOING. A Preston Sturges original that was slated for Turner and Gable but never made. Another was *To Please a Lady* which Gable filmed instead with Barbara Stanwyck.

1950: JEALOUSY. A romantic trilogy starring Spencer Tracy and, as the three disparate women in his life, Lana, Deborah Kerr and another top woman star.

KISS OF A MILLIONAIRE. A comedy about the off-screen amours of a movie siren ("the picture will not be biographical," insisted the press release).

1951: A LETTER FROM THE PRESIDENT. Shelley Winters eventually did the role and the film was retitled *My Man and I*. Mentioned about the same time was *Interrupted Melody*, the life story of opera singer Marjorie Lawrence (in 1955, Eleanor Parker played her).

THE LONESOME GAL. An unrealized project, the screenplay of which revolved around a real-life lady disc jockey with the sexiest voice in the world of radio. Dore Schary announced that the role would be played by either Lana or Ava Gardner "depending on which one is free."

1952: WHY SHOULD I CRY? Filmed a year later as *Torch Song* with Joan Crawford; and *Battle Circus* (June Allyson did the part).

ONE MORE TIME. An original comedy by Garson Kanin and Ruth Gordon with George Cukor directing and Armand Deutsch producing. Lana would have played a Korean war widow.

1953: HELEN OF TROY. In June 1953, an Italian production company announced that Lana was virtually set to star as their Helen. Her loanout depended on whether her MGM studio bosses approved the script which was on its way to them from Rome. Needless to say, it did not meet with their approval. This project, incidentally, bore no relation to the Warner Brothers *Helen of Troy* ('55) nor to *L'Amante di Paride*, the 1953 Italian feature with Hedy Lamarr as Helen.

MY MOST INTIMATE FRIEND. This was the much-publicized MGM project that would have teamed Lana and Ava Gardner. The story revolved around two female TV commentators who vie not only for the biggest audiences, but for the same man. Because of the potent star combination, *My Most Intimate Friend* is quite possibly the film Turner fans most regret never having been made.

THE KING'S GENERAL. Producers Irving Allen and Cubby Broccoli purchased this property for $125,000 from Sir Alexander Korda who owned the rights. A best-seller as a novel, it was a favorite story of Miss Turner's and was to have been filmed in London.

WEEKEND AT LAS VEGAS. This Joe Pasternak production, originally announced for Lana and Carlos Thompson, the studio's newest Latin lover, came to the screen three years later as *Meet Me in Las Vegas* with Cyd Charisse and Dan Dailey in the leads.

1954: THE COBWEB. Miss Turner, Robert Taylor and Grace Kelly headed the very ambitious cast of this film in its early production stages. Their roles were later

Rare shots of Lana's screen test for the role of Scarlett O'Hara in GONE WITH THE WIND. *Testing with her was Melvyn Douglas in the role of Ashley Wilkes*

played by Gloria Grahame, Richard Widmark and Lauren Bacall.

TACEY CROMWELL. This story of a dance hall hostess and a gambler almost became the first Lana Turner–Ross Hunter venture. Miss Turner liked the script but when the film was made, Anne Baxter wound up playing the part and the film was called *One Desire.*

Other films mentioned for Miss Turner in '54: *Rosalinda,* adapted from a Johann Strauss operetta with Kathryn Grayson as co-star, Gottfried Reinhardt as producer and Salzburg the location; and *Deep In My Heart,* the musical biography of composer Sigmund Romberg with Lana guest-starring as Gaby Deslys, the famed dancer (an abbreviated version of this role was later essayed by Tamara Toumanova).

1956: MY MAN GODFREY. This film was heralded as the first of a two-picture deal Miss Turner made with Universal shortly after she left MGM. It was to have co-starred the German actor, O. W. Fischer. Lana, however, stepped out of the picture because she was expecting a baby and when *Godfrey* finally went before the cameras it was with June Allyson and David Niven in the leads. Also in '56: *Love is a Long Goodbye,* a Henry Hathaway production from a Ben Hecht story for Miss Turner and Van Johnson; and *Miss Plymouth Comes Across,* an original comedy by Frederick Kohner that was to have been the initial production of the actress's independent company, Lanturn Productions.

1957: THE SOUND AND THE FURY. Producer Jerry Wald wanted Lana to follow *Peyton Place* with a similar mother-with-a-past role, that of Caddy in his film version of the William Faulkner novel. In the end, Margaret Leighton did the part. Other films mentioned for Lana that same year were *Pylon* (later filmed as *The Tarnished Angels* with Dorothy Malone); *Three Blondes,* an unrealized Joe Pasternak production based on a French novel by Pierre Dassete that (hopefully) would have co-starred Lana, Kim Novak and Jayne Mansfield; and *Maracaibo,* a Universal adventure yarn (bearing no relation to the Cornel Wilde-Paramount film of '58) that was called off because of hazardous weather conditions in Venezuela, the location site.

1958: ANATOMY OF A MURDER. Miss Turner made headlines when she withdrew from the feminine lead of this film after clashing with its temperamental producer-director Otto Preminger. She was replaced in the role by Lee Remick—and to this day she has no regrets about it. (Recalling the incident in 1975, the actress publicly stated: "God forbid that I should ever be so hungry that I would ever think of working for Mr. Preminger!")

1959: STREETS OF MONTMARTRE. Based on a novel by Stephen and Ethel Longstreet, this heavily-publicized Allied Artists project was to have starred Lana in the role of Suzanne Valadon, mother of Utrillo and the highly desired model, confidante and companion of such renowned painters as Toulouse-Lautrec, Renoir and Degas. It was to have been filmed in Paris with Louis Jourdan co-starred, but the long illness of director Douglas Sirk eventually grounded the project.

LUANNE ROYAL. Described by Ross Hunter as a "turbulent, exciting love story of a woman who falls in love with her doctor," this property was written by George Zuckerman, author of *Written on the Wind.* Reportedly, Lana turned down the script.

1960: THE COLONEL'S LADY. An original story by Stanley Roberts to have been produced by Roberts and Robert Arthur for Universal, it was a drama about a glamourous Broadway star who marries an Army colonel. Another film mentioned for Miss Turner in 1960 was *The Chalk Garden,* the Ross Hunter filmization of the Enid Bagnold Broadway hit (Deborah Kerr essayed the role instead).

1963: NOT ALL CATS ARE GRAY. This film never got beyond the talking stage but during 1963 its possibilities garnered a lot of space in the gossip columns. Supposedly, Lana would have played the still-sexy mother of Ann-Margret.

1966: Miss Turner announced in 1966 that she had optioned several properties for her own production company. The most interesting was titled *The Marriage of a Star* and was based on a novel by Alexandre Bisson, who wrote *Madame X.* The most exciting production news, however, came during the month of September, when trade papers printed that Miss Turner's Eltee Productions and Federico Fellini's FF Productions had entered into a co-production deal to make an independent film version of the Giovanni Mitti novel, *North to Brindisi.* She would have starred; Fellini would have directed—but the deal fell through.

1967: WEB OF FEAR (later called *The Tangled Web*). This was another European venture that ran into production snags. A romantic suspense thriller, it was to have been co-produced by Herbert Margolis and filmed in Italy.

LET ME COUNT THE WAYS. Jackie Gleason put out bids for Miss Turner and Ava Gardner to join him in his film version of Peter Viertel's book, *How Do I Love Thee?* The picture was released early in '71 under the latter title but with Maureen O'Hara and Shelley Winters in the female leads. Also mentioned for that year: *Sex and the Married Man,* a never-filmed comedy with David Niven for producer Alex Gottlieb at 20th Century-Fox.

1971: SHOCKING! This on-again, off-again project was on the production schedule of Filmways–United Artists for several years. An original suspense drama by Henry Farrell, who penned *Whatever Happened to Baby Jane?,* it was the story of two glamourous sisters who are trying to kill each other. Again, Lana Turner and Ava Gardner were the hoped-for co-stars, although just before the project fell through Rita Hayworth's name began cropping up in place of Miss Gardner's.

1975: DEADLOCK. This one had a woman-in-jeopardy theme and was heralded as Lana's first Hollywood-made movie in ten years. But financing difficulties followed by a legal fight between co-producers Leo Winter and John Lauricella put the project into limbo.

The following radio and television chronology does not include the literally hundreds of interviews Lana Turner has given throughout her career on both mediums —to disc jockeys like Fred Robbins or husband-and-wife teams like "Tex" McCrary and "Jinx" Falkenburg, for example. She has also made numerous appearances on local stations throughout the United States and abroad while on promotional tours for films (a practice that continued even into the '70s when she was touring with *Forty Carats*, her first stage venture).

There were also transcriptions made for the War Department; appearances at festivities like Hollywood's Santa Claus Parade; and ground-breaking ceremonies (the June 10, 1940 opening of the Palladium, the popular Hollywood ballroom, for instance).

Last but not least, there were dozens of "instant" interviews emanating from movie premieres, the first of which was heard when Miss Turner attended the locally broadcast (KFWB) Hollywood opening of *The Life of Emile Zola* in 1937.

This index consists solely of Lana's major network radio and television performances on what were either regularly scheduled dramatic, comedy or variety shows or those of a "special" nature.

RADIO

THE CHASE AND SANBORN PROGRAM (April 6, 1941, NBC). Edgar Bergen and Charlie McCarthy, Bud Abbott and Lou Costello.

LUX RADIO THEATRE (June 2, 1941, CBS). A dramatization of *They Drive by Night* with George Raft and Lucille Ball. In a casting switch, Lana played the wise-cracking hash-slinger (the Ann Sheridan screen role), while Ball was the sexy vamp. (Ball replaced Ida Lupino, slated to appear in her original film role but thrown out of mike action at the last minute by a heavy movie schedule.)

With Rita Hayworth on the SALUTE OF CHAMPIONS *special*

SALUTE OF CHAMPIONS (September 22, 1941, NBC). A special tribute to Uncle Sam's Armed Forces with Rita Hayworth, Pat O'Brien, Jack Benny, Sonja Henie, Paul Robeson, Joe Louis, Jack Dempsey, Gene Tunney, Leo Durocher, Dizzy Dean and others.

PHILIP MORRIS PLAYHOUSE (November 14, 1941, CBS).

NIGHT OF STARS (November 26, 1941, all non-major networks). A huge relief show emanating from Madison Square Garden in New York and featuring Mrs. Franklin Delano Roosevelt and a host of celebrities from stage, screen and radio (Danny Kaye, Groucho Marx, etc.).

THE CHASE AND SANBORN PROGRAM (December 14, 1941, NBC). Edgar Bergen and Charlie McCarthy, Bud Abbott, Mickey Rooney (subbing for an ailing Lou Costello).

NEW YEAR'S EVE DANCING PARTY (December 31, 1941, NBC). Coast-to-coast descriptions of New Year's celebrations with Lana tossing a pitch for the USO.

LUX RADIO THEATRE (January 19, 1942, CBS). A dramatization of *The Devil and Miss Jones* with Lionel Barrymore.

SCREEN GUILD PLAYERS (February 8, 1942, CBS). *Mr. and Mrs. Smith* with Errol Flynn.

HOLLYWOOD ALL-STAR USO RALLY (May 30, 1942, NBC). Deanna Durbin, Judy Garland, Mickey Rooney, Fannie Brice, Chico and Harpo Marx, etc.

PORTAND OREGON ROSE FESTIVAL (June 10, 1942). Lana did a sketch called "The Rose Is for Valor."

COMMAND PERFORMANCE (October 9, 1942, CBS). A special overseas broadcast for servicemen only with Bob Hope and Judy Garland.

LUX RADIO THEATRE (March 29, 1943, CBS). *Crossroads* with Jean-Pierre Aumont.

NIGHT CLUBS FOR VICTORY (September 29, 1943, CBS). Lana appeared on the program to help promote the sale of War Bonds.

PHILIP MORRIS PLAYHOUSE (October 1, 1943, CBS). An adaptation of the film, *The Talk of the Town*.

RADIO READER'S DIGEST (October 10, 1943, CBS).

LUX RADIO THEATRE (October 25, 1943, CBS). *Slightly Dangerous* with Victor Mature and Gene Lockhart.

ABBOTT AND COSTELLO SHOW (November 4, 1943, NBC).

COMMAND PERFORMANCE (November 13, 1943, CBS). Another overseas broadcast for servicemen only. Bob Hope and Betty Hutton were also on the show.

THE BURNS AND ALLEN SHOW (May 2, 1944, CBS).

THE STAR AND THE STORY (May 7, 1944, CBS). *Lucky Partners* with Walter Pidgeon.

THE FRANK SINATRA SHOW (June 14, 1944, CBS).

THE ORSON WELLES SHOW (July 5, 1944, CBS).

DEMOCRATIC NATIONAL COMMITTEE PROGRAM (November 6, 1944, all networks). One Thousand Club of America political rally on behalf of the re-election of President Roosevelt. Humphrey Bogart, James Cagney, Jimmy Durante and many others were on hand.

SCREEN GUILD PLAYERS (November 20, 1944, CBS). *Once Upon a Honeymoon* with John Hodiak.

DICK HAYMES' EVERYTHING FOR THE BOYS (November 28, 1944, CBS).

TAKE IT OR LEAVE IT (March 4, 1945, CBS). Phil Baker.

SUSPENSE (May 3, 1945, CBS).

LUX RADIO THEATRE (April 11, 1946, CBS). *Honky Tonk* with John Hodiak.

THE YEAR ONE (April 25, 1946, CBS). First anniversary of the United Nations Charter, broadcast from the Astor Roof, Hotel Astor, New York. The guests included Secretary General Trygve Lie, delegates from the Big Five—and Miss Lana Turner!

KATE SMITH SINGS (May 3, 1946, CBS).

SCREEN GUILD PLAYERS (June 17, 1946, CBS). *Marriage Is a Private Affair* with John Hodiak.

ACADEMY AWARD THEATRE (August 14, 1946, CBS). *Vivacious Lady.*

THE VICTOR BORGE SHOW (September 9, 1946, NBC). Benny Goodman was another guest.

THE 19TH ANNUAL ACADEMY AWARDS PRESENTATIONS (March 13, 1947, ABC). Lana presented the Best Musical Score Award to Morris Stoloff for *The Jolson Story.*

SCREEN GUILD PLAYERS (June 23, 1947, CBS). *The Postman Always Rings Twice* with John Garfield.

THE LOUELLA PARSONS SHOW (October 5, 1947, ABC).

THE EDGAR BERGEN–CHARLIE McCARTHY SHOW (November 16, 1947, NBC).

THIS IS NEW YORK (December 10, 1947, CBS).

On The
LOUELLA PARSONS
SHOW

With Clark Gable on SCREEN GUILD PLAYERS

On THE BURNS AND ALLEN SHOW

BROADWAY AND VINE WITH RADIE HARRIS (December 11, 1947, CBS).

THE BOB HOPE SHOW (April 13, 1948, NBC). This show was broadcast live from Lana's old alma mater, Hollywood High, as part of a benefit for the Hollywood YMCA Little Green Valley Camp Fund. Jerry Colonna, Vera Vague and Les Brown and his orchestra also entertained.

BROADWAY AND VINE WITH RADIE HARRIS (December 10, 1948, CBS). Miss Harris presented Lana the *Modern Screen* award.

LUX RADIO THEATRE (September 19, 1949, CBS). *Green Dolphin Street* with Van Heflin and Peter Lawford.

SCREEN GUILD PLAYERS (October 6, 1949, CBS). *Homecoming* with Clark Gable.

SUSPENSE (December 15, 1949, CBS).

SCREEN GUILD PLAYERS (February 8, 1951, ABC). A second radio adaptation of *The Postman Always Rings Twice*, this time with John Hodiak.

THE LOUELLA PARSONS SHOW (November 11, 1951, ABC). Taped at the Hollywood opening of *An American in Paris* (with Fernando Lamas).

MONITOR (March 20, 1966, NBC).

*With Richard Anderson, Edmund Purdom, Steve Forrest, John Ericson and chorus boys
on* ED SULLIVAN'S TOAST OF THE TOWN

TELEVISION

ED SULLIVAN'S TOAST OF THE TOWN (February 14, 1954, CBS). An hour-long tribute to MGM celebrating the studio's 30th anniversary of film-making. Film clips from past and present attractions highlighted the program along with live appearances by many of MGM's top stars. In addition to Lana, the players included Fred Astaire, Lucille Ball, Desi Arnaz, Lionel Barrymore, Ann Blyth, Cyd Charisse, Van Johnson, Howard Keel, Gene Kelly, Ann Miller, Walter Pidgeon, Jane Powell, Debbie Reynolds and Esther Williams. Dore Schary, then head of production at the studio, was a special guest. Assisted by chorus boys Edmund Purdom, Steve Forrest, John Ericson and Richard Anderson, Lana performed the "Madame Crematon" number introduced by Judy Garland in *Ziegfeld Follies* ('46).

THE 26TH ANNUAL ACADEMY AWARDS PRESENTATIONS (March 25, 1954, NBC [simultaneously aired on radio]). Lana and Lex Barker presented the winning cinematography awards to Burnett Guffey for *From Here to Eternity* (black-and-white) and to Loyal Griggs for *Shane* (color).

COLGATE VARIETY HOUR (*Modern Screen* Special Awards for 1955—November 27, 1955, NBC). Lana received an award as "the star who has appeared on the most fan magazine covers." Other winners present were John Wayne, Claudette Colbert, Rock Hudson, Debbie Reynolds, Kim Novak and Russ Tamblyn. Robert Paige was the host and special guests included Bob Hope, Gordon MacRae, Anna Maria Alberghetti, Louella Parsons and composer Jimmy McHugh.

THE 28TH ANNUAL MOTION PICTURE ACADEMY AWARDS NOMINATIONS SHOW (February 18, 1956, NBC). A ninety-minute special announcing the nominations for best actors, best actresses, best pictures, etc. of 1956 prior to the official Oscar ceremonies which took place on March 21 of that year. Fredric March served as "anchorman" and the list of "hosts" and "hostesses" who introduced the nominees included Lana, Barbara Stanwyck, Tony Curtis, Jack Lemmon, Deborah Kerr, Dick Powell, Fred MacMurray, June Haver, Robert Wagner, Claire Trevor, Lex Barker, Ann Blyth, Mitzi Gaynor, Celeste Holm, Aldo Ray and Edmond O'Brien. Eddie Fisher sang the five nominated songs.

CLIMAX!—The Louella Parsons Story (February 29, 1956, CBS). The life story of movieland's most famous newspaper columnist with Teresa Wright portraying Miss Parsons. Appearing as herself, Lana was a special guest along with Gracie Allen, Eve Arden, Jean-Pierre Aumont, Jack Benny, Charles Boyer, George Burns, Eddie Cantor, Dan Dailey, Howard Duff, Joan Fontaine, Zsa Zsa Gabor, Susan Hayward, Rock Hudson, Ida Lupino, Jeanette MacDonald, Fred MacMurray, Robert Mitchum, Kim Novak, Merle Oberon, Ginger Rogers, Gilbert Roland, Red Skelton, Robert Stack, Robert Wagner and John Wayne. William Lundigan was the host.

THE BOB HOPE CHEVY SHOW (March 10, 1957, NBC). This Hope show appearance garnered a lot of pre-airing publicity and since it was the most TV ex-posure she'd had thus far on the home screen, NBC advertised it as Lana's TV "debut." Miss Turner was first featured in an Enoch Arden sketch with Hope and Wally Cox as the men in her life. At the end of the hour, in a song and dance turn with Hope, she wore a skin-tight sheath for the benefit of the studio audience comprised largely of seabees. Rosemary Clooney was another of the show's guest stars.

THE 30TH ANNUAL ACADEMY AWARDS PRESENTATIONS (March 26, 1958, NBC [simultaneously aired on radio]). An Oscar nominee herself (for *Peyton Place*), Lana presented the best supporting actor award to Red Buttons for *Sayonara*.

WHAT'S MY LINE (March 22, 1959, CBS). On a tour promoting *Imitation of Life*, Lana was the show's "mystery guest."

THE DINAH SHORE SHOW (April 19, 1959, NBC). Along with another guest, singer Kay Starr, Lana was featured in songs and skits, the highlight of which had Turner, Shore and Starr portraying popular sister acts of the past.

THE MILTON BERLE SPECIAL (October 11, 1959, NBC), Lana sang "Just Turn Me Loose on Broadway" and "Taking a Chance on Love"; with Peter Lawford, she dueted "You'll Never Get Away"; and with Berle,

With Milton Berle, Danny Thomas and Peter Lawford on THE MILTON BERLE SPECIAL

With Kay Starr and Dinah Shore on THE DINAH SHORE SHOW

On THE SMOTHERS
BROTHERS SHOW

With the
Ernest Flatt
Dancers on
THE CAROL
BURNETT SHOW

Lawford and Danny Thomas, she was featured in *The Insulters*, a skit spoofing TV stars and shows.

THE BOB HOPE CHRISTMAS SHOW (January 16, 1963, NBC). Filmed highlights of Hope's 11th annual Christmas (1962) tour of overseas military bases. The 18,000-mile trip included stops in Japan, Korea, Okinawa, Taiwan, the Philippines and Guam. Hope's cast of entertainers included Lana, Janis Paige, Anita Bryant, Jerry Colonna, Amedee Chabot (Miss U.S.A.), Peter Leeds and Les Brown and his Band of Renown. One of the show's funniest sketches had Hope as a Chinese general brainwashing an American spy, played by Lana. Later on in the show, the Turner–Hope team displayed their dance floor agility in a Bossa Nova number.

WHAT'S MY LINE (February 27, 1966, CBS). Another promotional tour (this time for *Madame X*), and another surprise appearance as the show's "mystery guest." (Some of Lana's footage from this show reap-

With Lex Barker on CLIMAX!

On THE MIKE DOUGLAS SHOW

With George Hamilton in HAROLD ROBBINS' THE SURVIVORS

peared on TV nine years later—on May 28, 1975—on a special twenty-fifth anniversary tribute to *What's My Line*. An ABC network presentation, the show featured highlights from *What's My Line*'s quarter-century of broadcasting.

THE 38TH ANNUAL ACADEMY AWARDS PRESENTATIONS (April 18, 1966, ABC). Lana and James Garner co-presented the awards for best achievement in costume design. The non-present winners were Julie Harris for *Darling* (black-and-white) and Phyllis Dalton for *Doctor Zhivago* (color).

THE SMOTHERS BROTHERS SHOW (March 15, 1967, CBS). Lana and Robert Morse joined the Brothers for a series of blackouts and a spoof of TV viewer tests. One very funny sketch had Casanova (Tom Smothers) wooing the glamourous Lady X (Lana).

THE CAROL BURNETT SHOW (January 6, 1968, CBS). Accompanied by the Ernest Flatt Dancers, Lana sang and danced in a lavish production number built around the ballad "Greensleeves." In the show's second half, she was involved in a comedy skit that had Frank Gorshin portraying Bluebeard with Carol Burnett as his very nervous thirteenth wife and Lana as his mistress.

THE FIRST ANNUAL ACADEMY OF PROFESSIONAL SPORTS AWARDS SHOW (February 14, 1968, NBC). The first TV awards show to honor top performers in all categories of sports. A horse owner herself, Lana presented the Jockey of the Year award to Willie Shoemaker. Film clips showed all twenty-four nominees in action and among the other presenters were James Garner, Glenn Ford and Chuck Connors. Johnny Carson hosted and comics Don Adams and Don Rickles entertained.

HAROLD ROBBINS' THE SURVIVORS (Fall 1969 season, ABC). A multimillion-dollar, one-hour dramatic series about the international jet set. Advertised as Harold Robbins' "first visual novel," each weekly hour corresponded in structure to a chapter in a book. One of the stormiest, most publicized series in TV history, this expensive misfire, that lasted fifteen weeks on TV, took two years of planning, a proliferation of script writers, three producers and almost a year of shooting before the first episode was on film. The story centered around the jet-set family of banking tycoon Baylor Carlyle (Ralph Bellamy). Lana was Tracy Carlyle Hastings, his daughter, and George Hamilton was Duncan, the younger brother who disdains his father's business philosophy. Other characters involved were Philip Hastings (Kevin McCarthy) who married Tracy when she was pregnant many years ago on the agreement with tycoon Carlyle that he would have a career at the bank; Greek millionaire Antaeus Riakos (Rossano Brazzi), who nineteen years earlier, as an impoverished tour guide, unknowingly sired Tracy's only child; Belle Wheeler (Diana Muldaur), Baylor Carlyle's secretary, confidante and mistress; and Tracy's son, Jeff (Jan-Michael Vincent—then billed simply as Michael Vincent). Some of the players that appeared as recurring characters throughout the series' fifteen-week duration included Pamela Tiffin, Louis Hayward, Natalie Schafer (as Lana's dotty mother), Kathy Cannon, Robert Lipton, Louise Sorel, Robert Viharo, Celeste Yarnell, Jean-Paul Vignon, Richard Eastham and Carlos Romero.

THE TIM CONWAY COMEDY HOUR (September 20, 1970, CBS). In an opening sketch, Lana had some very funny moments as a hammy actress who wouldn't get offstage. Later, she and Dan Rowan were a wealthy married couple who hire a drunken detective named Danny Draft (Conway) to solve a murder.

THE JOHNNY CARSON SHOW (May 17, 1972, NBC). Lana's first late-night talk show appearance. Mickey Rooney, another MGM alumnus, and singer Vicki Carr were also guests.

THE DAVID FROST SHOW (May 18, 1972 [in New York City only; shown on other dates in different areas] Metromedia). A warm and consistently interesting ninety-minute interview with host Frost in which Lana discussed such topics as the star system at MGM, former co-stars, the films she loved, the films she hated —and even her mistakes in marriage. An absolute *must* for Turner fans, the show also presented film clips from a number of the star's films such as *Peyton Place* and *Imitation of Life*.

THE MIKE DOUGLAS SHOW (July 12, 1972 [in New York City only; shown on other dates in different areas] CBS). An interview done in Philadelphia with Lana's "favorite afternoon TV talk show host." Comedian Marty Allen and Hollywood columnist Shirley Eder were also present.

THE MIKE DOUGLAS SHOW (May 7, 1975 [in New York City only; shown on other dates in different areas] CBS). A return visit to the Douglas show to talk about the recent *Tribute to Lana Turner*, at New York's Town Hall. Douglas' other guests included singer John Davidson, comics George Carlin and Joan Rivers and publicist-author John Springer.

THE RUSSELL HARTY SHOW (September 5, 1975, London ITV). Although this show was seen in Great Britain only it is included in this index because of its very special nature. The first in a series of interviews tracing the career of a famous star, this one-hour special was devoted entirely to Lana who flew to London to appear on the show. In addition to a lengthy interview by host Harty, the show presented film clips from the most famous Turner movies.

PEYTON PLACE REVISITED (September 26, 1975, ABC). A light look at the Peyton Place phenomenon from the best-selling novel through the movie and the TV series. Host Peter Lawford chatted with the players from the feature film and the series. Among the stars participating were Lana (heard but not seen as she described a film clip involving herself and Diane Varsi), Russ Tamblyn, Mia Farrow, Barbara Parkins, Patricia Morrow, Christopher Connelly and John Kerr.

Note: Lana has also been seen on several TV shows via film clips. Among the more prominent appearances:

HOLLYWOOD AND THE STARS (October 14, 1963, NBC). A two-part segment of the series entitled *Sirens, Symbols and Glamour Girls*. Old film footage on Lana and other screen beauties was used to explore the changing image of movie queens.

HOLLYWOOD AND THE STARS (January 27, 1964, NBC). *Hollywood Goes to War* was the title of this segment which covered the wartime experiences of the stars. Among them: Clark Gable, James Stewart, Henry Fonda and Tyrone Power. Lana was seen entertaining servicemen on a *Command Performance* radio show.

THE ABC WIDE WORLD OF ENTERTAINMENT (June 14, 1974, ABC). On a special entitled *Warner Brothers Movies—A 50 Year Salute,* Sweater Girl footage of Lana from *They Won't Forget* appeared in a montage of the studio's best films.

With Bob Hope on the 1966 Academy Awards telecast

LANA

A
BEHIND THE SCENES
GALLERY

With makeup man Del Armstrong on the set of MARRIAGE IS A PRIVATE AFFAIR

Below: Robert Z. Leonard, director of MARRIAGE *(seated with back to camera), gets ready to supervise a scene*

*A coffee break between filming
of the famous entrance scene
from* THE POSTMAN ALWAYS
RINGS TWICE

*A propman applies red paint to
Lana's Irene-designed costume
for the scene in* SLIGHTLY
DANGEROUS *in which she is hit
with a bucket of paint*

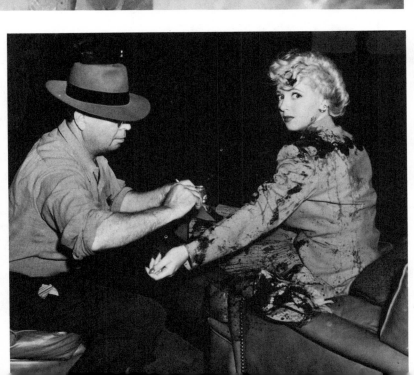

With Ray Milland posing for publicity photos for A LIFE OF HER OWN

Director George Sidney's candid camera catches Lana between scenes of THE THREE MUSKETEERS

Visiting MGM's still photo laboratory

Director Gurtis Bernhardt (seated on camera crane) guides Lana and Fernando Lamas thru the waltz scene from THE MERRY WIDOW

A last minute look before facing the cameras for THE PRODIGAL

Frank Veloz (of Veloz and Yolanda fame) coaches Lana and Ricardo Montalban thru a LATIN LOVERS *dance rehearsal*

On the same film, makeup assistant Mary Hadley applies Lana's body makeup

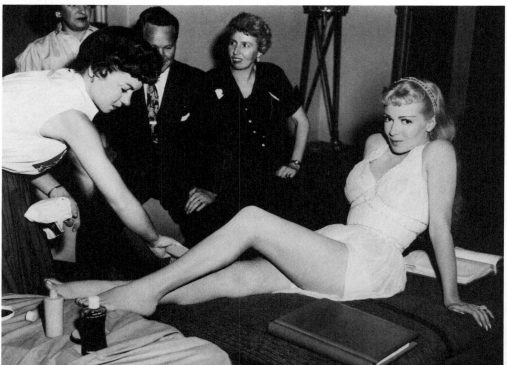

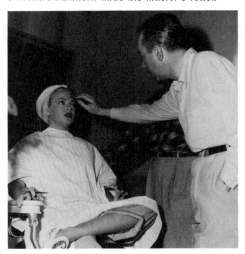

For THE BAD AND THE BEAUTIFUL, *director Vincente Minnelli adds his master's touch*

Boosting sales for Christmas seals between scenes of THE SEA CHASE

David Miller (white hat, foreground) directs a scene for DIANE *with Lana and child actors Ronald Anton and Micky Maga*

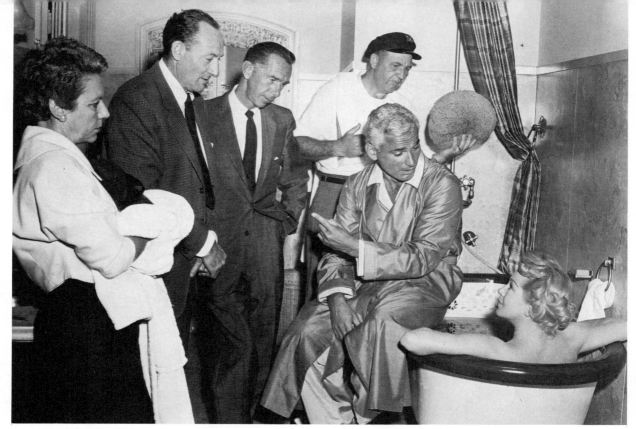

Immersed in a tub for THE LADY TAKES A FLYER. *Surrounding Lana are wardrobe attendant Martha Bunche, cinematographer Irving Glassberg, director Jack Arnold, propman Roy Neal and co-star Jeff Chandler*

Doing her own makeup for ANOTHER TIME, ANOTHER PLACE

During a break in the shooting of IMITATION OF LIFE

Douglas Sirk directs an IMITATION OF LIFE *love scene between Lana and John Gavin*

This is how the "intimate" love scene for By Love
Possessed *(illustrated on page 233) was filmed. Among
the interested onlookers are cameraman Russell Metty and
director John Sturges (foreground)*

281

Rehearsing a scene for MADAME X
*with John Forsythe, Constance Bennett
and script girl Betty Abbott (far left)*

*Martin Pendleton, a Paramount propman
who specializes in staging bathtub scenes,
gives Lana an unexpected visit after the
final take of her bubble bath scene in*
WHO'S GOT THE ACTION?

LANA

IN PERSON!

STAGE APPEARANCES

FORTY CARATS. Lana's first "live" venture. A ten-week tour (beginning June 8, 1971) on the Guber–Gross circuit throughout the East with stops at Washington, Baltimore, New York, Philadelphia and Chicago. The play, which first opened on Broadway on December 28, 1968, was adapted by Jay Allen from a French play by Pierre Barrillet and Jean-Pierre Gredy. Lana's role was that of Anne Stanley, a glamourous, forty-year-old divorcee who falls in love with a man eighteen years her junior. An excellent supporting cast included Peter Cofield, Louise Kirtland, Wallace Engelhardt, Honey Sanders, Kathleen Coyne, Constance Dix, Anne Russell, Dan Hogan, Michael Heller and Robert Kaye. John Bowab directed.

MILL RUN THEATER presents

LANA TURNER IN FORTY CARATS

AUGUST 3 — AUGUST 15

Tues. thru Fri. 8:30 P.M., Wed. matinee 2:00 P.M. Saturday 2:00 P.M. and 7:30 P.M. Sunday 7:30 P.M.

THE PLEASURE OF HIS COMPANY. Presented at the Arlington Park Theater in Illinois, this revival of the comedy by Samuel Taylor and Cornelia Otis Skinner starred Lana in the role that Miss Skinner played when the show premiered on Broadway on October 22, 1958. The story centered on a declining but debonaire playboy (Louis Jourdan) who returns home to see his daughter married. At the same time, he rekindles his love for his former wife, Katharine Dougherty (Lana), a happily remarried San Francisco matron. *The Pleasure of His Company* opened at the Arlington Park Theatre on November 14, 1975. It was originally booked for a three-week run but due to ticket demand the show was extended for an additional four weeks. John Bowab again directed Lana and the supporting cast included Allan Hunt, Marilynn Scott, Don Marston, Arsenio Trinidad and Sidney Breese.

arlington park theatre

Engagement Extended Pre-Opening!
DUE TO TICKET DEMAND, PLAYS THRU DEC. 28

PREVIEW THURSDAY

OPENS FRIDAY

LANA TURNER • LOUIS JOURDAN
In The Comedy "THE PLEASURE OF HIS COMPANY"

With Louis Jourdan, Marilynn Scott, Sidney Breese and Allan Hunt in THE PLEASURE OF HIS COMPANY

Neil Peter Jampolis

With Anne Russell, Kathleen Coyne and Peter Coffield in FORTY CARATS

Barry Kramer

John Bowab, who directed Lana in both of her stage ventures to date has this to say about the star: "Lana is this director's dream—an actress with respect for the author's words, her director's decisions and the casts' rights. She is the epitome of glamour tempered with vulnerability and a keen sense of humor—and the ability and discipline to draw on them at will."

On April 13, 1975 at Town Hall in New York
a standing-room-only crowd paid tribute to Lana.
The evening consisted of film clips from seventeen
Turner movies, after which the star herself
(introduced by John Springer) made an appearance to talk about her career and answer
questions from the audience.

286

A final bow
at Town Hall

Next on the Turner film agenda:
Bittersweet Love, in which Lana
plays a society woman whose
daughter has unwittingly married
her half-brother. In addition to
Miss Turner, the cast includes
Robert Lansing, Celeste Holm,
Robert Alda, Scott Hylands and
Meredith Baxter Birney. Sched-
uled for release late in 1976 by
Avco Embassy Pictures, *Bitter-
sweet Love* was directed by
David Miller for producers
Joseph Zappala, Gene Slott and
Joel Michaels. The original
screenplay was written by Diana
Maddox and David Colloff.

As Claire Peterson
in BITTERSWEET LOVE